D0914622

Blogging Heroes

Interviews with 30 of the
World's Top Bloggers

Blogging Heroes
Interviews with 30 of the World's Top Bloggers

Michael A. Banks

BICENTENNIAL
1807
WILEY
2007
BICENTENNIAL

John Wiley and Sons

Blogging Heroes: Interviews with 30 of the World's Top Bloggers
Published by
Wiley Publishing, Inc.
10475 Crosspoint Boulevard
Indianapolis, IN 46256
www.wiley.com

Published simultaneously in Canada

ISBN: 978-0-470-19739-4

Manufactured in the United States of America

10 9 8 7 6 5 4 3 2 1

For general information on our other products and services or to obtain technical support, please contact our Customer Care Department within the U.S. at (800) 762-2974, outside the U.S. at (317) 572-3993 or fax (317) 572-4002.

Library of Congress Cataloging-in-Publication Data is available from the publisher.

For Patricia, Betsy, Jerry, Roberta, Brandon, Dean, James, pushy James Patrick, Marj, Sharon, and the rest of the wonderful 1988 Worldcon Krewe.

Credits

Acquisitions Editor
Katie Mohr

Development Editor
Maureen Spears

Production Editor
Elizabeth Ginns Britten

Copy Editor
Kathryn Duggan

Editorial Manager
Mary Beth Wakefield

Production Manager
Tim Tate

Vice President and Executive Group Publisher
Richard Swadley

Vice President and Executive Publisher
Joseph B. Wikert

Project Coordinator, Cover
Lynsey Osborne

Compositor
Maureen Forys,
Happenstance Type-O-Rama

Proofreader
Candace English

Indexer
Jack Lewis

Anniversary Logo Design
Richard Pacifico

Cover Image
Michael Trent

About the Author

Michael A. Banks is the author of 42 novels and nonfiction books, most recently The *New York Times* bestseller, *Crosley: Two Brothers and a Business Empire that Transformed the Nation*. He has been a contributing editor for *Winmag, Computer Shopper, Writer's Digest*, and other publications. Online since 1979, Banks is a veteran blogger and web consultant. He can be reached at mike@michaelabanks.com.

Contents

Preface

"I've been too busy blogging to, well, talk about blogging."

—*Owen Thomas, Editor, Valleywag.com*

Projects that are simple in appearance usually turn out to be complicated. If you've ever built a deck or planned a cross-country trip, you know that.

This book is a good example. On the face of it, it seems simple enough: ask a bunch of bloggers questions about blogging, and then put the questions and answers into a book. But, as I knew going in, there was far more to it than that. Bare Q&A is rarely attractive. More often than not, it's boring—like reading a deposition. So creating this book would involve far more than putting a bunch of questions and answers into print. The interviews (one per chapter) would require editing. Each chapter would need an introduction, with background about the blog and relevant biographical material on the blogger. I felt confident enough about that part (the last biography I wrote made *The New York Times* bestseller list).

The book would also need an introduction, and various other front matter and back matter elements that go into any volume.

Knowing that, I could plan the book. I knew that the really difficult parts would come later, in the form of a seemingly endless series of complications, unforeseen events, and those special little problems that accompany the writing of just about any book.

Some of the more interesting aspects of putting this book together are described here. The whole process was almost worth blogging about.

Questions

I started the project as anyone would, by breaking the book down into groups of tasks, by category.

First up, what questions to ask? What to discuss with bloggers? Some questions were obvious—simple icebreakers such as, "How long have you been blogging?" and "Why did you get into blogging?" From there the conversation would work into more complex matters, such as getting traffic, maintaining quality, dealing with difficulties, and more. Gradually, a small list of questions evolved.

(I could omit blog statistics; easily accessible sources like Technorati and Alexa would supply those. Why copy material that was readily available for free? Besides, I was more interested in the people behind the blogs than in the numbers.)

Other questions would suggest themselves during the course of each interview. In other words, the shape of the interviews would be dictated by the interviews themselves.

Subjects

The next step was to find 30 people to interview. I looked around at who was doing what in the blogosphere. I consulted the Technorati lists, Digg, Alexa, and other resources to get an idea of which blogs were really popular, and which may have simply gamed the system to get on a list.

Sifting through the more active and popular blogs, I came up with a list of interesting blogs in several categories. I read the blogs to get an idea of each blogger's style and background. I also looked for buzz about other popular bloggers and their blogs. Links from some of the blogs I was reading pointed to additional candidates for interviews. Still more were suggested by my editors and the interviewees themselves.

The interviews were only the beginning of the process. I had to do extensive background research (more than simply reading blogs) for the introduction to each blogger. This often resulted in follow-up questions and revisions.

Contact!

Initial contacts were made via e-mail. I explained the book and my mission, and invited the subject to be in the book. I didn't always get an answer the first time, even though I was careful to make it clear that I was a legitimate author looking to interview people for a new book.

Sometimes it took two or three tries to get past spam blocks or to just get someone's attention. When the first message didn't get a reply and I really wanted to talk to the person, I switched to a more interesting subject header than:

> *May I interview you for a new book?*

Instead, I used something like:

> *I need to interview a blogger of great skill and cunning.*

or:

> *So-and-so tells me you are a crafty blogger with great powers.*

Those usually pulled in replies. Some were entertaining. Like one from the editor of Valleywag (http://valleywag.com), who replied, "I've been too busy blogging to, well, talk about blogging."

Logistics

The interviews would be conducted by telephone, because the book's schedule permitted no traveling. Why didn't I just ask questions via e-mail? Because it's too easy. And it happens that the ease of a task is inversely proportional to the quality of the product produced.

To clarify, interviewing someone by e-mail is too easy for the interviewer. At the same time, writing 3,000 to 4,000 words is *not* easy, but that is what a good interview requires of the interview subject. So I think it's something of an imposition to ask an interviewee to write the equivalent of a book chapter or magazine feature—and so do some interviewees.

NOTE

Only one of the interviews in this book was conducted by e-mail, at the interviewee's request. See if you can figure out which one it is.

Plus, there's a tendency for someone replying by e-mail to keep the answers short, whereas a good interview requires lengthy and detailed responses. The same thing applies to instant messaging.

But talking is easy. As easy as…well…talking. And a live conversation produces a spontaneous interplay that generates replies that would not happen in e-mail. There's also the advantage of audio cues. Tone, speed of speech, throat-clearing, laughter, and so forth add a depth of meaning to words that e-mail can never do.

So I worked e-mail, setting up interview appointments with a few people, and scoring promises from others to set up an appointment "some time next week." Okay, I thought, these are busy people, blogging day and night. Plus, the spring trade-show season had started.

While I was scheduling the interviews, I worked out the rest of the logistics. I had on hand a Sony digital audio recorder, a stable landline digital phone set, and a Radio Shack 43-1237 phone coupler, plus backup equipment. A USB connector would squirt the recordings to my PC's hard drive. Zip, zap, pow!

So I conducted my first interview. The hour-and-a-half conversation yielded some good material, interlaced with story-swapping and jokes. The rest of the interviews were much the same way.

Cancellations and Glitches

The system was in place. I had completed three interviews. Then my interview subjects began dropping like parity bits coming into a serial port. A couple of people cancelled, pleading lack of time. Others who had promised to set something up "next week" asked to set it up the following week, or the week after that.

For some people, it's difficult to conceive of being too busy to take an hour, or even a half hour, to chat. But more than one of this book's interviewees was in exactly that situation. When you have several million readers, and maybe a bunch of writers to supervise, it's sometimes difficult to break away. But several who really couldn't spare the time rescheduled something else—for which I will be eternally grateful.

But a number of interview subjects did cancel, and there was nothing for it but to dig in and line up more interview subjects. Fortunately there are lots of interesting bloggers who are good writers and have large followings. So I dug in and lined up more interviews. The book is actually the better for it, because I obtained interviews that I wouldn't have thought about if everything had just fallen into place.

Chasing down the interviews I did get was often a chore. Coordinating schedules—whether across continental time zones or the international date line—was the least of the logistical problems. Several subjects forgot about their interview appointments and weren't available when I called. Reschedule. On at least two occasions, I forgot a telephone appointment. Reschedule.

That wasn't the only human error. There were misaddressed e-mails and wrong numbers. Not all of the interviews recorded properly. Reschedule.

Many of the bloggers were using the latest telephone equipment, which of course meant that calls were dropped in new, leading-edge ways. All but one of the dropped calls—some of which had to be resumed at a later date—were in the United States. The only international call dropped was a Skype link to New Zealand. But we were able to pick up the conversation within seconds.

Other than that, there were the usual computer glitches, like file problems with a memory stick, and the laptop computer that would not turn off and refused to respond to the keyboard. Plus some screens to be re-shot.

What with the errors and cancellations, I found myself up against the deadline almost before I realized it. At that point, I called in someone to help by transcribing the final four interviews while I was getting the other chapters into shape.

Transcription

Once I had the first interview in the can, it was time to face the inevitable: transcription.

Transcribing someone else's words is tedious for writers. We're accustomed to pulling words out of our heads without routing them through our ears first. That extra step is time-consuming and often confusing. And the physical process of transcription—listen, pause, back up, listen, type, listen, back up—can be slow and maddening.

But several people told me that the audio interviews could be quickly and *easily* turned into text files with a voice-recognition program like Dragon NaturallySpeaking. Hmm...there was that "easy" thing again. I was suspicious. I figured only government outfits like the NSA had voice-recognition software *that* good. Still dubious, though hoping for a miracle, I sprang for a copy of NaturallySpeaking, recommended far and wide as the absolute best voice-recognition software.

NaturallySpeaking is indeed an excellent program. It does everything Dragon Software promises, and does it well. But they never promised that it would recognize more than one voice at a time. It transcribes any voice that it's been trained to recognize splendidly. But it handles only one voice at a time.

Faced with the tedium of typing and having spent $200 for the best voice-recognition software available, I still hoped for a shortcut—a way to get the words from audio to text format without pounding them into the keyboard.

I asked around a bit and found it. A blogger named Dan Brodnitz suggested dictating the interviews into NaturallySpeaking as I listened to the recordings. I tried it. I donned a headset-with-microphone and played an interview with Sony's Digital Voice Editor software (included with my Sony recorder). As I listened to the interview, I echoed back the subject's responses.

It worked! Trained to my voice, NaturallySpeaking faithfully transcribed the interviews. No stopping, no backing up. If the speech was too fast for me to echo, I slowed the playback. Quite often, just a few words would jog my memory of an interview enough that I could repeat entire sentences before I heard them.

Once the interview text was in place, I cleaned up the transcription errors (10 to 15 percent of the text). Then it was time to polish the text, culling out hesitations and misstatements, getting sentences into shape, and combining related sections of the text. I was careful to preserve the meaning, vocabulary, and speech pattern of each individual.

The Book

All of the virtual chasing around, telephone and e-mail communications, research, errors, and glitches, along with the solid writing, editing, and production, time resulted in the book you now hold. Along the way there was more than a little suspense for my editors, and for me after several cancellations left me wondering whether I would have time to do the replacement interviews, let alone all the writing and editing that each chapter required.

Although it took somewhat longer than I had intended (and what project doesn't?) everything came together okay. The editors, the publisher, and I hope you find this offering both interesting and entertaining.

—MICHAEL A. BANKS
Oxford, Ohio
September, 2007

Acknowledgments

Grateful appreciation is extended to all the bloggers who took time from their busy schedules to talk about blogging from their perspectives, and, in several cases, to introduce me to their peers.

Thanks are due to Joe Wikert for coming up with the idea for this book and bringing me into the project. Special thanks to editors Maureen Spears and Katie Mohr, who suffered through delays and backups as I figured out how to put this book together and dealt with the alligators in the swamp. Thanks also to Debbie Morner, who transcribed several interviews, thus freeing up time for me to concentrate on completing other chapters.

Introduction

"People now want to spread their presence around the world."

—*Esther Dyson*

Quick: What's a blog? A bunch of text (or audio or video) postings and comments, reverse chronological order on a web page? A collection of opinions? Topical news posts? Personal meanderings? Quotes of the day? An instant magazine with feedback?

If you want a pure definition of a blog, you should probably select the one that makes the most sense, or make up your own, because just what a blog *is*, or what a blog *should be*, is often a bone of contention. It is sometimes easier to say that a certain site is a blog than to define "blog."

But having picked up this book, you should have some idea of what a blog is. If you're uncertain, have a look at these sites:

- www.autoblog.com
- www.boingboing.net
- www.engadget.com
- www.internetducttape.com
- www.parentdish.com
- www.teleread.org
- www.thelongtail.com

Each is a blog. Each presents information, and often opinion. Some carry advertising. Some have multiple posters. Most allow readers to make comments on postings, which are normally brief and displayed in reverse chronological order. Most postings are primarily text, but there are blogs with graphics and sound. More and more frequently, there are blogs with video.

Why Blog?

There are already many ways to communicate online. Why add blogging? Because blogging is dynamic and flexible, and at its core, blogging is a communications tool that encompasses all communication models: one-to-one, one-to-many, many-to-one, and many-to-many.

A blog is also a means of establishing and maintaining a presence in cyberspace—which is exactly what social networking is about.

A BLOG IS LIKE A …

Online activities are often counterparts of real, physical world events, activities, or situations. In trying to come up with a counterpart to blogging to help define it, I talked with several acquaintances about it. We came up with a variety of possibilities: preachers on street corners, political discussions in cafés, rock concerts, riots, trade shows, and so on. We finally decided that trade shows were just about the best analogy for blogging, because trade shows are about maintaining a presence as well as dialogues on specific subjects.

And, according to pundit Esther Dyson, presence is what social networking is about. As she noted during a discussion on blogging and other forms of social networking, "People now want to spread their presence around the world."

Spreading their presence around the world is exactly what bloggers are doing. Whether the blogger is an individual or a corporation, government, or other institution, the idea is the same: establish and spread a presence. And those who visit a blog, like visitors to a trade-show booth, can exchange comments with other visitors, as well as with the proprietors of the booths.

Of course, the trade-show analogy goes only so far. Trade shows are confined to specific areas of interest, and they have a certain lifespan. Blogging has no limits, and no end.

Blog Roles

Establishing a presence can be gratifying, but presence is often a means to an end. Once one has established a presence, a blog can serve as a marketing platform or a research tool, as the interview with Chris Anderson illustrates. A blog can also serve as a pulpit or promote a cause, which is true of David Rothman's TeleRead blog.

Blogs like Gizmodo and Engadget serve as specialized news and information sources. Blogs for hobbies and special interests abound—Autoblog, AuctionBytes, ParentDish, and DIY (Do It Yourself) Life, to name a few.

Some blogs are personal, like Life in the Fast Lane. A few defy categorization, Frank Warren's PostSecret among them.

Some blogs have become books. Witness *The Long Tail* and *Naked Conversations*. And books inspire blogs that not only update the books, but also serve as extensions of their subjects.

The Cottage Industry of the 21st Century

In addition to giving voice to millions and enabling individuals to spread their presence across the world, blogs—or at least writing and editing blogs—are the cottage industry of the 21st century. Thousands of people make their living as bloggers. Some sell products and services, but it is becoming more and more common for bloggers to earn a living by creating content.

Interestingly, the majority of bloggers being paid for their writing are not preoccupied with search engine optimization (SEO)—held by many to be *the* "secret" to making money online. (The biggest proponents of this seem to be those selling the "secret.")

As you will learn from the blogging heroes interviewed in this book, there's much more to it than that. One of the real "secrets" is that you have to create original, high-quality content. Combine that vital element with a little SEO and the other valuable information the bloggers in this book have to share, and you'll be well on your way to building a huge readership and making money online—if that's what you want to do.

The bottom line: making money online doesn't require the possession of some mystical "secret" or a certain level of desire. All you need is what the blogging heroes in this book have to tell you, and some optional technical knowledge that you can pick up from the "Further Reading" at the end of this book.

Get Ready to Meet Some Interesting People

The blogging heroes interviewed for this book are an interesting bunch. In these pages you'll meet a woman who literally wrote her way into a job, and a man who gives away valuable content for free. Here, too, are professional journalists using blogs to develop and showcase a new kind of journalism.

You'll encounter people who have the dream job of writing about their hobbies, and at least one person whose online writing job is truly unique. There's a man whose blog is his career, and, oddly enough, a financially successful blogger who is *removing* ads from his blog because he feels that too many ads could be a bad thing.

These bloggers come from the ranks of blue-collar workers as well as professionals. There are several who grew up with computers, and a few who were never really "into" computers until after they finished high school or college.

Each blogger reveals his or her own personal approach to success—techniques for creating good content, finding subjects to write about, keeping the right attitude, and attracting a huge readership. You'll also learn about best practices, working habits, and more.

Among the many lessons you will take away from this book, the most important may well be that blogging can change your life...and that you can change lives by blogging.

Dave Taylor
The Intuitive Life Business Blog

1

"Blogging is guerilla marketing at its finest."

—*Dave Taylor*

Dave Taylor has a long history as an online pioneer. He first logged on to the Internet in 1980, when he was an undergraduate at University of California, San Diego (UCSD). While working at Hewlett-Packard (HP) in the mid-1980s, he served as a Usenet administrator and helped develop its domain hierarchy. He also found time to write the popular Unix Elm e-mail system.

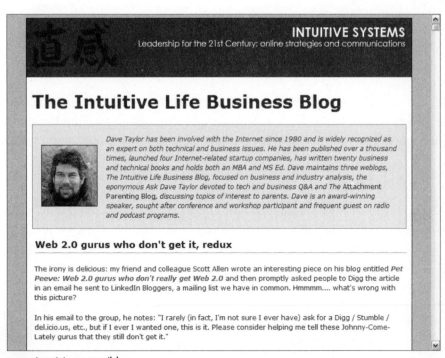

INTUITIVE SYSTEMS
Leadership for the 21st Century: online strategies and communications

The Intuitive Life Business Blog

Dave Taylor has been involved with the Internet since 1980 and is widely recognized as an expert on both technical and business issues. He has been published over a thousand times, launched four Internet-related startup companies, has written twenty business and technical books and holds both an MBA and MS Ed. Dave maintains three weblogs, The Intuitive Life Business Blog, focused on business and industry analysis, the eponymous Ask Dave Taylor devoted to tech and business Q&A and The Attachment Parenting Blog, discussing topics of interest to parents. Dave is an award-winning speaker, sought after conference and workshop participant and frequent guest on radio and podcast programs.

Web 2.0 gurus who don't get it, redux

The irony is delicious: my friend and colleague Scott Allen wrote an interesting piece on his blog entitled *Pet Peeve: Web 2.0 gurus who don't really get Web 2.0* and then promptly asked people to Digg the article in an email he sent to LinkedIn Bloggers, a mailing list we have in common. Hmmmm.... what's wrong with this picture?

In his email to the group, he notes: "I rarely (in fact, I'm not sure I ever have) ask for a Digg / Stumble / del.icio.us, etc., but if I ever I wanted one, this is it. Please consider helping me tell these Johnny-Come-Lately gurus that they still don't get it."

www.intuitive.com/blog

Taylor left HP a few years later to organize Intuitive Systems, a consulting firm that helps businesses develop Web marketing strategies. At the same time he turned to freelance writing and editing to put his technical expertise and industry knowledge to work.

In February 1994, research for a magazine article led Taylor to establish the Internet Mall™. Assigned to write a story about companies doing business on the Internet, he was surprised to find that there was no register of such operations available. So he put together his own and began publishing it as "a monthly list of commercial services available via the Internet." The text-only document started with a modest 34 entries, but it grew rapidly in size and popularity.

The Internet Mall was organized as a virtual multi-story department store, with each "floor" offering a different category of merchandise—books, music, and video on the first floor, personal items on the second, and so on. Individual retailer listings consisted of breezy descriptions, with instructions about how to connect to online stores using such arcane methods as Gopher and Telnet. Corporate underwriting helped support the list.

The endeavor was simple and effective—and *first*. (Consumer online services such as CompuServe and The Source offered online shopping, but they were not accessible via the Internet.) At a time when commercial activity on the Internet was of dubious legitimacy and frowned on by purists, the Internet Mall was radical. It has since been supplanted by search engines and mainstream advertising, but it has served as the template for Internet shopping ever since.

Taylor sold his online mall concept and trademark to TechWave, and a couple of years later he created another startup, iTrack.com—the first third-party auction search system, which has since been sold.

Just Ask Dave!

Today Taylor continues his consulting and writing activities, often combining the two in the several blogs he maintains.

Taylor is perhaps best-known for AskDaveTalyor (www.askdavetaylor.com) and The Intuitive Life Business Blog (www.intuitive.com/blog). AskDaveTalyor (his first blog, started in 2003) showcases and shares Taylor's tremendous technical expertise—and sometimes just plain common sense—as he answers questions on everything from cascading style sheets to search engine optimization, not to mention the plague of porn and spam on the Internet. The

Intuitive Life Business Blog is a center for information exchange and discussions on business blogging and real-world events that affect blogging and business strategy. Along with his wife, Linda, Taylor also maintains the Attachment Parenting Blog (www.apparenting.com).

Does blogging help Taylor's business? In addition to generating a healthy income through advertising, Taylor's blogs promote his books (he's written 20, and he currently offers a downloadable title) and boost his visibility in the technical and business communities. And high visibility, he maintains, translates into increased sales, whether you're selling a product or expertise.

Tell us why you started blogging. Was it out of curiosity or business-related?

It looked like an interesting tool to help me manage communications with readers of my books. With 20 books published, I had the same problem that many technical book authors have, which is that someone buys one of your books, and they think you're their free consultant for the rest of time. That means a lot of e-mail.

But the fundamental dilemma wasn't answering e-mails from people, which I like to do; it was that I'd get the same questions again and again. So the problem for me became how to be more efficient about this, and not have to answer the same question 10 times in a month.

The first stab I took at it was actually a web-based discussion forum, organized into subject categories and topic threads. But it didn't work real well, so the second time I tried it, I thought, "Let's just make it a blog, because this blogging thing looks like it is a very powerful tool." And that really hit some traction. The next thing I knew, I was getting more questions than ever—many from people who hadn't read my books.

It's obvious that blogging extended your interaction far beyond your original audience. Just how far has blogging taken you?

I have three different blogs that I pour attention into. There's the Attachment Parenting blog [www.apparenting.com], in which my wife and I address parenting topics. This is the most personal of my blogs. Then there's AskDaveTalyor [www.askdavetaylor.com], which now sees a million visitors a month. That one is basically technical and business Q&A. It was originally the support conduit for my books, but it has very much taken on a life of its own. I get a rather amazing daily waterfall of questions coming in. They range all over the map, from programming questions to the most rudimentary questions like, "How do I sign up for a screen name on AOL?"—and all things between.

Literally every single day, I get a question from someone saying, "I got an iPod; how do I put music into it?" I even get questions from kids asking about relationships, but I don't answer those. That's a little out of my bailiwick.

My Intuitive Life blog [`www.intuitive.com/blog/`] focuses on business and strategy. A lot of what I do is help businesses figure out how to tap into this (blogging) world. So I'm interested in things like how you take a good idea and make a real business out of it. How do you treat your customers so that they are delighted by how much you've exceeded their expectations?

I spend a significant chunk of my time consulting with companies on strategy, and hopefully, I reflect this in the blog. I'm not interested in breaking news. I'm not interested in talking about what everyone else is talking about. I'm really interested in just business questions—for example, whether it's a smart business strategy to let someone else run your server.

Some people have said that I march to the beat of a different drummer with all of that [focus on business blogging]. And that's fine with me, because I think there are important business questions that aren't asked in the blogging world, partly because as a general community, I think bloggers are somewhat reticent about earning money online.

They're not just unable to figure out how to make money. There's a large sub-community of people who think that you can't—that you *shouldn't*— earn money from your blog. In the online world, there's this sense of, "You offer the service for free and you get a lot of people who want to use it, and then you sell the company to Google, and that's how you make your money." Of course, that's not a sustainable business.

My AskDaveTalyor blog is more realistic, and a very profitable venture. It's a legitimate business, it gets a lot of traffic, and it adds value to the community. Tech support in companies like Microsoft and HP and Apple point their clients to my site to get answers. People tell me, "I was on the phone with Microsoft, and they said I should check you out."

But a whole lot of bloggers say, "Oh, that's not a blog. It's a business. It can't be a blog and a business." Or, it can't be a blog because I don't inject my own opinions. Or it can't be a blog because I'm not writing about the news that's happening at this very minute. So there's all this sort of arbitrary expectation in the sub-community, and yet at the end of the day, a blog is just a concept-management tool.

Blogging gives you certain capabilities, and there are certainly recommended practices and best practices, but there is no reason you can't use a blogging tool to create something that looks nothing like a blog.

BLOGGING GIVES YOU A VOICE ... AND MORE

A blog can help you establish a voice and identity online, can help you position yourself as the authority in your marketplace, and can give you a great avenue into learning more about what makes your customers tick.

Keeping up with three blogs—each with a different emphasis— would seem to require a lot of time. How much time do you spend blogging? Do you feel obligated to post every day?

On blogging itself I probably spend roughly 60 to 90 minutes a day. Sometimes I'll have two or three postings, maybe four or five, in a week, and other times I'll go for two or three weeks with nothing bubbling up.

> *"Instead of reacting defensively—or offensively—what you want to do is what any business needs to do when they encounter criticism. Take a deep breath, and then come at it from the perspective of 'How can I make this a plus?'"*

There are periods when I publish every day on AskDaveTaylor, but I don't *write* every day. A lot of bloggers think that [posting every day] is a huge mistake. You set expectations that you're going to write every day and then you're trapped; you have to write every single day.

For some people that works, but for other people, it's a bit of a treadmill. You end up diluting the quality of your work simply because you're writing for the sake of writing, not because you have something to say.

But one of the wonderful features of a blog is that you can schedule articles to show up in the future. So I can spend a day or two and pound out 6 or 10 or 15 articles. And often what I'll do is write two or three that are in somewhat of a series, and then I'll schedule them nonsequentially. The first will run the next Monday, the second on Thursday, and the third on the following Tuesday. And then I'll do another series, and I'll interweave them, so from the reader's perspective, I publish something on a different topic every day.

However you approach it, you have to create a lot of content. What inspires you?

It depends on the blog. On AskDaveTaylor, I have such a flow of questions that I won't run out for years. But I don't limit coverage of a topic to answering one question. I try to provide complete coverage of an area. If I have a bunch of questions on certain aspects of MySpace, for example, I'll go ahead and document other areas of MySpace so I can offer a complete set of instructional information.

With regards to the Intuitive Business blog, I read other blogs. I go to conferences. I talk to people. I have meetings with people. And I just wait for inspiration to hit.

Once you have the content in place, it's time to bring in the audience. Aside from the obvious—getting into search-engine results and e-mailing your friends—how do you attract readers to your blogs?

One big, big tip is [to] participate on other blogs. The metaphor I use is this: If I've just started college and I want to have the most successful party on campus, a really bad strategy is to just throw a party. That's because no one knows who I am. I'll end up sitting there with my house open and lots of alcohol and munchies, but no one will come. Or maybe two or three people will show up, and then leave.

The same thing happens if you set up a blog and just wait for people to come by. A few people might show up because they're your friends or you turned up in search-engine results, but mostly you'll just be waiting. So what can you do? You might try what some blog scammers do: Go to blogs, and leave comments that basically say, "Visit my site," and then hop away. Returning to the party metaphor, that's like going to other people's parties wearing a sign that says, "*I Have Really Interesting Things to Say—Come Home with Me,*" and then going home.

The correct strategy—the one that actually works—is to go to parties and engage in discussions. Whatever they're saying, you get involved in that discussion. Maybe you eventually lead into what you want to talk about, or maybe you don't, but you're interesting. You bring a bottle of wine as a thank you. You dance well. You help clean up afterwards. You're a good guest. You become popular. And because you've become popular, you can throw a party and people will show up.

Make yourself known in the blogosphere, and people will come to your party. It's a smart strategy, though not many people seem aware of it. If you look at the statistics, less than 1 percent of people who read blogs ever leave a comment. So you'll really stand out if you get engaged in other blogs.

After the party starts, so to speak, are there things to watch out for—common mistakes you see bloggers making?

Absolutely. I'll also say that what I see as a mistake, other bloggers you talk to will not see that way.

One of the mistakes that business bloggers make is that they write about what they want to sell, rather than writing about their expertise. If I sell outdoor furniture, and every single entry in my blog is about something I sell, no one's ever going to come back. But if I write about things like how you take care of lawn furniture, how you keep it nice, and how to get a bee's nest out of your umbrella, then people will come back to see what else you have to say. And they'll associate what you're selling with your interesting posts.

Another mistake business bloggers make is having a negative reaction to criticism of their product. Let's say you run a ski resort. Someone comes onto your site and posts that they had a really bad experience at your resort, you were rude, and your slope sucks.

And you just respond, right there, "Well what do *you* know? You must be some sort of amateur idiot!"

Instead of reacting defensively—or offensively—what you want to do is what any business needs to do when they encounter criticism. Take a deep breath, and then come at it from the perspective of "How can I make this a plus?"

So what do you do? You have the guy who runs the resort call this person and say, "I'm just so appalled to read about this experience you had! We would like to send you vouchers for a free weekend, including hotel. And when you're here, I'd like to go out and grab a beer with you because I want to find out exactly what happened, so we can make sure that no one ever has that experience again."

At a cost of maybe $200, you can convert a critic into your best evangelist. If they come back, and they get the wine-and-dine, red carpet treatment and feel like someone really listened, now they're going to tell 20 of their friends, "You know what? I had this bad experience, but these guys are so cool, they actually brought me up and paid for this fancy dinner, and I even got appetizers." The point is that not thinking of long-term ramifications and not being willing to accept criticism is a mistake. No business is perfect. No individual is perfect.

Yet another mistake is not allowing comments. There are some blogs out there where the blogger's attitude is, "Well, there's really no discussion around our product, so there's really no reason to allow comments."

To me, letting any random person who comes onto your site add their two cents is the magic fairy dust of this whole thing. That's what makes it so darned interesting. I don't want to read just your opinion. I want to read other people's responses to your opinion and, ideally, your retorts to them. And now it's a whole discussion that just happened to start with the person who wrote the original opinion. But it goes on, and maybe it actually goes somewhere. Or at least there are multiple opinions and multiple perspectives that are all exposed and debated, for better or worse.

Whether you're blogging for business or personally, I think it's very poor form if you don't have good grammar and good spelling. And I don't really like obscenities, although they may sometimes have their place. The problem is that they're used so often today that they have no value.

I also believe—and I might be in the minority here—that having some inherent level of respect for other people's opinions is in order.

The reason I say I might be in the minority is because there is, to me, a very alarming current in our culture toward sarcasm, hostility, and rudeness. Obviously, people get to run their blogs the way they want. But from my perspective, if I write about a particular way of doing something, and someone disagrees, I'd rather respond to "Oh, I don't agree," than to "You're an idiot!"

Just be professional. Even in your personal blog, be professional. Be mature. If someone disagrees with you, you can make them look far stupider by being calm and pleasant than by ranting or hurling insults.

You mentioned grammar and spelling as important elements for good blogging. Spelling can be fixed, but what can you say to people who aren't comfortable with their writing ability?

A blog is really cool in that regard because it gives you a publishing platform, and you can be as good or as bad as your skills let you. Also, you can vary your voice and tone over time. You can decide to try a more personal voice for a while. Or you might get the feeling that readers don't like it when you inject your opinion, and try not doing that for a while.

If you are indeed writing a couple of times a week, one hopes that over time you're getting better. As you write more, over time you find your voice and comfort level.

I'm a big fan of Peter Elbow. He wrote a great book (*Writing without Teachers*) that I read when I was an undergrad. [The message of the book] boiled down to, "If you want to learn how to write, just start writing."

DAVE'S BLOGGING TIP

If you are willing to share your experience, expertise, and insight into your own industry, you will gain readers and fans, and they will spread the word. Sharing my own insights and thoughts on business news and company offerings has significantly raised my visibility in the international business community and commensurately grown my consulting practice.

What do you find to be the most gratifying aspect of blogging?

The people who say, "You solved a problem I've had for a long time. Thank you so much." And I get that on a daily basis.

Another thing I really like is when someone says, "Thank you for having a thoughtful voice on this business instead of being just a knee-jerk person who agrees with everybody else."

And I'm careful not to have a knee-jerk reaction to things. In fact, I'll often take a contrary opinion to the majority, because I think that many people are sheep—even people who are in disguise as strong opinion leaders just echo what someone else says without really thinking through the implications. People tend to not remember the sheep of the world.

What are your plans for the future? Will you continue to expand your own personal blogosphere?

At AskDaveTaylor, I'm moving into Microsoft Windows Vista. I haven't yet covered Vista in a meaningful way, but I see that as a future trend. That's something I'm working on now.

And in terms of additional blogs, I have two that I'm sort of playing with. One will be movie reviews, and I'll invite anyone who has ability as a writer to be a co-contributor. Any money we make we'll just donate to the film preservation society. I think it would be fun to have an aggregation of good writers. I'm hoping we can get the Internet Movie Database [IMDb] to link to us automatically.

The other involves a book of mine that went out of print. I am hiring someone to turn it into a blog. It's a technical book, and 90 percent of it is probably relevant content. [That's] 600 pages just sitting there, so I might as well pour it out on the Web and let people comment on the chapters. And if they can update things, hopefully it will take on a life of its own.

What is your opinion of the blogosphere in general?

The beauty of blogging is in the eye of the beholder. There's a lot of noise and a lot of dribble out there. There are people who are just writing to see their words on the screen. And reading blogs can be like driving down the highway and looking at billboards—none really stand out, and the next day it's difficult to remember what you saw.

But you know what? That's fine! The forum for debate that blogging provides is unequaled, and blogging is the only outlet that many people have.

In the future, I think the concept of blogging as a distinct entity will blur. When you go to MySpace and send bulletins to your friends, it is not unlike blogging. And when you upload pictures from your recent vacation to Flickr, and your friends add captions, it's an awful lot like blogging. Blogging *per se* may eventually go away, but all that blogging *is* will be around for a while.

Points to Review

As a veteran of the pre-Web Internet and founder of the original Internet Mall and other important online businesses, Dave Taylor is someone to listen to. Here are some of the main points that Taylor makes in this interview that should be of special interest to bloggers:

- A blog doesn't have to look like a blog, and isn't limited to opinion. Taylor's first blog began as means of communicating with his books' readers. Today it hosts wide-ranging discussions on just about every topic imaginable.
- Can't write every day? Write when you're inspired, and write more than you need. Set up the extra material to post at later dates. From the reader's perspective, it will look as if you're posting regularly.
- Give your readers something extra. Don't stop with solutions— provide background or instructional information along with answers to questions.
- To bring readers to your blog, go to other blogs and engage in discussions. Don't just leave quickie comments so you can post your blog's URL.
- Don't write about what you're trying to sell—write about what you know. People will return to see what else you have to say, and they will take note of what you're selling.
- Accept criticism with a positive attitude.
- Don't block comments. You'll draw more readers if you show multiple viewpoints on topics.
- Cultivate good writing, and avoid obscenities.
- Think before you post. Respect others' opinions, and consider the future implications of your words.
- Blogging and business are not mutually exclusive. A business website can look like an informal blog or anything else a marketeer wants it to be.

Chris Anderson
The Long Tail

2

"Blogging is a way to make myself smarter."

—*Chris Anderson*

Chris Anderson is the editor in chief of *Wired* magazine, for which he was named Editor of the Year by *Advertising Age* magazine in 2005. Before joining *Wired* in 2001, Anderson held editorial positions in Hong Kong, London, and New York with *The Economist*; he's also held positions at *Science* and *Nature* magazines. Educated in physics, Anderson has also done research at Los Alamos National Laboratory.

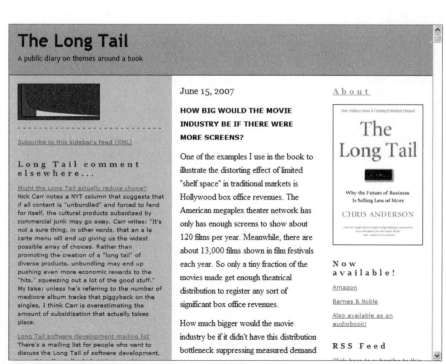

The Long Tail
A public diary on themes around a book

Subscribe to this sidebar's feed (XML)

Long Tail comment elsewhere...

Might the Long Tail actually reduce choice?
Nick Carr notes a NYT column that suggests that if all content is "unbundled" and forced to fend for itself, the cultural products subsidized by commercial junk may go away. Carr writes: "It's not a sure thing, in other words, that an a la carte menu will end up giving us the widest possible array of choices. Rather than promoting the creation of a "long tail" of diverse products, unbundling may end up pushing even more economic rewards to the "hits," squeezing out a lot of the good stuff." My take: unless he's referring to the number of mediocre album tracks that piggyback on the singles, I think Carr is overestimating the amount of subsidization that actually takes place.

Long Tail software development mailing list
There's a mailing list for people who want to discuss the Long Tail of software development,

June 15, 2007

HOW BIG WOULD THE MOVIE INDUSTRY BE IF THERE WERE MORE SCREENS?

One of the examples I use in the book to illustrate the distorting effect of limited "shelf space" in traditional markets is Hollywood box office revenues. The American megaplex theater network has only has enough screens to show about 120 films per year. Meanwhile, there are about 13,000 films shown in film festivals each year. So only a tiny fraction of the movies made get enough theatrical distribution to register any sort of significant box office revenues.

How much bigger would the movie industry be if it didn't have this distribution bottleneck suppressing measured demand

About

The
Long Tail

Why the Future of Business
Is Selling Less of More

CHRIS ANDERSON

Now available!

Amazon

Barnes & Noble

Also available as an audiobook!

RSS Feed

Early in this century, Anderson was struck with the vision that new efficiencies in manufacturing and distribution (particularly distribution via the Internet) will bring about fundamental changes in choice, creating niche markets that would not exist without the new technology. The opportunities to serve those markets promise a new world for small business—a world of trade unlimited by shelf space, price, and the other considerations that have, in the past, limited the portion of demand that can be profitably served by retailers.

The phenomenon promises long-term effects in economics, culture, and more. Anderson dubbed it "the long tail" because when graphed on a standard demand curve, the niche market of low-demand products looks like a tail hanging from the fat rump of best-selling products, or "hits."

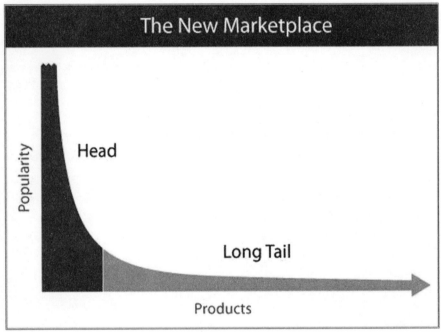

The Long Tail

Anderson began presenting this concept as a series of speeches in early 2004. On the basis of positive feedback, he turned his speeches into an article for *Wired*, which appeared in the September 2004 issue. Because the article became the most cited article *Wired* ever ran, Anderson decided to turn his speeches into a book.

Blogs Are the Long Tail of Media

By the end of the year, Anderson had closed a book deal, and his blog, The Long Tail: A Public Diary of Themes around a Book, was open for business. This was Anderson's first public blog, though not his last. The book, titled *The Long Tail: Why the Future of Business Is Selling Less of More* (Hyperion, 2006), would not be published for nearly two years. Meanwhile, the concept was out there (thanks to Anderson's speeches and the *Wired* article). To keep the Long Tail concept from being co-opted by others—and to keep interest in the book alive—Anderson turned to the Internet and blogging.

The Long Tail blog achieved far more than Anderson intended. As described in this interview, blogging helped him research and write the book, and provided a "beta test" and marketing platform for it, among other benefits.

More than a year after publication, the buzz about *The Long Tail: Why the Future of Business Is Selling Less of More* continues unabated. A *New York Times* bestseller, *The Long Tail* received the 2007 Audie Award as the best business information/educational audiobook, and the Gerald Loeb Award for Best Business Book of 2006.

Why the Long Tail? Why such a focused blog?

There are three reasons I started the blog. Not all three of them were obvious to me in the beginning, but in retrospect there are three reasons.

The main reason I started the blog was simply that there was going to be a two-year gap between the article and the book. And I just didn't want the momentum to fall off or the conversation to go on without me, nor did I want to lose ownership of the meme during that quiet period. So I really started the blog just to keep the conversation going and keep it going around me. It was really quite selfish, but meme ownership was the main reason.

In time it became clear there were two other reasons to have started the blog. The first is that the conversation I was having was basically me sharing my research and reporting—in progress—and my thinking and some of my analysis on a semi-daily basis. What happened was that the Long Tail blog established quite a large readership, which helped me with the research. They corrected my errors, suggested applications I hadn't thought of, and gave me feedback on what was working. They wrote the subtitle for the book, et cetera.

So it became kind of a distributed research project. I essentially open-sourced the book research to the readers. I gave them something for free, and they gave back much, much more to me for free. There were some people who thought that I was giving away my ideas, that it was highly inappropriate to share the details of a book before publication. But in the software business, you wouldn't release a program without beta-testing it. And in science, you don't release a paper without peer-reviewing it. So why would you release a book without doing the same? In retrospect, it seems obvious that, of course, you would write a book in public if you could, because doing so will make it a better book.

The third reason was only evident at the very end—which is that the community I built around the idea became the greatest marketing platform for the book. What I did was give an advance review copy to anybody who wanted one, anyone who had a blog and was prepared to review the book. We sent out hundreds of those, and got hundreds of reviews back in return. It was fantastic word-of-mouth marketing, which I could not have done had I started the book blog six weeks before the book's release. I had to build a community over time, because it took time for the blog to become an efficient marketing platform for the book.

And now the community is taking the idea far beyond *The Long Tail* concept, pursuing [new] concepts that weren't in the book.

Do you see the blog as a platform for other things, like your booktour.com?

Oh, yes. The blog is now my personal platform. You'll notice that at the moment I'm blogging about a little snafu we had at the company website [referring to a *Wired* advertiser's pop-up window misbehaving]. I'm using my blog to do that because that's where I communicate directly with people. I don't do it on the Wired.com site because that's not a personal platform—it's an institutional platform. Discussing the problem at the *Wired* site is really an exercise in being transparent, [which is] something I believe in. My posts are critical of certain rules in the company, and that might not work on the Wired.com site. So I believe a personal platform is transparent in a way an institutional one isn't.

I also use thelongtail.com to market my events. I use it to communicate with my audience. And it liberates me to not have to satisfy commercial interests.

So you aren't concerned with just pulling in readers?

I'm not trying to maximize my audience here. I'm trying to keep it focused on my interests. I feel that I don't have to worry about boring 90 percent of the audience—because [the audience for my blog] self-selected themselves as wanting to read this, I can be much more authentic and much more liberated to talk about what I really want to talk about, rather than trying to anticipate the needs of a scattered, diverse audience like a magazine has.

By the way, I find blogging ruins me for magazine writing. It's difficult to write for magazines right now, which is ironic given that I'm a magazine editor. It's difficult because magazines are a kind of one-size-fits-all product, and the audience is large, with differing interests. You have to write something that tries to satisfy all of [your readers] or many of them, whereas a blog is very self-selecting. If you're interested in what I have to say, fine. If you're not, that's great—go somewhere else.

The book is also self-selecting. If you're not interested in the concepts in the book, don't buy it. If you are, I'm going to go deep, and that's great. But books—and

> *"I think I do my best thinking via my blogs."*

blogs—are focused, whereas magazines are not. Obviously the magazine [*Wired*] is doing very well, so there must be something, some asset that satisfies a general audience. I'm just saying that my failing as a writer is that I don't do [magazine writing] well. I edit well, but I can't write for that platform well. So I don't write for the magazine very often.

But you are writing.

Yeah. I write a lot—more than I've ever written. You only know about one of my blogs. I have others—and I have a big audience. But when it comes to the magazine, I just edit. Different writers have different styles—it turns out that my style is better suited for books and blogging.

What are the other blogs?

One of them is group blog that I started called Geek Dad. And you can find it at geekdad.com. That is a *Wired* blog. And the other ones are geeky and narrow—not important to talk about yet. They're not meant for public consumption. They are public, and I'm not hiding them, but they are other aspects of my life that are really, really geeky—and if I have a readership of more than a hundred people, I am doing something wrong.

www.geekdad.com

You have a lot on your plate, what with editing, traveling, and all. Doesn't blogging require a significant time commitment?

You know, I don't spend that much time blogging. I feel guilty about how infrequently I post. I've got this massive backlog of draft posts for The Long Tail blog, for example, that I feel guilty about.

As you've heard from probably everyone you talk to, having a blog is this beast—a monkey on your back. It wants to be fed every day, but we all have jobs and it's hard to do. So I don't blog as much as I'd like. I try to post on one of my blogs every day. But that doesn't mean that on every single blog, I blog once a day. But I feel like I'm blogging all the time, and I also feel like I'm under-blogging.

Basically I devote an hour a day to blogging-related functions. That is, either writing posts, or editing other people's posts, composing drafts, or thinking about or pulling together research that will go into drafts. I wish it were three hours a day. I'd love to spend more time. It's a really satisfying process. I think I do my best thinking via my blogs. Because that is really what a blog is about: a blog is a scratch-pad, and a discipline to collect your thoughts, compose your thoughts, advance your thoughts, and do it in public in a way that can amplify your thoughts by not only reaching an audience, but also getting feedback on your thoughts. Blogging is a way to make myself smarter.

Blogging is incredibly satisfying. I'd love to be blogging full-time. But blogging is an avocation—I don't make a penny from it. I have to balance it with my day job. We have colleagues here at the magazine who have taken blogging sabbaticals, which is to say they've taken sabbaticals from work so they can blog more. I'd love to take a blogging sabbatical.

What is your most gratifying experience as a blogger?

The most gratifying experience is just seeing my idea, which I put out there on The Long Tail blog, resonate in communities I had no idea about. Watching the flood of e-mails about the long tail of churches, the long tail of crafting,

> *"The first rule of the blogosphere is not to generalize about the blogosphere."*

the long tail of travel, the long tail of warfare, the long tail of beer, etcetera. Who knew? Who *knew*? I had no idea!

What happens when you put an idea out there is that people receive it and then translate it to their own world. And they find resonances in their own experience that I never would have anticipated.

Looking at discussions on your blog and elsewhere, one sees many variations on the Long Tail theme—new ideas like the railroads being the long tail of the 1860s, and Wal-Mart having long-tail experiences.

Yes. All this stuff came from the readers. The book is richer, the blog is richer, and the idea is now, fundamentally, held collectively between me and my readers. That idea is richer because people mashed it up with their own experience.

Do you spend much time looking at other blogs?

I pretty much exclusively read blogs. I don't actually visit any of the blogs—I just get them in the feeds. I subscribe to about 220 feeds, almost exclusively blogs. There may be some exceptions, but I can't think of any offhand. Maybe 180 of those 220 are blogs.

Of course, what I'm reading on those blogs often consists of pointers to mainstream media, so I'm reading mainstream media via the blogs. But virtually everything I read is either blogs or micromedia sites that are essentially blogs—things like PaidContent [www.paidcontent.org], GigaOM [www.gigaom.com], or the Gawker site [www.gawker.com]. Those are what I call the micromedia sites, but they can be called blogs. They're kind of commercial blogs.

So the blogs act as a filter for mainstream media?

Yes. I use the blogs as a filter. I don't read any mainstream media directly. I don't subscribe to any newspapers. The magazines I subscribe to are not mainstream. We don't watch television. I never go to newyorktimes.com or wallstreetjournal.com by typing an address into the browser bar. I read a ton of mainstream media when the blogs point me to it. So I read a lot of stories from *The Wall Street Journal, The New York Times*, and many others, but only because somebody I trust brought them to my attention.

Do you get some feeling for the *gestalt* of the overall blogosphere from these feeds?

No. There is no one blogosphere. There is an infinite number of blogospheres. My 220 feeds are not your 220 feeds. Nobody shares my specific combination of tastes. I have no idea about what the blogosphere thinks. One of the things I've written about it is that the first rule of the blogosphere is not to generalize about the blogosphere. You can quote me on that. It is a cardinal error.

Any time someone generalizes about the blogosphere, it eliminates them intellectually, as being unwilling to have a kind of a nuanced discussion. If someone says the blogosphere is irresponsible, or the blogosphere is left-wing, or the blogosphere is right-wing, or the blogosphere hates anything—any time they say that, it means they don't understand. They don't understand a truly heterogeneous, unbounded marketplace of opinion, which is what the blogosphere is.

So, you know, I wouldn't *presume* to say anything about what the blogosphere thinks, or how it feels, or whether it *has* a *gestalt*, because my 220 feeds are a statistically insignificant sample that's randomly assembled.

Is 220 a manageable number?

It's too many. Once upon a time, I tried to keep it at a hundred. A hundred was manageable, but I kept finding great new blogs. The information they provide is all highly relevant to me, which means I can't just flip through it as quickly as I can *The New York Times*. I can glance at a couple of headlines and toss *The New York Times*, because it's not relevant, it isn't targeted to my interests. Unfortunately, these feeds are. They are all highly targeted to my interests, and I've got a lot of interests.

So I am suffering from too much information (I realize this is a somewhat clichéd complaint), and it is difficult to manage. In the same way it's taken us decades to perfect inbox management (which we still haven't gotten right), I think that what I call "bloglines management" or "feed management" is going to take us decades to get right, too.

Do you post on blogs other than your own?

No. Never.

Being editor in chief of *Wired* gave you a highly visible platform for launching thelongtail.com. Did you have a supplementary strategy for bringing in more readers?

Sure. I did the same thing everybody else does: I whored myself shamelessly. [Laughs] I'm joking. What I did was I e-mailed people.

You know there's sort of an underground economy of begging for links. We all do it: "I started a new blog. I thought you'd be interested." Or "Here's the post that mentions your post; I thought you'd be interested."

> *"Blogs are wildly imperfect, and therein lies their beauty, because they are wildly authentic."*

All bloggers do it—or all good bloggers to it. They market themselves. We teach it internally at *Wired*, with courses on self-promotion.

Bloggers shamelessly self-promote, but they do it in an appropriate way. They e-mail people they know, regarding things that really are of interest to those people, and ask for links. They're not just begging for a random link—they're actually adding value, because this link is in fact complementary to something the blogger they're e-mailing has already done.

Do you have any advice for somebody who's starting a blog?

I think the only advice I'd have is, "Have a focus." The one thing a blogster can do that mainstream media can't do is be in focus with laser precision on something—anything. It doesn't matter what—*something*. It's best that the "something" not be you.

[Pause] Actually, that's totally unfair; I take that back. Focusing on yourself is totally fine. It's not a good way to maximize your audience, but it's totally fine if that's what you want to do. But if you want to maximize your audience, it is best to focus on something else.

Maximum, by the way, doesn't mean 1 million. As I said, I've got blogs whose target audience is 100 people—the *right* 100 people.

Among your carefully selected feeds, do you see many posts that could stand improvement?

Sure! Every blogger blows it all the time. Everybody needs improvement. There are people I admire tremendously who occasionally ramble on too long, or whatever. Blogging is not perfect.

This imperfection is the difference between blogging and what I do in my day job. In my day job, we create this perfect object. It is polished to perfection. It is error-free. It is reviewed by professionals to be the best it can be. Blogging is not that at all. Blogging is a work in progress. Every post could be better, and the errors of omission are worse than the errors of commission—things that we're not blogging about, but we should.

Blogs are wildly imperfect, and therein lies their beauty, because they are wildly authentic.

Blogging is a Turing test for humanity.

Points to Review

As you can see from Chris Anderson's interview, you, too, can become part of the Long Tail phenomenon. To better serve the low-demand niche markets (or just to increase the quality of your own blog), consider these points:

- There is no one "blogosphere." There is an infinite number of blogospheres, each shaped by the tastes and experiences of individuals.

- A blog is a thinking tool, a means of collecting, composing, and amplifying your thoughts—while getting useful feedback. Ideas are enriched by the experiences of blog readers.
- A personal blog presents a better platform for communicating honestly and transparently than a company blog, where a writer is constrained by commercial considerations. However, remember that self-promotion is more effective when it includes a value-added element.
- A blog, especially one with a large community, can function as a distributed research project and become an efficient marketing platform.
- A carefully selected set of feeds can make blogs function as an information filter.
- When blogging, focus on specific interests. You don't have to appeal to an overly diverse audience. Focused blogs are self-selecting, in that they draw readers who have a legitimate interest in the blogs' subjects. Such readers are more likely to forgive errors and omissions, and will contribute more than someone just passing through.
- Every blog, and every blogger, can be improved. To maximize your blog's audience, focus with laser precision on your subject.

Gina Trapani
Lifehacker

3

"The blogosphere is filled with undiscovered gems."

—*Gina Trapani*

Gina Trapani is the founding editor of Lifehacker.com (www.lifehacker.com), a blog devoted to clever shortcuts and faster methods of completing software and personal productivity chores. Lifehacker finds and shares downloads, tips, and techniques that actually make you more efficient without costing you time. Whether it involves computing (Mac or PC), the Internet, or life and technology in general, there's always something at Lifehacker.com to make your day easier. And you don't have to be a computer whiz to benefit.

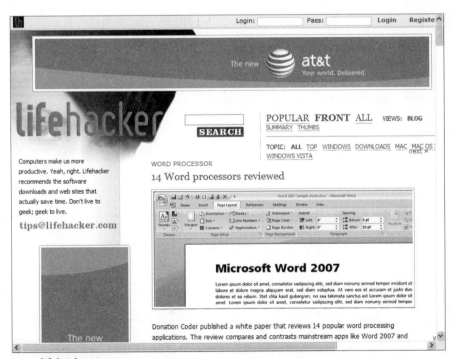

As the site's motto states, "Don't live to geek; geek to live!" Like many who work from home, Gina Trapani has a full schedule. Lifehacker.com is updated at least 20 times per day, which means she has to get an early start—a very early start. She lives on the West Coast and begins posting the day's tech news at 6:00 AM, because it's 9:00 AM on the East Coast and big news has already broken.

The news done, she catches up on e-mail and postings, and researches and writes her major posts. The day is otherwise spent communicating with her co-editors and writing less-important posts. She sometimes works during dinner and into the evening, but tries to avoid that as much as possible because "computer-free time is important." In fact, she characterizes herself as a big fan of being away from the keyboard.

As busy as it keeps her, Lifehacker.com isn't Trapani's only professional activity. She builds websites and Firefox extensions, and her writing has appeared in a several popular magazines, including *Wired*, *Time*, *Popular Science*, and *Newsweek*. Her column, "Easy Way," appears in *Women's Health* magazine every month.

Interestingly, Lifehacker was her first paid writing job. She did no magazine writing until after she began Lifehacker. Before all that, Trapani was a run-of-the-mill code monkey, working for various startups.

In 2006, Wiley published *Lifehacker: 88 Tech Tricks to Turbocharge Your Day*, by Gina Trapani. Like the website, *Lifehacker* the book empowers readers to apply technology creatively.

The idea of turning a blog into a book might seem to be a step backwards, moving content from the latest-generation technology to one that is centuries old. But as demonstrated by bloggers such as Chris Anderson and Frank Warren, it's a viable concept. As Trapani puts it, "A blog is a great way to test a concept and see if it can attract a large audience with a low barrier to entry. Whether in print or online, readers want compelling content."

Although she is pressured to turn out a lot of copy quickly, Trapani still finds time to check out her favorite blogs, among them Tricks of the Trade (www.tradetricks.org), 43 Folders (www.43folders.com), and A Whole Lotta Nothing (a.wholelottanothing.org).

Don't Live to Geek; Geek to Live!

Founded in 2005, Lifehacker received the 2006 Rave Award from *Wired* magazine and the 2007 Bloggies award for the Best Group Weblog. CNET listed

Lifehacker in their "Blog 100" in 2005. That same year, *Time* magazine listed Lifehacker as one of its "50 Coolest Web Sites," and in 2006 the blog made *Time's* list of "Sites We Can't Life Without." *PC Magazine* also listed Lifehacker in its "100 Blogs We Love" in 2007.

What attracted you to blogging?

I started blogging back in December 2001, mostly as a means of self-expression. I was always a writer—journals, stories, et cetera—and blogging allowed me to connect with an audience for that writing. I've blogged on several sites in the past six years.

> *"I think of Lifehacker as self-help for geeks"*

Today, primarily it's Lifehacker.com, a blog which is updated about 20 times a day by my three co-editors and me. Lifehacker's mission is to help people become more productive using the latest in software, web applications, and DIY [do it yourself] projects. Last year Lifehacker turned into a book [see www.lifehackerbook.com]. The site isn't there to support the book—just the opposite. The book complements the website.

I write, edit, and manage posts; moderate comments; answer reader e-mail; and work with our developers on site interfaces and vetting bug reports. I also code internal posting tools (bookmarklets and such) for myself and my editors, and I code software that we release on the website in our Lifehacker Code section [lifehacker.com/software/lifehacker-code].

Are you achieving what you set out to do with your blog?

I think of Lifehacker as self-help for geeks. Our goal is to help people, and I sure do hope we're achieving that goal! Based on reader feedback via e-mail and comments, we are.

What sort of background do you bring to blogging, as far as experience in mass communications?

I was an English major in college, with a concentration in creative writing.

Did you begin blogging with the intention of becoming famous or making money?

Not at all. I was interested in attracting a small audience for my writing, so I could get better at it. And when I started, making money at blogging wasn't a possibility. On my personal blog, which I post for my own pleasure and at my own pace, [making money is] not at all [important]. Lifehacker is a paid blogging job, so it is nice to get paid for my work there.

What else do you get from blogging?

The question is more like, what *haven't* I gotten from blogging?! The various sites I've written have gotten me jobs, a book deal, print magazine bylines, friends, professional contacts, and a tremendous sense of satisfaction and connection with readers.

What is the most difficult aspect of blogging for you?

Writing well *and* fast. After almost three years, I'm still learning how to post eight coherent and timely posts each day. Writing well is difficult when you have lots of time to think about it and self-edit! I often publish typos or wish that I'd written a tighter headline, well after the fact. I've gotten much better at it, but I still have much to learn.

> *"Lifehacker is a continuous back-and-forth conversation between the editors and our readers."*

Fortunately, my only job is to write the site. I get paid to post, so it's not an avocation. I spend the majority of my day posting to Lifehacker.com, and after almost three years of doing it, I've developed my sources and the ability to dash off several posts very quickly. Plus my three co-editors and an intern from Gawker Media [Lifehacker's parent company] who assists with moderating comments also help a whole lot!

Occasionally we get trolls in the comments, but it's pretty rare. Because our commenting system is registration-based, we're able to ban users who don't adhere to our commenting policies.

Do you ever get stuck when writing an important feature? What do you do to get unstuck?

Usually I'll step away from it and work on something else for a while. [If I get stuck], I'll abandon the idea entirely and go with something else. If a feature isn't coming easy, it's probably not the right topic to cover. The nice thing about running the blog is I can make those last-minute decisions myself, without having to check with anyone first!

Do you sometimes have to drop articles because they just don't go where you thought they would?

Yes. This happens more often that I'd like. If software turns out to be a lot less useful than I originally thought, I'll drop a post that I started on it.

What was your most gratifying experience as a blogger?

Getting a "Thank you" e-mail from a reader; [hearing] that something we suggested improved his or her life is the most gratifying experience I've had.

What inspires you, topic-wise? Do you simply browse the Web and work with what turns up? Do you set out to find material on specific subjects from time to time? How much do reader questions and input affect your choice of subject matter?

With Lifehacker, the topic at hand is software and personal productivity, so I choose posts that fit that topic. I subscribe to about 250 website feeds from various blogs, searches, and tech news outlets, which I check every day in my newsreader for post ideas. I also often use reader comments and e-mails (about 100 per day) to find story ideas and guide our coverage areas. Reader feedback counts a lot—Lifehacker is a continuous back-and-forth conversation between the editors and our readers. And there's the tips e-mail box.

> *"When I look out at the blogosphere, I don't see lots of inconsequential blogs; I see lots of possibility."*

I listen to family and friends, too.

Do you have any favorite blog tools or widgets?

I use a set of Firefox extensions and a couple of desktop applications to help me blog. In Firefox, I always have the Auto Copy, CoLT, NoSquint, and Greasemonkey extensions installed. For quick-post markup entries, I use Texter for Windows and TextExpander for Mac. I've also written a few bookmarklets and user scripts that streamline my posting process in Firefox and Movable Type. And I use TechSmith's SnagIt to do screenshots (because we write about software) and Adobe's ImageReady to edit images. To follow other blogs, I use Google Reader.

What kind of time does blogging require of you?

Because Lifehacker's my ¾-time job, I spend about six hours per weekday blogging and otherwise taking care of site matters (answering e-mail, researching stories, and communicating with readers).

You don't blog at Lifehacker on weekends?

I used to, and I may again in the future. Right now we have a weekend editor, Wendy Boswell. Once in a while if a story can't wait, or if I have a software release, I'll hop on and post something quickly on the weekends, but not very often.

Do you post on others' blogs?

Not right now, no.

What is your opinion of the blogosphere? Too many bloggers? Lots of inconsequential blogs?

Just the opposite—I think it's filled with undiscovered gems. Blogs are just coming into their own now—bloggers are learning how to write more skillfully and make their sites more relevant and useful to others. When I look out at the blogosphere, I don't see lots of inconsequential blogs; I see lots of possibility.

What sorts of mistakes do you see bloggers making?

> *"A successful blog is like a hungry pet that needs to be walked, fed, washed, cleaned up after, and loved regularly."*

Two things. First, revealing personal information without thinking about the long-term possible consequences. Second, not actively working on writing well. Most beginner bloggers aren't professional writers, and that shows—painfully, sometimes. I can appreciate the, "This is my site, I'll write how I like" stance, but if you're looking to come across well and attract an audience, it's up to you to pick up a copy of *The Elements of Style* by Strunk and White or *On Writing Well* [by William Zinsser] and apply the principles to your own work.

What's your advice for someone just starting a weblog? What do you wish you'd known when you started blogging?

I wish I'd realized what a big task maintaining a blog really is. It's not the sort of thing that you should start on a whim. A successful blog is like a hungry pet that needs to be walked, fed, washed, cleaned up after, and loved regularly.

To make it all easier, blog on a subject you really love. When you care about a subject, it shows in both depth of coverage and the quality of your writing.

Any tips on getting the word out about your blog, and driving more users to your site? To what do you credit your large readership—are there techniques you use to bring in readers?

The key to getting more visitors to your blog is to post useful, original, well-written content. If you feel you're doing that but no one is noticing, send a link to one of your great posts to blogs that write about similar things, and when they link it, you'll see traffic, and readers will subscribe to your site. If they don't link it—try, try again. A good blog is a large collection of posts, not just one essay.

I believe we swap ad space with partner sites, but I'm not sure of the details or which sites right now—it constantly changes, and the sales department handles that side of things. (Note: Lifehacker is published by Gawker Media.)

> *"Connecting with readers is my favorite part about writing the site."*

Can you gauge whether the Lifehacker book has increased traffic?

Our traffic has grown consistently before and after the book's release, so it's hard to say whether or not it's affected traffic.

Where do you see yourself in five years? Will you still be blogging?

I'm not sure where I'll be in five years, but I will most definitely be blogging, if I can help it!

Lifehacker is slowly transitioning from a traditional blog to a community site. We've amassed a huge community of registered users, and our plans are to roll out more ways for readers to connect with each other, and us, and track their favorite people and posts on the site. Connecting with readers is my favorite part about writing the site, so I can't wait.

Points to Review

Dubbed the "most organized of all the bloggers" by fellow Gawker Media blogger Brian Lam, Gina Trapani's obsession with organization and quality is a major factor in the success of the Lifehacker book and blog. If you want to emulate her success, keep these points in mind:

- Blogging is an ongoing learning process. If you're looking to come across well and attract an audience, it's up to you to improve your writing style.
- When you get stuck writing a post, step away from it for a while and work on something else.
- If a feature doesn't come along easily, it's probably not the right topic for you to cover.
- When possible, use blogging tools and widgets to streamline posting.
- Reader feedback *does* matter.
- The key to getting more visitors to your blog is to post useful, original, well-written content.

Ina Steiner
AuctionBytes

4

"The best blogs are ones where bloggers use their own voice, their own style."

—*Ina Steiner*

AuctionBytes (www.auctionbytes.com) is where serious online sellers go in search of news, tips, opinions, and products geared to support their online businesses. Founded in 1999 by Ina and David Steiner, the site hosts an ever-growing sheaf of services for sellers. The Steiners are authorities on the companies and products that are used in in online auctions and marketing; publications such as *The Wall Street Journal, The New York Times, Smart Money Magazine,* and *Fortune Small Business* frequently consult with the Steiners.

Ina Steiner, who serves as editor for the site, has written a number of articles about online auction research and technology, and her research has been published by International Data Corporation (IDC) in Framingham, Massachusetts. She holds an MBA with highest honors from Simmons School of Management.

Steiner is the technical editor of the book *eBay: Top 100 Simplified Tips & Tricks* (Wiley Publishing, 2004) and is the editor of *Snappy Auction Photos: The Online Auction Seller's Guide to Digital Photography* (AuctionBytes, 2003). Her credits also include numerous radio and podcast guest appearances, and the book *Turn eBay Data into Dollars* (McGraw-Hill, 2006). She is a member of Investigative Reporters and Editors (IRE) and the Online News Association (ONA).

Blogging, Bidders, and Sellers

In addition to providing daily news coverage of the online auction world, AuctionBytes provides its readers with the latest information on online tools and other resources, regular columns by auction experts, and online discussion forums. In 2005, Ina Steiner added blogging to AuctionBytes' collection of services.

When did you start blogging?

I started a personal blog in 2001. I've always been interested in trying new things, and that was a big motivation for creating the blog. At that time, as I recall, blogs really were diaries for the most part. Not to get too introspective, but I never kept a diary as a child because I had three older siblings who would have teased the molasses out of me if they had ever gotten their hands on such a thing, which might explain why I'm self-conscious about diary-style jottings. So I found I really wasn't interested in writing about my life and my thoughts for any and all to see.

> *"I've always been interested in trying new things, and that was a big motivation for creating the blog."*

Besides, I did so much writing for AuctionBytes, I could never motivate myself to write much on my personal blog. It lacked direction—who would read it? Did I even want anyone to read it? I had no clear-cut mission.

Then, in June 2002, I wrote a posting specifically to record my thoughts on the first eBay Live conference held in Anaheim, California. The words flowed very easily, and it was so much fun bringing the experience to people who couldn't attend in person. That gave me a necessary focus.

Still, I didn't think of the blog as a business opportunity. I created it separately from AuctionBytes, but I used my name and the tagline, "Ramblings from Ina Steiner, editor of AuctionBytes newsletter." I created an entry and rarely went back, although in the spring of 2004, I started blogging about matters relating to journalism. That too was short-lived because of time constraints and the question of whether I was really creating value for anyone.

When did you begin considering a blog connected with business? What was your motivation?

When I blogged on AuctionBytes about the 2002 eBay conference, I was highly motivated. I knew I had an audience, and I wanted them to see what I was seeing. Blogging about doing something for the first time is also much more interesting than writing about the daily grind. The excitement of the event and sharing it with others was the main source of motivation. In thinking about it, I realized the importance of having a mission, to sustain both the blog and my interest in it.

By 2005, I was pushing for a regular blog on AuctionBytes.com. In this way, I could leverage my time by writing about the industry I was already writing about. I could push out content that wasn't quite "article-worthy." Readers would have a forum to respond, *and* we could burn more page views, increasing our ad

> *"The best thing about the blog is the instant feedback from readers, and the fact that the blog can spark conversations."*

revenue through our banner advertising program. In order to do that, we developed a custom blogging program, and by 2006, I was off and running.

Did the custom blogging program give you any advantages? Several other bloggers in this book have found custom programs to be less utilitarian than they had expected.

The advantage was that if we could put it on our site, it would be integrated with our site and run out ads from the site. The bad thing is that it really doesn't take advantage of some of the Web 2.0 features.

Are you achieving what you set out to do with your blog?

Yes. It provides a place where I express my opinions about things going on in the industry and is another way to publish compelling content, in addition to our newsletters and columns. We have a good base of readers, and the blog posts are picked up by the search engines on their news channels, such as Google News. And, of course, the additional page views help AuctionBytes because we generate revenue through advertising.

What are the benefits of the AuctionBytes blog?

The best thing about the blog is the instant feedback from readers, and the fact that the blog can spark conversations. It puts more power in readers' hands, because their comments—just like the posts themselves—are read by eBay executives, analysts, and other online sellers. This is an age of user-generated content, and I like that people's opinions can be heard.

> *"I get to write things in the blog I couldn't write anyplace else."*

The blog is also a way for me to communicate in a less formal, more timely way with readers than I can with the newsletter articles. It gives me the freedom to speculate and editorialize more. Plus, there's a lot of information that comes my way that isn't very article-worthy, but is a perfect fit for the blog. I get to write things in the blog I couldn't write anyplace else. So in that sense, I hope it also serves readers.

We're also finding that the blog's RSS feeds can be a better way to deliver content than newsletters.

In what way?

The challenges to e-mail delivery are getting greater. Spam filters mean that legitimate mailings are sometimes mistaken for spam and get deleted or greatly delayed. People who subscribe to the RSS feed don't have to contend with any filters like they do to get their regular e-mail.

It sounds as if the blog is pretty much a necessary component of AuctionBytes. Does keeping up with it take a lot of time?

It definitely varies. I probably average around three hours a week, which is just as well, because maintaining the site and producing newsletters and columns takes a lot of time.

I do at least two postings a week. If there's a rush of news or something like eBay Live is happening, I'll blog more often.

Is twice a week enough to keep people coming back?

It works for us. A lot of people get the blog through RSS feeds. We use our newsletter to let people know when there are new blog postings. This lets people who don't get the RSS feeds keep up with the blog. [AuctionBytes publishes two newsletters—one goes out twice a month, the other three times a week.]

Keeping up with the site and its newsletters would seem to leave little time for reading. Do you spend much time reading other blogs?

I read tons of other blogs, and some very useful ones have sprung up in the online auction industry in the last year or so that keep me on my toes. They are excellent sources of information, too.

I also read "geek" blogs. Here are some of the folders I have set up in Bloglines [www.bloglines.com]:

- Auction Blogs
- Blog Blogs & Geek Blogs
- Ecommerce (These are actually product searches I have set up to alert me to new items.)
- IP Patents Trademark Etc.
- Media
- Miscellaneous
- News
- Travel

It is interesting to note that, in the course of reading blogs for several years, you can get a sense of who people are. This is especially true for the A-listers: who has the big egos, who's a little kooky, who brown-noses the A-listers, etcetera. And in the course of exploring, I've discovered communities of blogs. For example, there is this echo chamber of Silicon Valley bloggers who would all link to each other and post on each other's blogs. This started out as a community and a way to share information and have a dialog, but then turned into a way [for the bloggers] to promote themselves and get visibility.

Of course, all this takes time, and I try to manage my time carefully. Sadly, if someone posts too much, I tend not to read them, because I just can't keep up with all their posts. Once a day, good. Ten posts a day, forget it!

Yours is a rather specialized community. In reading all those blogs, what sorts of contrasts do you note between the AuctionBytes blog and other business blogs?

I would say the biggest difference between our blog and other business blogs is the prevalence of anonymity. Sellers are afraid to speak out using their own names. Online auctions are a very monopoly-like industry, and the sellers fear there will be retaliation if they speak out. Whether this is true or not doesn't matter—the fear is enough. I recently had a seller post a comment on my blog, and then send an e-mail an hour later saying, "Would you please remove my eBay user ID off my comment?" He was afraid eBay was stalking him.

> *"I'd rather people at least have a voice, even if it's anonymous."*

When I read the mainstream blogs, I get the impression that everyone wants to be known, to get links and increase traffic. But in our case, it's unique in the sense that sellers in this industry rely on their eBay revenue for part or all of their income.

If they want to post anonymously, I think it's great. No one really comes to my blog to cause trouble. They're usually saying, "Here's what's happening to me," and explaining a challenge they've had. I think it's different if you're making a political statement—sure that's fine, use your name. But if you're criticizing a company on which you depend for revenue, you really have to be careful. I know it's unusual, but I don't think it's a bad thing. I'd rather people at least have a voice, even if it's anonymous.

Do you post on other blogs?

No. I know that I could get more visibility by posting comments in other blogs, but it doesn't come naturally to me.

What has been your most gratifying experience with this blog?

Although eBay is a young company, it has a corporate mindset, particularly when it comes to public relations. And it's old-fashioned for a technology company. But it tries to be innovative in communicating in ways other than just making announcements. A blog called The Chatter (www.ebaychatter.com) is one conduit for this.

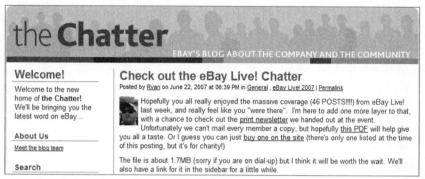

www.ebaychatter.com

eBay recently started using the blog to react to other bloggers, including me, to clarify and publish their own viewpoint. And that's a very good thing—eBay should be using its blog to talk to users beyond the press releases and announcements they make.

I feel my own blog has contributed to eBay's decision to push the envelope in its communications strategy, and that is very gratifying. The day an eBay spokesperson or executive makes a direct comment on my blog will be a banner day, but I don't expect it will happen any day soon.

What's the most difficult aspect of blogging for you?

Finding the time to do it, because I have to push out so much content for AuctionBytes' two newsletters. I also have a problem with writing short items. I take everything I write very seriously, which means I can't always just dash off a posting. So it's difficult for me to write short, quick pieces of the kind that fit the blog format so well.

> *"I feel my own blog has contributed to eBay's decision to push the envelope in its communications strategy, and that is very gratifying."*

The reason I take my writing so seriously is that people in the online auction industry look to my writing as authoritative. So I have a responsibility to be careful about the facts and how I present them. I've always been aware that news and information can have an impact on people's decisions about their lives and businesses. And because eBay is a public company, some Wall Street analysts read my blog, which is another reason I want to take time with my blog posts. Equally important is the need to always get the facts right, so as not to lose credibility with my readers.

Was there a time when you almost packed it in, quit?

Never. I have experimented with other projects and quit. The personal blog didn't work out, and my idea for video blogging [vlogging] hasn't really panned out. I find video works best for events like the eBay Live conference. But the AuctionBytes blog is definitely in for the long run.

Is there more experimentation in your future?

Right now I'm podcasting, and that is going much smoother than the video. I think it's all good content, just delivered in different ways—hopefully ways people can digest at their convenience and on their terms.

Do you have any favorite blog tools or widgets?

> *"The reason I take my writing so seriously is that people in the online auction industry look to my writing as authoritative."*

I am a huge fan of Bloglines, and I don't understand why 100 percent of online users don't use it. It's a web-hosted feed reader, and it's a lifesaver for keeping up with all the blogs and news sites I track.

By the way, I don't think people understand that feeds can also be used to track product listings on ecommerce sites. I have a search set up on some marketplaces and classifieds sites for a rare China pattern I collect, and as I'm scrolling through my Bloglines feeds, it tells me if there are any new listings. I can't say enough good things about Bloglines!

What do you see other bloggers doing "right" or doing "wrong"?

It's hard to call blogging "right" or "wrong," because it is a unique publishing platform. The best blogs are those where bloggers use their own voice and their own style.

Do you have any advice to share with other bloggers?

Be very careful! Use your blog to share your expertise and show your professionalism (which is different from being formal—something not necessarily required in a blog). That applies to online sellers, too. Think about a potential shopper and how they will feel about buying from you after reading your blog.

In my field, business bloggers mean online sellers, who already publish content—in their auction descriptions and letters to customers answering questions. Many have also written [content for] eBay Wiki and eBay Reviews & Guides on a variety of topics. They are turning to blogs not only to share information, but to help them gain visibility with potential shoppers.

One eBay seller I know writes a blog devoted to mugs, and he includes pictures, descriptions, and advice on the interesting mugs he finds. This is a great way to serve his customers by providing content that's of interest to them. In addition, he builds up a following of people who are more likely to buy from him in the future, and shoppers doing searches for those types of products will find his blog—and his listings.

Show potential shoppers that you are a professional who knows the ins and outs of the products you sell, and they will feel more comfortable shopping [on your site and buying] from you. But if you're publishing for clients or customers, avoid politics and religion—save that for your personal blog.

I've seen companies announce new blogs, but then end up abandoning them. Rather than try to build up a lot of expectation and excitement in advance, launch your blog and then start getting the word out. Don't announce it until you are sure you're going to stick with it.

If you are blogging as a company representative or authoritative figure, keep the ranting and sarcasm to a minimum. No one likes a whiner.

And yes, it's good to post on other blogs to get visibility. Just don't look needy or be obnoxious about it!

> *"Use your blog to share your expertise and show your professionalism."*

Points to Review

In making the transition from a directionless and sporadic blog to an effective, professional blog that supports a major website, Ina Steiner has become an expert on key aspects of successful blogging. Here are some of the most important lessons from Steiner:

- A specific focus or mission is necessary to sustain a blog.
- Be mindful that people in your industry may be using your blog to help make business decisions. Before you post, think about how a typical buyer will view what you have to say, and its potential effects on buying decisions.
- For online merchants, blogs can be a way to increase your visibility with potential buyers. You can use your blog to showcase your product or industry expertise so shoppers will feel comfortable buying from you.
- Wait until after your blog is established to promote it.
- RSS feeds can be more efficient in delivering content than e-mail newsletters.
- If you have a website in addition to your blog, cross-promote whenever possible. Consider ways that you can keep those who don't use RSS feeds advised on blog postings.
- Although it's impossible to read everything, keeping up with competitors' blogs is a necessary part of business blogging.

Mary Jo Foley
All about Microsoft

5

"No other company in tech space matters as much as Microsoft."

—*Mary Jo Foley*

Mary Jo Foley must be setting some kind of record for Microsoft-watching. A technical journalist since graduating from Simmons College in 1983, she first interviewed Bill Gates for a cover story in *Electronic Business* magazine a year later. It was her first Microsoft story and, at the time, she confesses she didn't know much about software or operating systems. But she quickly got herself up to speed. She joined *PCWeek* (now *eweek*) in 1991, and the mag-

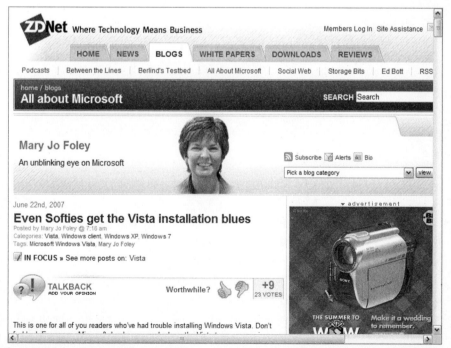

http://blogs.zdnet.com/microsoft/

azine moved her to San Francisco. Foley was asked to take over as the magazine's Microsoft reporter when the previous reporter quit. She agreed and moved to Seattle in 1993, where she has been a full-time Microsoft watcher ever since.

Over the years she has interviewed nearly all of Microsoft's top executives, and broken a number of important stories. Living in Seattle during the 1990s, Foley was invited to Microsoft's campus on a regular basis. "Given my age and casual dress, I looked like one of the employees at Microsoft, and people saw me on the campus so much that no one ever thought I wasn't an employee." Foley rode the corporate shuttle to buildings. A couple of times, employees let her in because they thought she was one of them.

But she was not always as welcome at Microsoft. After she broke a story reporting that the release version of Windows 2000 had 63,000 bugs, Foley was barred from executive interviews at the Windows 2000 launch and blacklisted by certain Microsoft groups for several years. Some Microsoft executives refused to speak to her for "ages."

Foley's Microsoft activities have inspired several legends—including one that she was seen disguised as a Microsoft cafeteria employee, flipping burgers to gather intelligence. Rumors of "Mary Jo sightings" on and off campus abounded. People broke off conversations in restaurants for fear she might be listening. Foley denies most of the stories, although she admits that she got into a couple of events "illicitly"—all in the line of journalistic duty, of course.

There have been fewer sightings since she returned to the East Coast in the late 1990s, but she tells a story that demonstrates that her reputation has not diminished: "One day, I was walking to work through Madison Square Park in midtown Manhattan. I noticed a guy was matching me step for step.

"Without missing a beat, he mumbled sideways out of his mouth: 'So, when do you think Orcas is really going to ship?'

"I did a double-take, and he said: 'Well, you're the Microsoft watcher, aren't you?' He had read my blog and recognized me from my picture. You can run, but not hide, from folks connected with Microsoft."

One of her most memorable moments covering Microsoft came during that first interview with Bill Gates, which was held in the open at the Microsoft booth at COMDEX (Computer Dealer's Exhibition). The interview was interrupted when Steve Jobs, whom Foley did not know, came up to Gates and started chatting with him. Foley waited and waited, and finally told Jobs that she was trying to do an interview and suggested that he come back later. Jobs walked off, at which point Gates asked Foley if she knew who she had just sent away. She didn't. "He's the head of Apple," Gates told her.

A more pleasant memory has to do with Windows 95. In the months leading up to its release, her job with *PCWeek* required her to write a story about "Chicago" (the code name for Windows 95) every week. It was an intensive and exhaustive series, and the day Windows 95 was released, she bravely completed a print story reporting that Microsoft had released the product to manufacturing—without receiving confirmation from Microsoft. Along with a tremendous sense of accomplishment over providing blow-by-blow coverage of the development of Windows 95, Foley was relieved that her intuition was validated.

Through rumors, legends, and blacklisting, Foley has provided more than two decades of distinctive Microsoft coverage for a variety of publications and organizations. In the late 1990s, her ZDNet column "At the Evil Empire," moved her into the vanguard of online journalism. It also earned an award from the American Society of Business Press Editors (ASBPE) for Best Original Online Column, which is just one example of the recognition her work has received.

Blogging about Microsoft

Foley's professional online activities expanded into blogging when she established Microsoft Watch (www.microsoft-watch.com) for Ziff Davis. She was almost immediately given the nickname "Microsoft Watcher."

In 2000, CNET bought ZDNet from Ziff Davis, and Foley was part of the deal. Late in 2006, she left the employ of Ziff Davis (and her affiliation with the Microsoft Watch blog, which is still published by Ziff Davis) to work as a full-time freelance writer. One of her original clients was CNET's ZDNet, and her All about Microsoft blog (http://blogs.zdnet.com/microsoft) went online not long afterwards.

Foley was trained primarily as a print journalist, but she has also done podcast and video work, including guesting on several ZDNet podcasts and producing a number of ZDNet whiteboard video podcasts. One of her first podcasts covered Windows product code names—which is appropriate given that Foley knows more about Windows code names than anyone else on the planet. (She once joked about putting "Codename Queen" on her business cards.)

Although she emphasizes that she is "just one of a flock" of Microsoft watchers, Foley has certainly earned the title, "An unblinking eye on Microsoft."

In addition to her blog, other Microsoft watchers will also want to look out for Foley's new book, *Microsoft 2.0: Life After Bill Gates* [Wiley, 2008]. The book gives insight into what will happen after Gates retires from his daily duties at the company he founded. In *Microsoft 2.0*, Foley projects where Microsoft will go next—and why—in terms of its products, people, business models, and strategies.

Today you're a full-time freelancer, but you started blogging when you were still with ZDNet. How did that happen? Were you given the blog as a job assignment?

I was not assigned to blog—I asked to blog. [From] 2001 to 2002, I saw blogging as a growing and interesting phenomenon. I asked my employer [at the time], Ziff Davis, to allow me to try setting up a blog. The result, Microsoft Watch (www.microsoft-watch.com) was the first [Ziff Davis] blog.

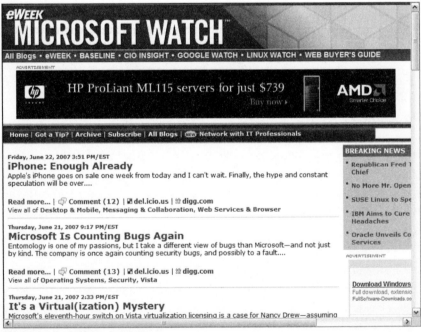

http://microsoft-watch.com

You have a degree in communications, and you've been a working print journalist for nearly 25 years. How do you contrast blogging with print journalism?

Blogging allows us writers to state our biases and admit them, thus bringing more honesty to the things we write. That's why I was really attracted to blogging. We can finally admit what's true: we all are biased.

> *"For me, blogging is the future of journalism."*

"Journalists" pretend that you can write without bias, but it's impossible. I've always been a journalist, and I was always interested in it, but I feel it's so disingenuous to pretend that we're not putting our bias in articles. Read any news article—the reporter's bias is in the article. There is no such thing as an unbiased article.

For me, blogging is the future of journalism. I say that a lot, and every time I [do], I always get people [replying], "Oh, come on, it's not. You're competing with journalism, not contributing to journalism."

I strongly disagree with that. To anyone who thinks they might want to do journalism as a career, I strongly suggest that you get into blogging. Start blogging now, and I think you can make a great career for yourself. This is especially true for technology subjects.

Do you have a mission?

My mission with All about Microsoft is to provide my readers with interesting, timely information about Microsoft—its products, people, and strategies—in order to help them do their jobs better. All Microsoft, all the time. I provide Microsoft news, interesting rumors, useful tips, and pointers to other interesting stories.

What is the return on blogging for you?

Getting personal e-mail from readers saying I helped them get a thorny issue resolved, or gave them information they needed to make a tech decision. Or just made them laugh and have a nice day. Those are the best! I love blogging. I feel like my whole career was reenergized by blogging. As a blogger, it's your reputation, your personality. You have more of a vested interest in making it interesting, fun, and a good read than you do in a news story.

> *"I post about whatever interests me. I try to find items to blog about that are a bit off the beaten path."*

And it's fun to break news. It keeps me going! I still love it after doing it for 24 years.

Monetarily, I get paid for every page view—that's the ZDNet blogs model. And, immaterially, I get a lot of pleasure from learning about technology and communicating [what I've learned].

And being self-employed—that must be a plus.

I like it. I've done it before. I did it in the mid-1980s when I was going to graduate school. It's a tough way to go, but it's a fun way to go.

I'm also free to say what I want, without having to be concerned over commercial issues. I don't really feel a difference as a freelancer, though. No one at Ziff Davis [which publishes Microsoft Watch] ever told me what I could or couldn't write. Ditto here at CNET's ZDNet (publishers of All about Microsoft).

Do your postings reflect your personal interests, or are your topic selections driven by news or sources?

I post about whatever interests me. I try to find items to blog about that are a bit off the beaten path. I don't try to do the same stories about Microsoft you can read anywhere. I try to bring a new perspective or a new "scoopy" piece of information to my readers every day.

I'd say about ⅓ to ½ of my posts are comments on things I find around the Web. The rest are things I unearth myself.

Some of the unearthing must involve confidential sources.

I have a constantly growing list of sources that includes Microsoft employees, Microsoft partners, Microsoft customers, Microsoft competitors, and others who are interested in what I write. Some of my sources are people I do not know, who send me tips via e-mail. I confirm every tip three ways before running with it—so even when I don't know the tipster's identity, I make sure the tips are real. Confirming a tip with three independent sources was a journalistic rule hammered into me at *PCWeek*.

Does the fact that you're blogging, as opposed to writing for a magazine, have any effect on your sources?

I'd actually say I've gotten more tips and sources since blogging than when I just did print. The exposure and range of potential contacts are so much greater.

Having been blacklisted, do you feel that some people at Microsoft may go out of their way to keep information from you?

Yes. But they are just doing their jobs. They are trying to maintain secrecy for competitive reasons. My job is to expose information as soon as I can [in order to] help customers, partners, and competitors make better decisions.

Do you ever feel overwhelmed by that—by the fact that your blog influences decisions in many businesses, large and small?

No. I doubt seriously that any company of any size would base their buying decisions on anything I said. [She smiles.]

As I often remind folks with whom I'm conversing, I am a journalist, not a trained technologist. I am not a programmer. I have never taken a computer science or engineering class. I see my role as helping to make public, in a fairly understandable way, information that hopefully will help my readers make better tech decisions. But I firmly believe I am just one of a number of sources of information they'd seek out. So that keeps me from taking myself *too* seriously.

> *"I confirm every tip three ways before running with it—so even when I don't know the tipster's identity, I make sure the tips are real."*

What's the most difficult aspect of blogging for you? Do you ever get stuck for something to write?

The hardest part about blogging is that it takes over your life. The more I do it, the more I want to do it. It's not a 40-hour-a-week job. It's more like 24/7. It will eat you alive if you let it!

I do take vacations and vacation days. What I do is probably what everyone does. I save up some posts and have WordPress launch [them] at a set time while I'm gone. And I post a couple of items wherever I am on the road and/or wake up early. But I try to make sure that I spend time offline every day, and don't get too crazy about not [getting] every or any story.

Everyone's at a loss for something to write, sometimes. When I can't think of something to post about, I go read my RSS feeds. There's always some food for thought somewhere out there that gets me riled enough to do a post.

And some posts I come up with are "evergreens." Not everything is spurred by news. Sometimes I get insights that I can save for a rainy day.

Do your readers ever make it tough on you? Do you sometimes get tired of blogging?

Being attacked for something—accurate or inaccurate—that you write is tough. It's tougher when you're wrong, obviously.

But I've built up a progressively thick skin over the years. So even the overzealous Mac zealots and Linux fanboys haven't made me think about throwing in the towel. It is tough to be called a "Microsoft shill"—something dedicated readers know I'm not, since I'm seldom on Microsoft's list of "favorite people." But, again, none of this has made me think about quitting.

Do I get tired of blogging? No. I find it rewarding—and humbling—that people read me daily. That keeps me going.

All about Microsoft must involve a tremendous time commitment.

I blog just about every day. I spend at least four hours a day reading, researching, and writing blog posts. I subscribe to a lot of RSS feeds. I subscribe to all the Microsoft RSS feeds, all the MSDN and all the Technet blog feeds they have—which is like 4,000 bloggers. And then I [also] have other Microsoft-related bloggers in my RSS feeds.

> *"My biggest criticism of the blogosphere is that so many posters and commenters opt to be anonymous."*

I'm getting really good at just skipping through them really fast, based on either the headings or the first paragraph. If I don't like the first paragraph, it's, "Oh, no—I don't like that one."

That doesn't leave much time for comment elsewhere. Or do you comment on others' blogs?

My contract with ZDNet specifies I can only blog for them. I can write about anything I want, including what I blog about on ZDNet, for anybody. They don't care who I write it for, but I can't do posts or guest blogging for any other site.

Because part of your income is tied directly to the number of visitors to your site, do you take an active role in attracting readers?

ZDNet does a good job of promoting me, but I do radio, TV, and speaking appearances to try to reach folks who might not know about my blog. I also guest on ZDNet podcasts and do a regular print column in *Redmond* magazine [www.redmondmag.com] every month. That also brings in readers who might not have found me via online channels.

What do you see when you look at the blogosphere? Are there too many bloggers, some who shouldn't bother?

I don't think there are too many bloggers. There's someone for everyone out there—and that's good. Who says the "A-list"—or "B-" or "C-lists"— are the only ones who should or do matter?

My biggest criticism of the blogosphere is that so many posters and commenters opt to be anonymous. Hey—I'm not anonymous. Stand up and be counted for who you are! It makes blog-inspired discussions far more interesting.

I think many people are afraid [of posting with their real names]. They either work for a company that doesn't approve of them posting or weighing in, or [they] want

> *"Be yourself. Don't try to imitate someone else's style or voice."*

to pretend to be impartial when they aren't. Some also just want license to say things anonymously that they'd never dare say in person or via e-mail. I've noticed when I e-mail some of the anonymous posters ([when] I can find a working e-mail address for them), they are relieved to be chatting and come around to revealing their true identities.

Do you have any advice you'd like to share with already-established or would-be bloggers?

Be yourself. Don't try to imitate someone else's style or voice.

Admit when you've made a mistake. It'll make your readers like you more.

Don't be rude—when blogging or commenting on blogs. I try to answer even the rudest, snarkiest commenters civilly. Remember the adage: You can attract more bees with honey than vinegar. And [you] can get more people to consider your products with compliments than insults.

Don't be ageist, sexist, or caught up by credentials. Some of the best bloggers out there are *not* journalists. Many are teenagers. (I am not. I am 45 and not ashamed of that.) To me, age, gender, and college degrees are irrelevant. When I started covering technology, there weren't very many women journalists doing technology coverage, and I think I had to kind of prove myself. Once I proved myself, there wasn't any discrimination because people realized I could do the job.

Don't steal—link! This seems obvious to me. But I see so many of my posts rewritten with no links that I guess it's not obvious to others. Link love is reciprocal; if you provide it liberally, it comes back to you. If you don't, you'll turn into your own walled garden.

Points to Review

Mary Jo Foley's training and experience as a print journalist helped make her one of the premier technical journalists, and continue to serve her as a professional blogger. There is much one can learn from her experiences. Here are some of the highlights that will interest bloggers of all types:

- Blogging is unique in that it offers a platform where one is free to admit biases, rather than trying to hide them as most conventional journalists do. In this sense, it promotes complete honesty.
- As a blogger, you have more of a vested interest in making your posts interesting and fun than a journalist writing a news story.
- Coming up with something to write about every day can be difficult. Store up posts that aren't news-driven, for the times when you don't have anything new to say.
- It is important to take time away from blogging; otherwise, you'll limit your perspective.

- Look for opportunities to promote yourself and your blog, and don't ignore cross-media promotion. When possible, create promotional opportunities.
- Unless you have a good reason, don't hide your identity in blogs. You're more likely to receive a better reception as yourself.
- Instead of imitating other bloggers, be yourself. If you're tempted to steal someone's post, link to it instead.
- If you make a mistake, admit it, accept it, and move on.
- Be polite. Avoid ageism and sexism in posts. You'll get more people to consider your product or viewpoint with compliments than insults.
- Credentials aren't necessarily an indicator of quality in blogging.

David Rothman
TeleRead

6

"Try to reward readers for the time spent visiting your blog."

—David Rothman

David H. Rothman might be thought of as a televangelist, in the sense that he has a cause and promotes it through electronic media. And he is as dedicated to his cause as any fire-and-brimstone preacher ever was. But don't worry: you won't find him pushing religion or calling for offerings. Rothman promotes e-books, e-book standards, and digital libraries. His medium is the Internet, and his podium is the TeleRead blog (www.teleread.org/blog), a nonprofit operation

www.teleread.org

that accepts neither donations nor advertising. It has been online in one form or another since 1993, when it began on CompuServe.

What exactly is TeleRead? As the site itself explains, it is a plan and group that supports putting e-books in American homes through a well-stocked national digital library system and small, low-cost e-book readers based on a standard (yet to be determined) that is accepted and used by publishers—print and electronic—everywhere.

TeleRead's purpose is not to establish libraries or dispense e-books. Instead, it serves as a clearinghouse for ideas, discussions, and proposals involving e-books, e-book media standards, and digital rights management (DRM). Of course, the site's activities can always change to take advantage of the site's mission.

At times it is a struggle to keep the TeleRead blog (which is often referred to as the TeleBlog) in operation. As noted, TeleRead doesn't accept donations and has no income, not even for advertising. Rothman has wrestled with the question of registering as a nonprofit corporation, concerned that he would have to give up complete freedom of expression in exchange for a tax break. (In connection with this, he heartily recommends the Sinclair Lewis novel *Gideon Planish*, which in part dissects the world of charitable foundations.)

And Rothman does at least 85 percent of the posting and management, with volunteers filling out the rest. So the driving and supporting forces behind TeleRead are truly in Rothman's dedication to the cause.

In addition to TeleRead, Rothman works on several complementary projects, including LibraryCity (www.librarycity.org). This is a project that will put thousands of e-books and other electronic resources online to make them available to librarians, learners, teachers, and readers in general. As the site notes, "Honoring the Carnegie tradition, we intend to reduce the correlation between personal income and access to the best books and other items for self-improvement."

The E-book Cause

In an online world where blogs that aren't personal hobbies or supported by organizations are focused on generating money or fame, the TeleRead blog is a rare example of pure dedication. Read on to see why.

Did you start blogging as an extension of promoting your cause?

Yes. I started TeleRead.org to promote the cause of well-stocked national digital libraries and related matters, especially e-books. The e-book–focused blog happened because no one else was covering the issues—technical, legal, you name it—in the depth and manner that I wanted.

I'm also interested in stimulating people to provide answers to problems, in a collective process.

Are you achieving what you set out to do with the TeleBlog?

TeleBlog is doing its share, and it is achieving visibility. It helps that we're included in many blogrolls, including *The Wired Campus* blog of *The Chronicle of Higher Education.*

TeleBlog has been a leader in the area of e-book standards, [which are] very important to the future usability of e-books. E-books aren't going to really become as popular as, say, CDs or MP3s until there is a standard. And I'm talking about one the big publishers are comfortable with, as opposed to simply distributing e-books in ASCII or HTML. That's why John Noring and I started OpenReader [www.openreader.org]. I doubt OpenReader will end up being the final standard, but it has influenced the thinking of the International Digital Publishing Forum [www.idpf.org], and they have taken e-book standards a lot more seriously as a result of OpenReader, which arose from TeleBlog.

Our traffic is pretty good for a specialized site. It's hard to pin down the number of readers because many read us on RSS. The number of unique visitors per day is typically in the region of a thousand.

> *"I learn from interaction with my readers."*

But there are times when the accesses are well above one thousand.

We are interested in sponsors, but they have to be people who won't try to influence the content of the site in ways that could be very harmful to our credibility.

Again, though, please understand I didn't start TeleRead to make money. The talk about donations or other support is simply a matter of sustainability. We have avoided appeals for small donations except for a quick experiment with an Amazon tip jar.

How much time do you think you spend on the blog?

It can vary all over the place. Sometimes it'll be just a few hours a day. Sometimes I'll just bang out something and focus on a book or whatever else I might be up to.

But some days—and this is where I need badly to find the right business model—sometimes it can take up most of the day, or a working day and then some.

As I've implied, for now the blog is financially a disaster. But the operative words are "for now." I'm convinced that something good will happen. If nothing else, possibly the LibraryCity project will work out, and that can be a source of income for me and for others.

What is your source of inspiration for postings? Do you read many other blogs?

Basically I combine news items with my years of writing about e-books, and come up with connections that might elude other people. I get some great ideas from readers, but basically I do a lot of surfing and a lot of RSS-ing.

As for other blogs, I look at them directly and I follow them through RSS feeds. I have hundreds in my reader. I'm not claiming to read every weekly item from the hundreds of blogs I follow, but I'll read RSS on my desktop, I'll read it on my tablet, I'll read RSS even on my Palm TX PDA.

My ambition is to be in a position where I'm reading fewer rather than more feeds. I'd much rather be reading books than RSS feeds. This is the way in which the blog is a time sink, in that you can't do a good job without keeping up with the rest of the world, and that takes time. But the mainstream people don't care sufficiently about e-book–format standards and other important topics. And more than a few are clueless on topics such as draconian DRM. So I work to bring information to the public.

Do you have time to do much posting on other blogs?

I do occasional posts, and every now and then I attempt to get slashdotted, but I generally stay within the confines of the TeleBlog, because I feel that I have so much to cover for the blog that I just can't take time out to be all over the net.

I know it sounds hypocritical, but because the blog has become such a centralized hub for the e-book world (it's not the only one out there, but it's one of the major sites), people are posting not only in their home blog, but also coming to us with some real gems. I love it when they share. And they in turn get greater exposure in most cases. I figure that by tending my own little garden, I can better fertilize the ground for other people.

What do you do to bring in new readers?

I'm not doing anything special to attract readers, other than trying to provide a quality site and blog. Normally, readers and the media just find me. This is a concern for me. I'm very frustrated that I can't clone myself, so that one David can do the blog and the other promote it.

I have been fortunate to have gotten media attention over the years. I get quoted in publications like *Newsday*, and I've been mentioned on the National Public Radio (NPR) website. In the past, TeleRead has been included in *The New York Times* site list, and *The Washington Post* has linked to TeleRead.

Ironically I'm often outdrawing http://libraryjournal.com, according to http://alexa.com, although neither of us would be in the big leagues.

Do you have any favorite blog tools or widgets you use with TeleBlog?

WordPress provides much of the functionality we need. Its disadvantages are many, but it works. I use a wide variety of plug-ins. A recent addition was MyBlogLog, a reader community tool that displays photos of its members. It is helping us reel in visitors. Various other additions provide pictures in postings and the display of recent comment excerpts in the blog's margin. We are currently looking for a new translation service.

> *"I see some blogs that are nothing more than disguised outlets for news releases, and this is unfortunate, as those blogs could be offering fresh information and raising questions."*

That last is really useful, because 40 to 50 percent of our traffic is from overseas—Eastern Europe, in particular. I think people in other countries see e-books as a way to drive down the cost of reading.

What is the most difficult part of blogging for you?

My main problem is time. And I would like to see more participation in the blog by readers. We're not doing too badly, but we could do better.

But the biggest frustration is the lack of a decent business model. If I charged for membership, then people would just gravitate to free sources of e-book news and views. Advertising? It's a possibility, but keep in mind that I've tried hard to keep TeleRead a noncommercial site.

Another frustration is not having enough volunteers to help with the writing and other tasks. I'm very thankful to Robert Nagle for pitching in with hosting and technical services. Still, I do maybe 85 percent of the posts myself.

And yes, I think about quitting from time to time. And yes, it's possible that I might take some of the things I'm doing with the blog and use the same skills in a more commercial way. But when I get discouraged, people come to me with things to post and that prods me on. We get some great ideas from people who are reading the blog, and it actually can be very interesting to have thousands of different editors looking at posts.

Do you consider bloggers journalists?

I think it's going to vary according to the blog. Some blogs just pass along news releases, but others really are interested in informing the reader, so I'd like to think that TeleBlog is practicing journalism, though it's not traditional journalism in the sense that the coverage is influenced by the cause.

What was your most gratifying experience as a blogger?

Helping David Faucheux get his blog into TeleRead. David is a blind librarian who holds a Master of Library and Information Science degree and has written both fiction and nonfiction reviews for *Library Journal*. He used his blog, Blind Chance [`www.teleread.org/blind`], to build an online portfolio. When Audioblogger disappeared without explanation, I helped him move Blind Chance to TeleRead. I later convinced Audioblogger's new corporate owners to restore the audio on company servers.

Blind Chance has been on TeleRead since May 2004, and provides both audio and text versions of David's postings.

Your blog isn't for money or notoriety, but you put a lot of time and energy into it. Is there any benefit that you, personally, derive from the blog?

Well, certainly I get my share of fame within the e-book world. Just about everyone who's anyone in the industry knows of me, so it has been good in terms of being famous and infamous and whatever. But the main benefit is that my activities promote the cause.

I learn from interaction with my readers. They tell me when I'm right and when I'm wrong, and this is so much better than the usual journalistic situations, where readers don't feel as free to comment. My quest for dialogue is also one reason why I'm so keen on interactive e-books. The blog gives me a far, far better understanding of interactivity than books and academic studies could.

What do you think of the blogging world at large?

I see bloggers as being able to assume a unique role in the scheme of things. Some blogs try to provide news, to function just like a newspaper, though usually specialized. But I see a different potential for bloggers, a role in which bloggers raise questions. But a blogger typically doesn't have the time or resources to get the final answers to those questions. This is where traditional journalism comes in, to answer those questions.

Yes, it's true that bloggers have "answers" in terms of their opinions, but in terms of answers on specific issues, there ought to be a synergy between the mainstream media and the blog world.

> *"I'm not just interested in providing answers. I am interested in stimulating people to provide answers themselves."*

Not a lot of bloggers appreciate how much energy is involved in newsgathering for the mainstream media. It's true that you can get a lot of information from documents. I did reporting, for example, under a grant years ago from the Fund for Investigative Journalism, and a lot of my work involved interpretation of documents. But that is not all that's involved in gathering news. A lot of what the media does involves interaction either over the phone or in person with newsmakers. And because most bloggers blog in their off hours, they're not going to have the same interaction with newsmakers that members of the mainstream media have.

On the other hand, the members of the mainstream media are so busy gathering news that they may lack time for reflection, and they may be so interested in immediate details that they fail to connect the dots.

But if a synergism is established, the media will notice the questions raised by bloggers, and some good hard news stories will result.

So I'm not just interested in providing answers. I am interested in stimulating people to provide answers themselves, in a collective process, though I'd like to think that the TeleBlog is practicing journalism. It's just not traditional journalism in the sense that the coverage is influenced by the cause.

I see some blogs that are nothing more than disguised outlets for news releases, and this is unfortunate, as those blogs could be offering fresh information and raising questions.

I also have to say that, as a group, the major e-book and publishing-related blogs, and others associated with publishing and writing, tend to be better than blogs as a whole. This is true not just in the writing, which is to be expected, but in the overall organization and quality.

And there is the integrity issue. If I find adverse information about e-books, I'm going to put it in the blog. In fact I *want* to put it in the blog, so people can think about answers—whereas a lot of people who might have a cause to advocate will let that limit the kind of coverage they do.

Do you have any specific advice for other bloggers—to do a better job, to attract readers, whatever the positives may be?

My biggest advice is to work to get people information that is relevant to them. Don't just come up with arguments; provide information along the way. It's a way to reward people for the time they spend visiting your blog. A newsy approach is always better than a static, pamphleteering one.

Points to Review

David Rothman's dedication is sincere, as evidenced by the energy and time he puts into TeleRead and his other projects. It also shows in the depth and quality of TeleBlog's posts and comments. The success of TeleBlog is largely due to that dedication, along with these considerations:

- Combining news with one's personal background and perspective can make for more interesting blog posts.
- An important role of bloggers is to raise questions and encourage others to provide answers in a group setting.
- Give readers something extra in the way of information as a reward for visiting your blog.

Frank Warren
PostSecret

7

"Don't start blogging for money; start blogging because of your passion."

—Frank Warren

Nearly everyone has heard the story of Frank Warren's community art project, PostSecret. How, in late 2004, he started handing out stamped postcards with his address on them. The cards were blank, and as he gave them to random strangers at Metro stops and elsewhere around Washington, D.C., he invited them to anonymously send him a secret—any secret. He further

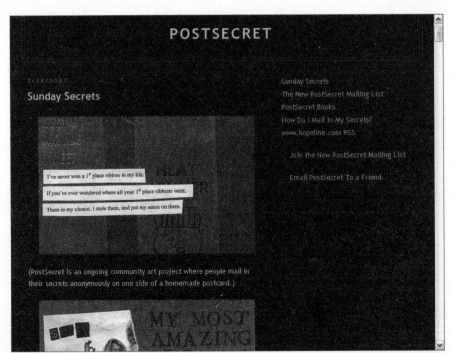

http://postsecret.blogspot.com

explained that the cards would be part of a community art project, and secret submitters were encouraged to decorate the cards however they wished.

The project culminated in a display at an art gallery in Washington, D.C. The display was gone after four weeks, but the postcards kept coming. Hundreds every week.

What to do with them? Inspired by a blog called FOUND (www.foundmagazine.com), which displays images of small pieces of lives that are literally found on the streets of the world (shopping lists, personal notes, parking tickets, and so on), Warren decided that he would place the postcard secrets on the Web in a blog.

By this time, he had thousands of postcards, and there was no way he could post all of them. Not without overwhelming visitors and discouraging them from coming back or telling their friends.

But a limited exhibit could be comprehended and provide something people could take with them. Handled properly, it would leave visitors wanting more and certain to return. So Warren came up with the idea of a 20-postcard exhibit that changes every week.

Thus began PostSecret (http://postsecret.blogspot.com). Every Saturday night, Warren chooses 20 postcards in a painstaking process. Those 20 secrets are culled from a thousand or more, a typical week's haul. On Sunday, he loads the new postcards onto the blog's page, replacing the preceding week's set.

The secrets that Warren receives cover just about the total range of the human experience. Most are works of art in miniature—many rough, some collages. A few are photographs. "I quit karate because of a panic attack," one person confesses. We assume the writer is a woman because the words are written across a photo of a woman in a karate gi, her face obscured. Another contributor assures the world, "I no longer look out for high places to hang myself from when I walk down the street." An image of a Norman Rockwell painting is labeled, "My prom date was gay. I pretended not to know." Mysteriously, an early photo of the Beatles is captioned, "I sometimes still wish I had had an abortion." Pick a card, any card: It could be heartbreaking, terrifying, disgusting, inspirational, or hilarious. Or it might be lustful or incomprehensible. Each one tells a story—often, more than one.

Although it is made up of secrets, Warren's blog is anything but secret. He has been interviewed about it by *The Washington Post*, *The New York Times*, the *San Francisco Chronicle*, and most of the rest of North America's major newspapers. Scotland's *Daily Record*, *The Times* in London, the *Asahi Shimbun* in Japan, and other European and Asian newspapers have also noted PostSecret with

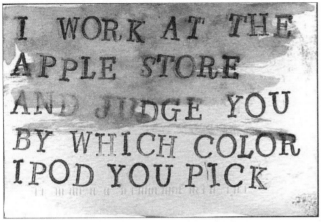

iPod color matters

Karate anxiety

Fortune-cookie bliss

Accountant confessions

interest. And Warren has been a guest in such radio and television venues as National Public Radio (NPR), *20/20*, CNN, Fox News, and MSNBC. Magazines love his secrets, too, as stories in *Time*, *Newsweek*, *Cosmopolitan*, *Marie Claire*, and others indicate.

With this kind of publicity, you might expect PostSecret to have a lot of visitors. And it does—the blog registered 100 million hits in less than two years. It's the kind of traffic that attracts ad agencies, but Warren is quick to point out that PostSecret is "not a commercial site, not a business." He has turned down more than one advertising deal, citing that advertising is not in tune with the nature of the blog's community and that is counter to the respect with which he handles the secrets entrusted to him.

Even though Warren eschews advertising, there is some real-world return for his efforts. He accepts invitations to speak at college campuses, bookstores, and museums.

There have been four PostSecret books, each a collection of hundreds of secrets that didn't appear on the PostSecret blog. Cards that appear in books and presentations are selected at the same time as cards put on the website. Decisions as to which cards go where are based on special criteria for each medium. Warren's newest book is *A Lifetime of Secrets* (William Morrow, October 2007). This volume contains previously unpublished secrets from people as young as eight and as old as 80. (In case you're wondering, full-size images of the actual postcards received grace each page.)

Warren has also received quite a few honors. The blog was one of *Time's* "50 Coolest Websites" in both 2005 and 2006. In 2006 the site won six Bloggy Awards, and was recognized as Weblog of the Year in 2007. It made *Advertising Age's* list of most popular blogs. Forbes.com included Warren on The Web Celeb 25 list of the biggest, brightest, and most influential people on the Internet. According to Forbes.com, "These are the people who are creating the digital world from the bottom up."

An Accidental Artist

"I think of blogs in the highest sense as a virtual community that you can grow and nurture," Warren says. "I think they're creating the opportunities for new kinds of conversations—conversations that can offer healing, that can offer a greater spiritual sense for us, that can offer wisdom or learning. I really feel as though these new modes of communication, and these new kinds of conversations, can uncover hidden elements of our common humanity—or perhaps, truth, humor, or art in places where we don't normally look for those things. And I find that very exciting." The following interview certainly reveals Warren's own secrets—his thoughts and experiences of running this unique blog.

PostSecret started as a physical display, a community art exhibit. Why put it into a blog?

I like to show the immediacy of secrets. When I put secrets on the blog, they are *living* secrets. When you visit the blog and read a secret, you know that somebody is carrying that burden or dealing with that issue in real time, at that moment. I think that shares the secrets in a special way that's medium-dependent.

Another thing PostSecret and the web environment provide is the opportunity for me to explore something more in my life. I feel like I am finding a greater sense of purpose or meaning in being able to help facilitate this community. That's why, when I talk to people about blogging, I talk about how it's about passion, about finding something you want to share with other people, and maybe just [getting] more familiar with yourself.

And I like the way that PostSecret connects these two very dissimilar communications technologies. The postcard, which is so old and antiquated, is connected to the blog, the most technically advanced mass communication technique we have right now. I like the way this blog marries the old communications technology with the new one.

But I really think of PostSecret not as a blog or a book, but as a collection of secrets that I share with people in different ways. I think of the blog as a display of living secrets, and I think of the books almost as an archive. I think of each book as telling a story about us, through our secrets. When I talk about the project at college campuses, bookstores, or museums, I really love being able to share these stories. I think they're very inspirational stories—some are funny, some are haunting, some are inspirational, but there are so many moving stories and vignettes behind these secrets.

An interesting element I try to introduce at such programs is projecting huge images of these postcards on a screen, a building, or what have you. It's utterly fascinating because there's a sort of dialogue between the micro and the macro size.

When you first started the PostSecret blog, did you do things to boost the number of visitors to the site, like posting on other blogs or search-engine optimization?

I did very little of that, and certainly spent no money on any of it.

I think the way I structured the blog was more critical [than publicity efforts] in affecting how the community has grown. There is a kind of strict minimalist style to PostSecret. It's not cluttered, and there are no ads—just those two factors alone make it look different from other blogs. They make it look more pure, in a sense. And so it's easy to navigate, because it's almost pure content. It's simple, and it compels people to return.

I recently read a magazine article about the most popular blogs on the Web. It said most of them have two things in common: either they've been around forever, or they have connections to huge numbers of popular websites that funnel in traffic through links, or blogrolls.

Interestingly, PostSecret has neither of those elements. It's a relatively recent blog, and I connect to no other blogs. Its only links are to a suicide-prevention hotline, and to information about PostSecret books or signings.

So, most of the early traffic was generated by word-of-mouth?

> *"For me, blogging is about passion. It's about finding something you want to share with other people, and maybe just getting more familiar with yourself."*

Yes. Even before PostSecret went on the Web, people found out about the address and the postcards and secrets, and it just spread, kind of like a joke spreads. Then it went to the Web. So it was almost viral before it got on the Web.

The whole concept was self-reinforcing in a lot of different ways, especially with young people, Web-savvy people. It is amazing, the kind of currency PostSecret has with young people.

You've received some enviable media coverage, too.

Newspapers, magazines, television, and radio have increased awareness. There were some important websites that talked about PostSecret favorably, and that helped. And there was an MTV music video called "Dirty Little Secret," by The All-American Rejects, which used PostSecret postcards. [Note: Warren's fee for the use of the postcards was a $2,000 dona-tion to the National Hopeline Network.]

What inspired PostSecret's simple design?

It turned out that there is no way I could physically put all the postcards on the blog. I have well over 100,000 of them now. If I updated the blog every day and left the postcards on day after day after day, there would eventually be tens of thousands of postcards on the blog, and I think it would almost overwhelm people. There would be so many that people would get sick [of them] and not want to come back [to the blog].

So I came up with the idea of dis-playing selected postcards on a schedule. The way it's structured is almost like your favorite television show, or like church services. It's a

> *"It turned out to be a good idea to just let the content rule."*

once-a-week event. And you have a mental bookmark that reminds you on Sunday that you might want to see the new postcards.

When I started the website, I used to add my own commentary, telling little backstories behind the secrets. But then I realized that the postcards and the voices speaking through them were really what made this site special, powerful, and poignant. So I've tried to stay as much out of the blog as pos-sible. It turned out to be a good idea to just let the content rule.

BLOGGING THERAPY

I get many e-mails about people being alone in their basement going through the postcards and either laughing out loud or finding themselves in tears. There's also something very interesting about people having mean-ingful relationships with these artifacts on a computer screen. The fact that we can make that kind of connection through a computer, through a blog—I think that hints at the kind of great potential that's out there in years to come.

PostSecret is the largest advertisement-free blog on the Web. Why do you not accept advertising?

For me, blogging is about passion. It's about finding something you want to share with other people, and maybe just getting more familiar with yourself.

And I don't think of PostSecret as a commercial site. I feel like there is a sense of trust that allows strangers to send me their most personal secrets. Because of that, I think of those secrets as something beyond a business site, something attuned to the community.

Finally, ads would clutter the site. PostSecret's minimalist style and lack of ads make it look different from any other blogs. It has a pure look, in a sense, [and] it's easy to navigate—it's like pure content. So, I have never accepted a single dollar in paid advertising, though I have had some lucrative offers.

In this book, most bloggers have talked about what inspires them. For you, it's obvious that you have tapped into a self-renewing source of inspiration.

It is more than that. The secrets I post every Sunday influence the secrets that I receive the next week. For example, if I posted all pornographic secrets, that's what I'd be getting. So there is this give-and-take between me and the community that allows us to grow the community and the project in a way that satisfies most of us.

> *"If you go into blogging because you have a passion about something you want to share or explore, I think you're going to succeed, because that's the nature of it."*

Sometimes the responses express trends or themes. For example, after posting Father's Day postcards, I got a lot of endearing vignettes from inside families. You might have seen some on the Web, where fathers would have these white lies that they tell their children, some of them involving long family trips in the car. These illustrate an interesting aspect of PostSecret—that it turns up trends that allow you to see things in our hidden common environment that normally you don't see.

Once, after I posted Mother's Day postcards, all these young people started sending me pictures of their bedroom doors that had been damaged by their parents trying to break in. That was their response to Mother's Day.

One postcard like that and you go, "Hm…that's interesting." But then you post it and dozens of others send the same kind of card, and you think, "Wow, there's some sort of trend here—there's something statistically significant about what's going on here."

SEARCHABLE SECRETS DATABASE

I would like to eventually donate PostSecret to an institution. It would be really nice, I think, to create a database and make it keyword-searchable. So, for example, you could type "bulimia" and see a thousand secrets on that issue pop up.

So little hidden realities can be uprooted or illuminated by PostSecret.

How much time do you put into blogging?

On selecting and posting postcards? I select the postcards to post on Saturday night. Usually I have about a thousand postcards that I go through for the blog. I arrange them on a coffee table I have down in my basement. As I do it, I almost imagine myself as a film editor, taking these scenes from people's lives and trying to knit them together into this cohesive narrative that is, I'd like to think, hopeful.

I probably rearrange them 20 to 30 times when they're on the coffee table, and then I'll rearrange them a dozen more times when I have them on the website to see how they are flowing and affecting and speaking to each other. I really do feel as though the secrets are talking to each other. I feel like it's a conversation, and I have to get the flow just right. And in doing it, I use all these different techniques. I use literary techniques. I try to juxtapose some secrets. I try to build up to a punch line with other secrets. I try visual cues.

And every week, I try to somehow link the first postcard with the last postcard. The arrangement also includes total randomness, so people can project their own connections to the cards and maybe learn something more about themselves.

The whole process, from beginning to end, I guess takes about three hours. I never really know because time always just vanishes.

So you spend three hours or more every Saturday night selecting postcards, and then scanning and posting them. But there are other tasks associated with PostSecret, aren't there?

Oh, yeah. Going through several hundred postcards every weekday takes up time. And I get a lot of postcards, but I get even more e-mail. I get so much e-mail that I can't put my e-mail address on the blog, because I would just get far too much to even read. So going through e-mail takes up time. So does deciding which comments to add to the blog, and posting them.

There is traveling to various towns to give talks. I'm involved with putting books together and mounting a traveling PostSecret exhibition. And those things take time as well. It's easily 30 to 40 hours a week.

It appears that PostSecret is in some ways analogous to an iceberg, with maybe 10 percent of it visible on the Web, and the other 90 percent extending out into the real world.

I agree with that. One example of PostSecret reaching out into the real world occurred last year when an important organization was in dire financial straits. My friend Reese Butler, who founded the National Suicide Prevention Hotline, 1-800-SUICIDE, sent me an e-mail to tell me that the hotline was in financial trouble and needed a quick infusion of cash just to stay afloat.

I tried to do what I could, but it wasn't enough. So I posted his e-mail on the PostSecret blog. Within one week, over 900 visitors raised over $30,000, saving this national suicide prevention hotline.

I love to cite that example because it shows how virtual communities can make an impact in the real world. In fact, over the years, PostSecret has raised over $75,000 for the hotline.

What is your most gratifying experience as a blogger?

Let me give you two gratifying experiences. The first one continues to be receiving the postcards every day and going through them. I can get two or three hundred postcards in a day and go through all of them, and when I get to that last one I still wish there were more to see.

The other greatly satisfying part in this journey for me has been traveling to college campuses and making presentations about the project, and having discussions and conversations about the secrets and the stories behind them. I get to talk to people about their experience mailing in a postcard, or maybe seeing their secret expressed on a stranger's postcard, and the effect that had on their life.

I also enjoy giving presentations. We held a PostSecret "event" in Toronto, Canada, and drew more than a thousand people. This speaks to the universal appeal of PostSecret, that something that is primarily "American" would draw so many people.

But the best is still going through those cards on Saturday night. For me, that's the most creative part of it.

What else do you get from PostSecret?

When I started PostSecret, I knew in my heart that there was something kind of cool there, that people had these rich interior lives [and] if I could build this relationship of trust where they feel like they could really share their soulful secrets with me, I could create something that I would find very special and precious. And it came to pass. The big surprise was that so many other people found value in there, too.

I really wanted it to continue to grow and develop. And it is growing. If you look at the statistics for the site, you'll see that every quarter, there are more returning visitors than first-time visitors from the [previous] quarter. And that's for two and a half years. Usually blogs will peak, but PostSecret continues to grow and grow.

PARENT/CHILD SECRETS

When I give a PostSecret presentation, I'll have parents with their sons and daughters coming up, and they'll joke around about, "Yeah, I've asked him to tell me that secret, and he tells me he never will." And I tell them, "Well if you want to hear his secrets, the first thing you have to do is tell him one of your secrets."

Do you spend much time looking at other blogs?

I have a few favorites I like to go to. I like the Wooster Collective [www.woostercollective.com]. I guess that's a blog. They share street art. People from all over the world take pictures of street art—graffiti, murals, and videos—and they send them in to the Wooster Collective. I like BoingBoing [http://boingboing.net]. Those are about the only two that I regularly check.

And of course there's *Found Magazine*. I think of it as an inspiration for PostSecret. It started five years ago, when Davy Rothbart invited strangers to mail him items that they found. He posts scraps of paper, love notes, shopping lists, and the like on a blog [www.foundmagazine.com].

Do you use RSS feeds, and do you post comments on other blogs?

> *"I treat the secrets with respect on the website. I don't edit [them], and I have no commercial on the blog."*

No, I just jump around on the Web. I don't post any comments on other blogs. I have been mediating the comments on PostSecret, which means that sometimes I pick out an e-mail to post on the blog in response to a postcard.

I recently allowed visitors to post unmediated comments on PostSecret for the first time. We got close to 2,000 comments in about three days. A lot of people are telling me that they don't want the comments. I might have to revise that.

The PostSecret idea has been copied. Does this bother you?

The PostSecret idea has been copied many times. There's a commercial campaign based on it. There have been some books and movies tied into the idea. A Dutch newspaper has a copycat site, and now they're coming out with a PostSecret book. This just underscores the international, universal appeal of the project.

It never really bothers me that much. I feel like people come to the website and think, "This is such a simple thing—all we have to do is ask people to share their secrets with us."

But they don't get it. What they don't understand is what makes PostSecret special: it is this precious relationship I have somehow been able to develop with strangers who trust me. I think part of why this happened is the way I treat the secrets with respect on the website. I don't edit [them], and I have no commercials on the blog.

Another reason for this trust is that I've told a secret first. I've made myself vulnerable in a sense by putting my home address on the website. So I am taking that first vulnerable step in a relationship, which makes people feel like they can trust me with something that makes them vulnerable.

SIMPLE IDEAS ARE THE BEST

Sometimes when people find out I am the PostSecret guy, the first thing they say is, "Oh, I wish I got your mail!" And the next thing they say is, "You're a genius."

I always say, "No, no, no—there is no genius idea here. The idea is very simple. I just invited strangers to mail me their secrets. If there was any genius to it, it was the faith I had in the idea early on, when everybody else thought it was crazy and weird."

Then I go on to say that I hope someone listening to me is the next person to come up with a crazy idea and believe in it, sacrifice for it, and execute it in such a way that it becomes the next grand community or a project that really allows people to look at life, to look at themselves in a new way, and to feel more connected to people they never met.

What is your overall opinion of the blog world?

I think blogging is in its infancy. I think it's really messy. But I think it's really exciting, and I think we're just scratching the surface now. One of the true beauties and powers of blogs is that they can give voice to people who are not heard.

An example of this was the presentation of the Blooker award [a book award given to a book that's based on a blog]. to an American soldier in Iraq who was blogging about the war, and voicing the perspective of the foot soldier to people back in America.

There are many more examples of this in secrets from young people, women, and religious or ethnic minorities who might not feel comfortable expressing their true feelings or thoughts in an open way where people can judge them and there might be consequences. Enabling such voices can facilitate empathy. It can really make you feel more connected to the stranger you walk by on the street or the person who sits by themselves in a movie theater.

But there are some dark linings, too. I am aware of a business out there that links advertisers to bloggers in what I feel is an underhanded way. There is a website where budding bloggers can go and pick up key phrases, ideas, sentences, or key words, and if they use them in their blogs, they get paid for it.

I see this as being insidious, and it could undercut one of the greatest strengths of blogs—their authenticity.

Any advice for other bloggers?

I think I would just probably voice the common cliché: Don't start blogging for money; start blogging because of your passion.

But you do need to focus, and the focus should be something you can feel passionate about. It shouldn't be money. If you go into blogging to make money, you're going to fail. If you go into blogging because you have a passion about something you want to share or explore, I think you're going to succeed, because that's the nature of it.

BLOGGING MAKES YOU A BETTER WRITER

I always recommend to writers that they blog. I think it creates a great opportunity for consistent practice. It also gives you this great community of feedback. If you can reach that tipping point where people comment on your writing, you'll find out what people appreciate, what works for your writing, what doesn't work, and what gets a reaction. It creates the kinds of feedback mechanisms which I think can not only grow a community, but also make somebody a better writer than they were before.

Points to Review

PostSecret is a one-of-a-kind phenomenon that offers useful lessons for bloggers of all stripes. Frank Warren's success is based on honesty and respect, as well as an intuitive, transcendent understanding of communication. From those tenets come the following basic rules that can be applied to any blog:

- A blog offers an immediacy that is not available in any other form of individual media.
- Treat comments from others with respect, and they will reciprocate in future comments.
- The strength of successful blogs is their authenticity. Let content, rather than personality, rule your blog.

- If it is to succeed, a blog must focus on something the blogger is passionate about.
- If you make posting a regular event, people are more likely to return.
- A simplistic page design is usually better than a complicated design. Try to make your page as close to pure content as possible, and avoid overwhelming your readers with too much content at once.
- Comments to blog posts can be used to spot trends.

Mike Masnick
Techdirt

8

> *"It's great that anyone who wants to have a voice can do so with a blog."*
>
> —*Mike Masnick*

Mike Masnick started blogging almost before it was called blogging. His Techdirt blog officially launched in 1998, which makes it one of the oldest business blogs online. Its mission then was to provide technology-industry news analysis, and it continues to focus on that mission today.

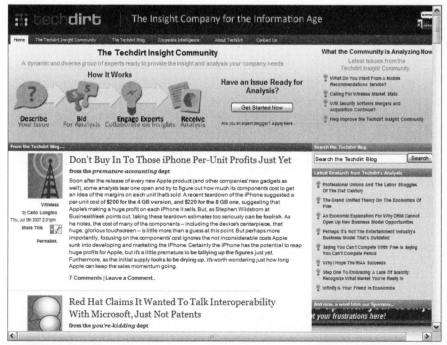

www.techdirt.com

Techdirt has an unusual ancestry. It started as a newsletter, and then it became a website, which in turn inspired a blog. And from that blog grew a company, Techdirt Corporate Intelligence.

And today the blog remains an integral part of the company's strategy. This is all highly appropriate for an organization that blends expert analysis with advanced technology to provide custom corporate-intelligence services for Fortune 500 companies. As the company's own website notes, "Our clients receive private, customized, tactical analysis of news and information in a context specifically relevant to their needs, delivered daily in an easy to read blog format."

Insight from Techdirt's analysts can be sampled on the public blog, which is widely quoted and respected.

Before beginning the process that led to the founding of Techdirt, Masnick worked in business development and marketing at Release Software and in marketing at Intel. In the mid-1990s, having already earned a bachelor's degree in Industrial and Labor Relations at Cornell University, he made the decision to return to Cornell and earn an MBA.

Fired by Enthusiasm

Interestingly, the groundwork for Techdirt was laid years before anyone had even heard the word "blog." Fired by his enthusiasm for the ever-evolving world of technology in the mid-1990s, Masnick's habit of sharing information became the inspiration for the blog that would become his career.

How did you get into blogging?

It started with a technology newsletter. During the mid-1990s I was in business school at Cornell University in Ithaca, New York, and I was trying to build an e-mail newsletter about technology space—about the technology industry and startups.

Why a newsletter? Was it a course project?

No. I did it because I thought it would be fun. And writing about it would be a good way for me to keep up with technology, and to help other students keep up with it.

Something like this was almost a necessity for someone who wanted to stay abreast of developments in the rest of the world, because Ithaca is so isolated.

In fact, the standard joke is that the town is "centrally isolated." It took at least half an hour to get to a major highway.

But people were definitely interested in the technology world, and I was interested in the technology world. So I started that e-mail newsletter.

At first it was solely for students, but I put a link at the end with a note saying, "If you would like to subscribe, send an e-mail to..." and I included my e-mail address.

This was business school, so most people were returning from a few years out in the industry. Students started forwarding the newsletter to people they knew back in the industry, so the subscriber list grew very quickly. This is something I wasn't expecting at all.

> *"We never did anything to try to get more readers, other than to just keep writing what we hoped was interesting and compelling content."*

The next logical step was to put up a website for the newsletter, and from that came the blog.

It sounds like a natural progression. What was your initial exposure to blogging?

Honestly, what inspired me was seeing Slashdot, in 1997 or 1998. It had just come on the scene, and there was no other blogging software. I recognized that it would make a fantastic tool for the kind of quick news updates I was doing.

The original Techdirt was based on Slashdot code. This was before they had officially released Slashcode. We had Slashcode 0.3, which was a very, very early and very, very messy code. It took us a couple months to figure out how to use it. But we based Techdirt on their original code, and then built it from there.

The Techdirt blog started in 1998. You could say that I started blogging before it was called blogging. There were a few other blogs then, but certainly not many.

What was it about the software that made you want to start a blog?

I think what attracted me most to blogging was that it was just a really effi-cient way of communicating online. My mission with Techdirt was and is to provide what is hopefully intelligent insight and analysis of news that relates to innovation, and generate additional discussion based on that. Blogging is the best way to reach the maximum number of people, and enable them to participate in a dialogue.

In the beginning, did you make an effort to get readers to come in? Do you today?

To be honest with you, we never did anything to try to get more readers, other than to just keep writing what we hoped was interesting and com-pelling content.

Of course, when I started the website, I already had the e-mail newsletter going, and I was able to move people from the e-mail newsletter to the website. So I had this small core audience for the blog going in.

From there, we just kept writing and it kept growing.

Do you think being an early adopter helped?

> *"If we think we have something to add to a story…then we'll write about it. If we have nothing to add, we'll skip the story."*

Well, there were only four or five other tech blogs in the same arena as Tech-dirt. There was not a lot of competi-tion. So, yes, it was easy to be found on the Web back then. Unfortunately, all the others are long gone. Through luck, attrition, or whatever, Techdirt built up an audience and kept going and going.

Today, of course, there's something to be said for longevity. You can accu-mulate a lot of new readers every year just by existing.

So you've never been preoccupied with building readership?

That's right. We've never done anything proactively. Sometimes a reporter mentions us in an article or we get picked up by other media, but we haven't done anything actively to encourage new readers.

Do you pursue search engine optimization (SEO)?

We certainly didn't in the past. We have more recently, now that we're larger. We have a technology staff, and they've done a few very minor things to optimize for search engines—making sure the post title is in the title and things like that. But that was very late in the game.

How does the Techdirt blog serve your company?

In our case, the company Techdirt Corporate Intelligence grew out of what we were doing with the blog. So the blog is an integral part of our strategy.

I imagine it serves as a marketing tool, too.

Yes. It does a variety of things. It gets us attention. There aren't that many small businesses that can say they get so many visitors to their homepage every day. So that's really helpful.

And the blog lets readers see us at work. Our business is providing analysis and insight. To prove we can do that, we're out there every day with at least some analysis. Certainly it helps build our credibility and our name recognition. And it gets attention, so it's been a very, very helpful part of the business.

You post on a wide range of subjects, from baseball, to eBay, to privacy issues. Do these reflect your personal interests, or are your subject selections driven by news or posts on other blogs?

Our rules for what we write about are pretty simple. We follow news having to do with technology and innovation, and if we think we have something to add to a story in the way of insight, analysis, or opinion, then we'll write about it. If we have nothing to add, we'll usually skip that story.

Techdirt might be a little bit unique because we have so many stories, yet we keep everything tied to a specific news story. We try to establish an ongoing thread. A lot of our posts link back to previous posts, to establish the thread and to explain what's going on. Readers appreciate this kind of continuity—there is a progression of information that can be tracked.

What about sources?

I guess you could say our sources are everywhere, on the Web and off the Web. We pick up news from traditional sources (magazines, newspapers, radio, and television) as well as the Web, and from private sources, people we talk with.

And like your original newsletter, the blog continues to serve as a way for you to keep up with technology.

Certainly. It forces me to pay more attention and to read a lot more than I would otherwise. Just the act of writing about something forces me to think about it more, and also remember it better.

The design of your page is very smooth, very flowing. The first thing one notices is that you seem to have very few ads on the site.

Yes. And ads are relatively recent for us. I had never been that interested in doing advertising, so we were one of the very last to go into advertising. That's because it's really not our business—the blog is here to promote our business, to showcase what we do.

But, of all things, we started doing advertising because we had some clients who were interested in the online advertising space. And it turned out to be a way for us to get some experience with something new, and at the same time make some money.

And do something for the client. It sounds like a win-win situation, with a bonus.

Yes. It was a very good learning experience. Once we set up the client's ad, we understood the process. Given that, there was no reason to leave the money on the table.

We're very careful, though, about avoiding anything that might lessen the reader experience. We avoid ads that are overly intrusive.

And, again, you hadn't done any advertising before one of your clients asked for help with it? That's a perfect example of organic growth.

Right. The amusing thing, honestly, is that before we had advertising, we actually used to get e-mail from people who were—I don't want to say angry—but people who were confused. They were saying, "Why are you doing this? There are no ads on your site. I don't get it!"

In turn, we were confused; we didn't understand what the fuss was about.

Interestingly, once we finally had advertising in place, we didn't get any complaints about having ads on the site. In fact, we were complimented. When people saw an advertisement from a big company like Microsoft or IBM or HP [Hewlett-Packard], they were impressed. Many wrote to say, "It almost adds legitimacy to your site—that those companies are willing to advertise on your site."

This was something I had never even considered. I wouldn't have expected that kind of reaction.

Looking at the logistics of blogging, is there an average number of stories you post per day or per week?

We have no hard-and-fast rule about posting. We just do what feels right. There are times when we'll have more than 20 stories a day. When there were fewer tech blogs out, there we might've been doing more stories. But these days, we are settled in at somewhere around 12 stories a day.

We don't want to overwhelm readers. And if other blogs are covering a story and doing a good job with it, and we have nothing to add, there is not much benefit in us covering it.

How much time do you spend blogging?

I don't keep track, actually, so it's tough for me to say.

Do you comment on other blogs very often?

I try to. If there's something interesting in tech news, I read other blogs and comment. It depends on the situation and how much time I have available. Sometimes I have to make a judgment call whether it's more effective for me to comment on a post on another blog, or carry the discussion to Techdirt.

> *"Almost every one of our posts expresses an opinion."*

What's the most difficult aspect of blogging for you?

As the blog grows larger, there are lots of expectations from readers about what we should and should not do with the blog. Sometimes people are critical if we don't take a certain direction, or if we do.

Does that include the content?

Yes. It depends on the story. Criticism is more frequent with controversial topics. And I personally tend to write a lot about the patent system and intellectual property law, which is a subject of fascination for me and for a lot of people. People will take exception to some of my analyses and suggest things that are factually incorrect, so we tend to have a lot of discussions in that area.

Well, certainly patent, trademark, and copyright law are contentious topics.

I enjoy those discussions. It keeps me sharp. Even when I feel like I'm going over the same argument for the thousandth time.

My viewpoint is that, if people continue to argue with me on a subject, it really implies that I haven't done the best job of explaining my position—because if I've done a good job of explaining my position, I've explained away all the potential objections.

So it forces me to keep thinking things through. Could I have better explained something? Is my viewpoint right? Have I made an assumption that's wrong? And how have I squared the different thinking? It makes me continually rethink my position, and I try to explain it better.

There are cases where people take exception to the angle we're taking on a story—meaning our opinion. They seem to think that we shouldn't have opinions. The funny thing is that we do not identify ourselves as reporters. We're always expressing an opinion. Almost every one of our posts expresses an opinion. So I find it somewhat amusing when someone accuses us of not adhering to journalistic objectivity.

We don't ignore facts. It's important to us that we back up our opinions. We back up our opinions with facts that are accurate.

There are times when people send us something sensationalistic with facts that are totally taken out of context, and we will not write about those. We're not trying to push anyone's agenda. We'll write our own opinion, but we're not going to take things out of context.

Some people may accuse us of doing that, anyway. But we try to be careful to not take things out of context, and to be able to back up everything we say because if we don't—if we can't—we will get called on it. And that's fine. If we get something wrong, and our readers call us on it, that's good—we will learn something from it.

But we work to prevent this sort of problem. We'll have discussions before some posts go up, where we say this is how commenters are going to respond, and we need to have something in here to cut that off. We want to be able to say that our opinions are supported by the facts, and present our analysis of why an opinion is valid.

I suspect that your enjoyment of these discussions is also your most rewarding experience as a blogger.

It's always nice to see something we've helped stir up turn into a larger discussion.

I wonder if some of the negative elements carry over into e-mail. Do you get a lot of e-mail about the blog, or do people stick with posting comments?

Certainly some people send e-mail. The distribution of communications is that we get the most comments in the blog. Next in frequency are people talking about us or our subject matter on other blogs. Lots of other bloggers will write about the same subjects and link back to us. E-mail is less common.

An interesting pattern we've noted is that people who are negative—people who really dislike what we have to say—they'll go with blog comments, in public. Not everyone who comments is a negative, of course, but if a reader has a really negative observation about us, they'll put it in as a comment. They don't send it in e-mail—maybe e-mail is too personal. Our e-mail comments are 90 percent positive.

> *"Pay attention to other bloggers. Link to them, Connect to their sites. Assuming you're writing about a subject that other people are interested in, and you communicate well enough, people will find you."*

It sounds as if you have a good number of potential editors out there. Do they correct typos, too?

Well, certainly if it's grammar or spelling mistakes, we hear about those pretty quickly. We try, but some things just slip through. People write with corrections, but some people see it as an opportunity to slam us for not understanding proper English or grammar.

Along with the discussion, disagreement, and corrections, do you get spammed much?

We get a ton. There's comment spam. There is PR [public relations] spam. There is e-mail spam. I feel bad about this—there are people who legitimately want to talk to us, but sometimes it becomes very difficult to sort them out from the spam.

What is your opinion of the blogosphere?

I think the question may be too broad. There are tons of blogs. There are tons of really insightful bloggers. There are some that aren't very insightful, but that doesn't bother me. It's great that anyone who wants to have a voice can do so with a blog.

Do you have any advice you'd like to share with bloggers or would-be bloggers?

Just write what you're passionate about.

You had a ready-made user base when you established your blog. What about people who don't have a readership waiting? Do you think it's important to try to build readership, or should bloggers wait for it to happen?

It's hard to say. It depends on what your goals are. It doesn't hurt to try to develop some traffic. But it is important to find the balance between trying to build traffic and begging for traffic.

A lot of people beg for traffic, and I think that's counterproductive. We get people begging for traffic all the time, and it's a turnoff. They post some little line just to get traffic. Anything that enables a discussion works better. I think it comes back to the whole thing about being passionate, where, if you are passionate about a subject that you're writing about, people will find out about it.

Beyond that, if you link to others and you respond on their blogs, you will see a kind of natural growth. You may not become a top-100 blogger, but you can draw more traffic in a much more comfortable way without begging.

So, pay attention to other bloggers. Link to them. Comment on their sites. Assuming you're writing about a subject that other people are interested in, and you communicate well enough, people will find you.

Points to Review

For Mike Masnick, advertising is not a major source of income. Nor is it the reason his blog exists, which is the case for many of the 80 million blogs in existence. Masnick moves in a somewhat different world than most bloggers. Instead of using blog content as a lure to expose readers to advertising, he sells that content. And in the best tradition of someone with a good product, he gives away free samples daily.

Those free samples draw an enormous readership (paying customers are a minority), which suggests that he knows what he's doing, and that he's someone to pay attention to if you want to learn about blogging success. Here are a few pointers to keep in mind:

- Not all blogs start out as blogs.
- In some circumstances, blogging can be used to showcase a product or service, without pushing to sell it.
- Blogging can make you pay closer attention to a subject, think about it, and remember more.
- Try to blend advertising in with content, rather than allowing it to intrude on content.
- A certain kind of advertiser can add prestige to a blog. Big-name companies advertising on a blog tend to make it appear more "legitimate" to readers.
- Want to get more readers? Write about something for which you have passion.
- Avoid begging for links—it's counterproductive.
- Don't spam other blogs with invitations to your blog—stick to legitimate comments that add to or begin new discussions.

Mark Frauenfelder
BoingBoing.net

9

"You'll find an audience if you write what you're passionate about."

—*Mark Frauenfelder*

Mark Frauenfelder has worked as a mechanical engineer, an editor, and a publisher, but he is probably best known as a writer, an illustrator, and a world-class technology evangelist. Currently the editor-in-chief of *Make* magazine, he has also been an editor at *Wired* and is the author of such books as *Rule the Web* (St. Martin's Griffin, 2007) and *The Computer: An Illustrated History* (Carlton Publishing Group, 2007).

www.boingboing.net

Frauenfelder is also responsible for the number-one blog on the Web—BoingBoing: A Directory of Wonderful Things (www.boingboing.net). Known as "the most popular blog in the world, as ranked by Technorati.com," BoingBoing won the Lifetime Achievement and Best Group Blog awards at the 2006 Bloggies ceremony.

It's Better to Be Accurate than Cute

Billed as a weblog of natural curiosities and interesting technologies, BoingBoing.net is a direct descendant of *bOING bOING* magazine, which was founded in 1988. (Yes, it was named with a cartoon sound in mind.) Published by Frauenfelder and his wife, Carla Sinclair, *bOING bOING* was concerned with pop culture and having fun with the rapidly evolving and highly affordable leading-edge technology of the 1980s and 1990s. Its contents ranged from "The Evolution of M&Ms" and "The Worst Videos of All Time" to a study of *Mad* magazine's Dave Berg. At its peak, this extremely specialized publication achieved a circulation of 17,000. (*bOING bOING* is, alas, no longer published, having been superseded by the Web.)

BoingBoing.net was Frauenfelder's first blog. Of course, his many and varied interests wouldn't let him have just one—he is also co-founder of a blog devoted to the ukulele (Ukulelia, at www.ukulelia.com), and runs a blog devoted to his personal interests called the Mad Professor (www.madprofessor.net).

www.madprofessor.net

Tell us a bit about *bOING bOING*.

My wife and I started it because at the time we were interested in things like cyberpunk science fiction, comic books, and technology. Especially interesting was the way technology was becoming affordable to individuals, and how they were starting to do really creative things with them. [Not unlike the focus of *Make* magazine today.] All sorts of exciting things were happening with computers and culture and more. There were magazines out there like *Creative Computing*, and Alexander K. Dewdney was writing the computer recreations column in *Scientific American*, which he compiled into a book. These and other things inspired us to start the magazine.

Naturally, when the Web came along, we thought it would be fun to have a website for these emerging technologies. The website, BoingBoing.net, started late in 1995.

bOING bOING, Number 8, 1991

When did it occur to you to add a blog?

In 1999, I wrote an article about blogging for a magazine, *The Industry Standard*. At the time there were only a few hundred blogs, but I got really excited about the idea of blogging. I could see that it was a really powerful publishing tool.

What most impressed you about blogging when you first encountered it?

The most important thing about blogging was the instantaneous publishing you could do with it. I also found the fact that the web posts were in reverse chronological order very interesting, very different.

Equally amazing was the content on the front page. A lot of web pages at the time required you to wait while a screen loaded. Then the screen would say "Click here to enter." And then there would be another screen. It was like a magazine cover. But it was crazy—sometimes you would have to go through several different screens to get what you wanted. But with blogs, everything was there on the first screen, in a long strip that was arranged with the newest stuff right at the top.

That just really appealed to me, and I started blogging soon after that, in January of 2000. I took to it immediately. Later, I was preparing to go on vacation in Hawaii, and I invited Cory Doctorow to blog for me because he'd been sending me ideas for the blog all the time, suggesting sites and so forth.

While I was gone, he cranked up the postings to something like 10 times what I was doing. That brought in tons of readers. The more he blogged, the more readers came. So when I got back, I said, "Why don't you just stay on board and do this?"

EARLY INSPIRATION

When I was 11 or 12, my dad worked at IBM and he brought home a Hewlett-Packard calculator. I think it was the HP 41-C. I'd never seen a calculator, much less one that had these little magnetic strips you could run through it. And there were programs like the Lunar Lander game, where you have to calculate the exact amount of fuel to burn to land safely on the Moon. And you could write programs for it. To me it was the coolest thing ever. That got me going in the world of technology.

He thought that was a great idea. Later, I invited a couple of other people to blog with me—David Pescovitz and Xeni Jardin. I find that it's easier to work with other bloggers, and the four of us were a tight group, almost like the members of a band. We each bring our own thing and do it, but we also have similar tastes. And it works out very well.

That's a rather compelling metaphor.

Yes. We also have a "band manager," which is what we call our business manager.

Management became important when you started carrying advertising on BoingBoing.net. When was that?

When BoingBoing started taking off and getting tens of thousands of readers per day, our bandwidth bills started to get expensive—about $1,000 a month. That was around 2002. We were splitting the cost among the four of us, and we thought maybe we could sell a few ads on BoingBoing to cover the costs.

So I called my friend John Battelle, who had started *The Industry Standard* and had a lot of experience with this kind of stuff. I asked him, "Do you think you could help us sell advertising for BoingBoing?"

He said he could do that. And I told him that all we wanted was to cover our bandwidth bill. To which John replied, "Well, you know, if you want to sell advertising, you'll probably make a lot more than covering your bandwidth bill, because any ad salesperson is not going to want to limit themselves to just $1,000 a month. So you'll probably make some money."

We had no objection to that, and told him to go ahead. I believe John started selling ads himself at first. Then he hired other people, and it worked out really well. He used BoingBoing as a testbed for some ideas he had, and eventually he started a business called Federated Media, based on selling advertising online. He now sells advertising for dozens of blogs, and he does really well. Federated has a lot of the big blogs, sites like Digg, TechCrunch, and Fark.

He's doing a really good job, and we're really happy that we're working with the company.

Has the business element changed blogging for you?

Now that BoingBoing is kind of a business, I feel obligated to post every day, and I have to fight the urge to blog stuff that I don't think is great, just because I think I need to get something out there. I'd prefer to not blog unless I'm really excited by what I'm writing about. So, one of the hard things is not having any good ideas to blog, but feeling obligated to do it anyway.

One of the good things about blogging is also one of the tough things, and that's the ability to instantaneously publish something to the world without really reflecting on it. Sometimes I'll write something and blog it, and then regret it for a variety of reasons. Maybe it's something as simple as thinking I could have worded it differently. Or I'll realize that I could have said something more interesting if I'd sat back and thought, but I was so excited by this idea that I just churned the thing out and hit the publish button.

It would be good if I forced myself to wait 10 minutes after writing something, before I published it, so I could think about it for a little while.

Doesn't the same thing happen when you're writing for print magazines?

Sure, but then you can call or write your editor and say, "Wait!" And there is usually plenty of time to make that change before anyone sees it. With the blog, thousands or tens of thousands of people may read the post before I edit it.

At least you have tools to make changing text easy, almost as easy as changing your mind. You mentioned that you used Ecto as a Movable Type front-end.

Yes. Ecto is really nice, and it works for Movable Type. The thing I like about it is that it has all sorts of little keyboard macros that let me format things in a certain way, add text quickly, and reformat and resize photos. It's just a nice front-end for most blogging software. For me, it's a lifesaver.

Sounds like it really speeds things up.

Yeah, it definitely does. And it's easy to edit stuff that you've already written, which is good because I make a lot of typos.

And I use it to go back and fix things when people point out errors. [This] happened recently, when I posted something that said it had to do with Fox News [Channel]—and people pointed out that it was NBC. So I just went into Ecto and made that change, including a note [that said] no, it wasn't Fox; it was NBC.

Do you always cite the earlier error?

If we make a small typo, we just fix it. But if it's a factual error or of any importance or significance, what we do is strike out the incorrect information and add the correct information. This way, people don't think we're trying to revise history. It's our way of acknowledging our errors.

When you were publishing *bOING bOING*, your audience was measured in thousands. How does it feel to have an audience in the hundreds of thousands and know they're out there and looking at everything you post—some of them at almost the instant you post it?

It's amazing. It's kind of impossible for me to conceptualize the fact that there are hundreds of thousands of people reading the posts. I just imagine it to be 40 or 50 people. My brain can't accommodate a larger audience than that.

> *"I love being able to communicate. That's part of the reason I started blogging in the first place, because there are ways to share cool ideas or to share even better ideas."*

Speaking of audiences, there is a lot of talk nowadays about search engine optimization (SEO). Do you use SEO to try to bring in readers?

No, I don't really do that. Probably it's a good idea, but I think that my efforts are better spent finding the most interesting stuff I can and writing about it. SEO is kind of a second-order thing. If I have a lot of time, I might look into it, but I would rather focus on the content of the blog itself instead of worrying about metadata or other things like that.

What do you do to bring in readers?

I always put a link at the end of my blog posts to the source of information. When I do that, the other bloggers appreciate it and will return the favor, linking to BoingBoing. And it's just a nice, sharing kind of thing that works really well. It was a big help to BoingBoing in the early days. It's kind of scratching each other's back.

What else do you find gratifying about blogging?

I would have to say meeting people online and in real life—in particular, meeting people who have told me they have the same interests, and they want to share ideas, something that adds to what I posted. I love that—I love being able to communicate. That's part of the reason I started blogging in the first place, because there are ways to share cool ideas or to share even better ideas.

For example, I posted something about how our neighborhood dealt with someone playing "mailbox baseball" and knocking mailboxes over. I took pictures of mailboxes that had been upgraded with homemade fortifications—like bricks.

People started sending me photos that they'd saved through the years of amazing mailboxes they'd come across. And somebody, inspired by my blog posts, started a blog about fortified mailboxes. They invite people to send in photos. And that kind of stuff is really great.

Another example: John Hodgman, who played the PC in the Mac-vs.-PC commercials, is a really funny writer and performer. He did this thing called "700 Hobo Names." He had made up names like Todd Four-Flush, Stick Legs McOhio, Boxcar Ted—those kinds of names. He read them all out into this really long song that he posted online, and I posted it on BoingBoing.

> *"Be interesting, think about the news, and express your opinion clearly—that's the secret to success."*

I said, "Wouldn't it be fun if all the cartoonists who read this could draw pictures of the 700 hobos?" And believe it or not, they did it. Somebody started a website called The 700 Hoboes Project" [http://e-hobo.com]. And now all 700 hobos have been illustrated several times over. They're great drawings that are just so entertaining and funny.

John Hodgman wholeheartedly supports this, and he is really active in it. It started a whole movement. Seeing that just makes me feel happy to know that I was in some way responsible for it—for inspiring all these really talented people to get together online.

It's also gratifying to be able to investigate any neat things I want.

You have quite a bit going on, with the blogs, your family, *Make* magazine, et cetera. What kind of time do you have to spend on blogging? You mentioned some time back that you blog maybe three or four hours a day.

Yes, I would say that's a good average. Sometimes if I'm really busy working on the magazine or something else, even half an hour [with the blog] is too much. Other days, I go up to maybe five or six hours if I'm really on a roll.

Do you get much of a chance to leave comments on other blogs?

I do once in a while, especially if it's somebody who has blogged about something I've written. I may want to make something clear, or just thank them for commenting.

What tips or advice would you like to share with bloggers?

I think it's really important to write a good headline. It's better to be accurate than it is to be cute or clever. When you make a post, do a little summary of what it is in the headline, because a lot of people read blogs through RSS and go to the headline first to see what's going on. It can make a difference in whether you get read.

As for the blog post itself, if you're writing about something out on the Web, give a good short description of *why* it's interesting. When I see something I want to talk about, I outline some of the questions that readers might ask, like, "Why is this interesting?" or, "Why is this important?" I write down the answers, and then I post.

In effect, do you think like your audience, putting yourself in their place?

Yes. I like to think that everything I've created is media that I myself would like to consume. And with BoingBoing, I've made a blog that I'd like to read. Being honest with yourself is really a good way to ensure that you write a really high-quality blog.

Also just writing about what you're interested in helps make sure you find an audience. It might not be the largest audience, but you'll find an audience if you write what you're passionate about. What you write will ring true. If you copy someone else's blog, it won't be the same.

Do you have any additional thoughts to share?

New bloggers should *not* concern themselves with trying to be the first to report on something—[that's] very unlikely. That's not a game that is easy to win.

What's easier to win, and better, is to have something interesting to say about news. Let other people try to scoop it. Be interesting, think about the news, and express your opinion clearly—that's the secret to success. Even if people disagree with you, when you express your opinion in an arresting way, they'll come to see what you have to say. It's okay to have people disagree with you—it's part of the conversation. And that's what's so great about the Web and blogs—it is part of a big conversation, and all day long I'm e-mailing people who have things to say about what I'm posting. And it's a lot of fun.

Points to Review

During my interview with Mark Frauenfelder, it was obvious that he channels a tremendous amount of energy into his projects. That energy is the result of his enthusiasm and passion for his subjects. Here is a summary of tips inspired by the interview:

- Write about your passions.
- Resist the urge to write a post just to get something out there. If you think before you post, you won't have to edit your posts later.
- Put yourself in your reader's place before you write. Ask yourself what a reader will find interesting about your topic, or why the topic is important. Write down the answers and use them as a guide when you are writing the post.
- Write a descriptive headline for every post. Many readers browse headlines (especially those who use RSS) and won't stop to read a post that isn't clearly described.
- Always link to sources of information in your posts. This encourages others to link back.
- Don't worry about being the first to report something new. It is unlikely you'll be able to do that. Instead, focus on expressing your ideas clearly and with enthusiasm.

Robert Scoble
Scobleizer

10

> *"Google is the reason blogging continues to have power."*
>
> —*Robert Scoble*

Robert Scoble is the spark behind one of the Web's most influential technology blogs, Scobleizer (`http://scobleizer.com`), which offers a personal and sometimes controversial mix of discussions on technology and business, with occasional forays into other subjects. Scoble characterizes himself (and his blog) as being "in the business of having something to say about things before anyone else has something to say."

http://scobleizer.com

Scoble began blogging in 2000. At the time, he was uncertain whether blogs had any value, but two friends talked him into giving it a try. He started his blog a few weeks later, and was surprised to learn that so many people followed blogs. There was obviously some value to be found in blogging.

That value was underscored in 2003 when he was offered a job with Microsoft by an executive who had been reading his blog. While with Microsoft, Scoble helped produce the company's Channel 9 MSDN videos about its people and products.

From the beginning, Scobleizer was an independent blog. It carried no advertising, and Scoble expressed his opinions freely. He continued in this fashion during his tenure at Microsoft, criticizing the company when criticism was due, and praising deserving products from competitors.

Thanks in large part to his independence, his blog has enjoyed exceptional growth; Scobleizer sees around 3.5 million visits per year.

Scoble left Microsoft late in 2006 to become vice president of Media Development for PodTech (`www.podtech.net`). At PodTech, he continues to produce interviews with important technologists, tours of companies, and other videos of events, people, and products at technology's leading edge.

Scoble's work has appeared not only in blogs, podcasts, and videocasts, but also in print. With Shel Israel, Scoble co-wrote *Naked Conversations: How Blogs are Changing the Way Businesses Talk with Customers* (Wiley, 2006). Appropriately, the book was written on a blog, with lots of help from the blog's readers.

Naked Conversations

As Scoble notes in *Naked Conversations*, a good blog is "authoritative and passionate." A Google search for "blogging+passion+authority" brings up nearly 1 million results. Substitute "blog" for "blogging" and you get more than 1.5 million hits. Obviously, a lot of people, like Scoble, approach blogging with passion and authority, and in fact are blogging with passion and authority.

Pay attention as Scoble speaks of passion and authority in this interview— these elements are keys to blogging success.

You've been blogging for most of a decade. Has your blog changed much over the years?

It's changed in that I have an audience. When I started it, I was publishing to two people. And it was a little easier back then just to write to two people, than with 20,000 people a day reading it.

What got you interested in blogging?

I was a conference planner, doing conferences for web developers back in 1999 and 2000. One of the conferences was the 2000 CNET Builder.com Live! conference. Every year, I asked the conference speakers what they thought we should cover in the next year's conference. Two of our speakers that year, Dave Winer, editor of the Scripting News blog, [www.scripting.com] and Dori Smith [co-author of the Backup Brain blog, www.backupbrain.com], suggested that the next conference address blogging.

I wasn't sure if blogs were important enough; I could only find a couple hundred on the Web. But they did talk me into setting up my own blog.

I started blogging on December 15, 2000.

What sort of audience did you find?

At first I was just writing to Dave Winer, and telling him what my life was like, who I was seeing, and what I was thinking about. After about 10 days, he linked to me, and sent me 3,000 people—not bad for one link. And that's when I realized that, wow, there are lot more people reading these things than writing them.

Did you work at increasing readership?

No. I didn't really go after it that way, because to me blogging was like writing stories, or telling two or three people what you thought. Looking at it that way helped me write.

If I was trying to [create] a business [from] it, I don't think I would have done a blog. That points to one of the reasons why blogging became

> *"Great content beats SEO."*

popular—because it wasn't CNET, it wasn't *The Wall Street Journal*, and it wasn't *The New York Times*. Those people worry a lot about audience growth, audience acquisition, and advertising revenue. I really didn't care.

I still don't care. Not having to be concerned with getting a large audience is one reason I avoided advertising, even though I probably could make a pretty good amount of money with advertising. But this way, I don't have that influence forcing me to care about the blog as a business.

So you're not distracted by tracking traffic and SEO (search engine optimization)?

I do look at my stats and my referral logs. But mostly that's because I'm looking for who's talking up to me or about me, or making fun of me, like the Fake Steve Jobs.

> *"We wrote the entire book on the blog."*

But it is important to remember that, in the long term, most of your readers will come from Google. The more you help Google find you, the more traffic you'll get. It's not just Google—Microsoft and Yahoo! work the same way.

But in a way, SEO doesn't matter. What matters is that you get links—because if people link to you, then you get the SEO anyway. You don't have to work at SEO.

In other words, great content beats SEO.

You just have to be there with good content, like a meritocracy?

Well, it's *mostly* a meritocracy. There certainly is gaming [influencing search engine results] going on. But if you're a better networker, you're going to get more links. It's all about links.

If you convince people to link to you even if you might not have quite as good a news offering, or you're 15 minutes late, you're still going to get the traffic.

Somebody else might be better than you in terms of getting things out sooner, or a little bit better-written, but if they don't get the links, it doesn't matter.

Then networking is, in effect, part of the merit system?

Yes.

What's it like to have so many readers?

It's a lot of fun. I can ask a question and get 20 responses in a few minutes. It's really great when you're having problems with technology, like when I had a problem with Firefox and I thought it was just my computer. But I went online and asked whether anybody else was having problems. In two minutes, 30 people came back and said, "Yeah, I thought it was just me, too." So we knew the problem was in Firefox.

How much has blogging affected the sales of your book, *Naked Conversations*?

A lot—going back to before it was published. We wrote the entire book on a blog set up for that purpose. We posted chapters as we were writing them, before they went to the editor.

There were two important effects. First, the readers—the audience on the blog—fixed our words. They fact-checked for us, and they copy edited. One guy went through every word and improved the grammar. The book would not be the same book if we had not done it in the public eye. It was dramatically improved.

The result is that we've outsold all the other blogging books combined. None of the other authors of blogging books did a book blog in this way.

The second thing is, because we were in the public eye, the book became a public thing that people linked to, right from their blogs. Bloggers would talk about the book. They would say, "Hey, Scoble and Shel Israel just released a new chapter of their book, and I think it sucked," or, "I thought it was great," or whatever. And they linked over to it.

That increased our Google juice, and that meant that we got a better Google PageRank over time. It kept us at number seven or eight on the link list for "naked" for a long time.

And the blog benefited too, I'm sure.

Yes. We got a lot of continuing traffic from the Google word.

A lot of people in business don't really understand that Google will bring a trickle of traffic to you forever, as long as you own a word. So if you're a plumber in San Jose and

> *"Google will bring a trickle of traffic to you forever."*

people are searching "plumbing San Jose" because they need a plumber, as long as you're on that page you're in business.

Remember that blogging is the best way to get on Google. And that's one reason [blogging] continues having a lot of power in the world.

The power that blogging has is also the reason it hasn't been reduced to the status of a fad. I've heard over and over that blogging is a fad. When I first started blogging, my best friend said, "We won't be doing this for very long, because it's just a fad," et cetera, et cetera. But it's not a fad.

So Google continues to give blogging its power, even though Google has turned down [reduced] its influence on blogging. The PageRank algorithm has been getting better and better, and that means blogs are not able to game the system the way they used to be able to do. But blogging is still a pretty powerful way to get high on Google.

With Google driving Internet users to blogs, it would seem that Google ought to be trying to find a way to harness some of that power itself.

Google fired a blogger a few years ago, and that caused Google's corporate culture to avoid blogging for quite a while. It seems people there are skittish about or not understanding of blogging. There is nobody there who is really a great blogger. Matt Cutts [www.mattcutts.com/blog] is probably the closest thing to a great blogger they have.

What kind of time do you spend on your own blog?

> *"Blogging doesn't care about bias, as long as you disclose your bias, or your conflict of interest."*

You could say I spend every waking minute of every day thinking about my blog and thinking what to put up. But I choose to write only when I have something to say. I usually write up a post in 10 [to] 20 minutes. I never spend two hours straight on my blog.

So thinking about the blog is part of the blogging process.

Yeah.

Do you spend much time looking at other blogs? Do you comment on other blogs?

I look at 700 blogs on an average day. I'm the number-one Google Reader user in the world. It shoots me 1,800 items an evening. And I share about 80 of those on my blog.

I participate as a commenter on hundreds of blogs.

Does looking at so many blogs every day give you a good overall picture of the blog world?

Oh, yeah—that's one reason I read so many blogs. I want to make sure that I keep up with it all, because someone that nobody reads could break a major news story—and if you're not reading his blog, you won't know about it.

That's important to me, because I am in the business of having something to say about things before anyone else has something to say.

I'm sure you're never at a loss for something to write about.

Sometimes I am. But sometimes it seems to just come to me. An example: I just went out to the grocery store and ran into Mark Graham, senior vice president at iVillage online [www.ivillage.com]. He was showing me his new iPhone. So I went home, and in about 10 minutes, I wrote up a post about this.

Even when you think you don't have something to write about, usually somebody has an interesting story to tell.

Do you see bloggers doing dumb things that drive readers away?

Well certainly you see people get fired for blogging—for writing stupid things on their blogs that turn out to have consequences they didn't foresee. That is the best example of somebody shooting themselves in the head with a blog.

Anything you do that tells your readership that you're not credible is bad. Say, for instance, that you start running advertising copy on your blog without disclosing that you're taking money to write stuff. When somebody figures that out, you're going to lose credibility, and that will mean loss of readership and getting exposed on Valleywag [www.valleywag.com] or elsewhere.

Credible bloggers don't like that kind of behavior, because it reduces the credibility of the entire blog world.

Blogging doesn't care about bias, as long as you disclose your bias, or your conflict of interest. We're not hard-core about it like *The New York Times*—that is, that you're not allowed to own stock or you're not allowed to take money for things. But we are hard-core about disclosure. If you're taking money for some reason, disclose it and put "advertising" on it—say "This is advertising," or "This is a paid blog," or something like that.

I don't have a problem with somebody selling their words like that, as long as they are disclosing it, and making it real clear so that everybody can understand where their biases are.

Don't think that you can just do this without people knowing. Word gets around, and we start comparing notes on people. How good a writer is this person? Is he worth linking to?

We compare notes on the credibility and authority level of each other. And people are talking about us all the time. So if you ask Michael Arrington, "What do you think about Scoble?" he should have an answer, and tell you that he's good at this and not good at that.

All of that translates into linking behavior, partnership behavior, and all sorts of other things.

You must find sharing knowledge and opinions with such a large audience rewarding at times. What was your most gratifying experience as a blogger?

I think it's when I told Steve Ballmer that he wasn't leading the company in a good direction, because Microsoft pulled its support from a gay-rights bill. Within a week, Ballmer changed his mind and put support back behind the bill, and the bill passed within a year.

This was a state bill?

Yes, up in [the state of] Washington. A small church was pressuring Microsoft to pull support from this bill, and it was quite public. It wasn't just me, but I was one of the more public people saying it was wrong to pull the support for this bill. Microsoft had supported it for eight years prior to this, even thought it was unpopular.

What is your advice to someone who's starting a blog?

Have something interesting to say. That's easier for some people than others. If the real Steve Jobs started a blog, he would instantly have hundreds of thousands of readers, without even trying. It wouldn't necessarily have to be interesting—you would just want to read Steve Jobs to see what he's saying, right? But if a normal person who doesn't have the kind of position in life that draws attention starts a blog, people don't automatically flock to it.

For those people, I have a whole raft of tips. Use images. Go above and beyond, and be more thorough, more in-depth in your topic coverage. Use video instead of just text. Be a better networker. Be a better reader—read more blogs than I do. If you want to beat me, you've got to be competitive.

And if you're thinking about competing with someone in a certain subject area, see if you can find an angle that person doesn't cover. If you plan to compete with TechCrunch [www.techcrunch.com], for example, don't try to be the world's authority on everything to do with Web 2.0. Just pick one aspect. Become the world's authority on some part of Web 2.0.

Examples of that are several Facebook blogs that recently popped out of the woodwork. They became very popular because they cover a smaller niche than TechCrunch is covering. But they're doing it better. They cover everything Facebook, whereas Techcrunch can only cover Facebook once in a while. Now anyone who wants to really keep up with the Facebook world reads these blogs.

THE FACEBOOK-BLOG CONNECTION

It is interesting to note that Facebook [www.facebook.com] showed me some readers I didn't know I had. A couple of weeks after I got on Facebook (in 2007), thousands of people joined my Facebook account, based on the blog where I'd talked about Facebook. I'd never seen comments from most of these people, but they knew me from the blog.

This begs the question: Do you think blogs might be heading toward specialization, a whole bunch of blogs in niches?

Unless you're going to be a better writer, a better photographer, or a better videographer than Mike Arrington and all the other top bloggers on the Web, you need to consider finding a niche.

Points to Review

Although Robert Scoble uses Google to draw readers, he is not preoccupied with SEO or gaming the system in the same way so many other bloggers are. Instead, an emphasis on social networking—interacting with other bloggers—has been a major factor in his success as a blogger. At the same time, he has focused less on building an audience than on creating quality content which, he notes, "beats SEO." Scoble recommends bloggers keep in mind the following:

- Focus heavily on building an audience can be detrimental to a blog's content.

- Blogging is heading toward more niche themes.
- In the long term, most blog readers are referred by Google or other search engines.
- Links from other blogs are more valuable than SEO, because those links give you the effect of SEO.
- If you're a better networker, you'll get more links.
- Google will bring a trickle of traffic to you forever.
- Google gives blogging its power, because blogging is the best way to get on Google.
- Don't risk damaging your credibility.
- Good content beats SEO.

Peter Rojas
Engadget

"It's not as easy as it looks."

—*Peter Rojas*

As cofounder and editorial director of Engadget, Peter Rojas is responsible for keeping millions of blog readers up-to-date on the latest in consumer electronics, personal technology, and gadgets in general.

Rojas, who is a graduate of Harvard and the University of Sussex (U.K.), has an extensive background in print journalism. Among other publications, he has written for *Popular Science, Fortune, Food & Wine, Slate, The Village Voice,*

www.engadget.com

Money, *Wired*, *Business 2.0*, and many other magazines. He has also served as editor for *Red Herring*.

In addition to being editorial director of Engadget, Rojas is the chief strategy officer for Weblogs, Inc. As a result of AOL buying Engadget and the rest of Weblogs, Inc. in 2005, he's also a programming director with AOL. Rojas is a frequent commenter on technology for several television and radio programs.

Engadget was not the first blog Rojas created. As a freelance writer in 2001, he started a personal blog, in part as a public notebook for article ideas. One year later he founded Gizmodo (www.gizmodo.com), a weblog that focuses on the latest in technology.

The Meritocratic Blog World

In 2004 Rojas created Engadget as a move toward his vision of what a dedicated team of bloggers can accomplish. His blogging experiences have made him a believer in the power of niche blogging and enthusiasm. In the interview that follows, he relates some of his personal experiences.

What inspired you to start your first blog?

At that point [in 2001], there was almost nothing that wasn't a personal blog—there were just blogs. Mine was a personal blog in that I wrote it—[but] it wasn't necessarily a blog about me. And it wasn't a business. There weren't any blogs that were businesses then, at least as far as I know.

I started the blog just after I was laid off from my job at *Red Herring* magazine, where I was a technology journalist and editor. Forty other people lost their jobs the same day as I did. The technology industry had sort of melted down in California.

I had a good friend who was an editor at *Wired*. He was sort of playing around with blogs, and he suggested that I start a blog. "Here's your chance to get your writing—and your voice—out there," he said, "and at the very least, you'll be writing and coming up with ideas for stories that you can pitch."

And so that's originally what my blog was—sort of a public notebook of ideas for stories that I wanted to pitch to magazines. I never was very good at the personal blog. I didn't write for it very often. Because I was freelancing, I spent a lot of time writing pitches for magazines and newspapers, which cut into my blogging time.

You weren't in it to make money?

When I started blogging with my personal blog, it was definitely not to make money. I got into it very early, when it wasn't clear that there was any money in blogging. The idea that someone would advertise on a blog seemed kind of absurd. It was just unknowable.

And the idea that advertisers would want to associate themselves with something so loose, free-form, and chaotic—the consensus was, "People will never advertise on blogs, at least not on a large scale. You will never get big advertisers, because they won't trust it, they won't want to be associated with that kind of stuff."

But people came around. When you have seven or eight million readers, it's kind of hard to wonder where your audience is.

And blogging grew up a little bit. People started to trust it. They realized that just because it's free-form doesn't mean that there aren't sites that are more trustworthy, have better reputations, and have better concepts than others. As the medium grew up, people started to see the nuances, and it became less black-and-white and more gray. And that's when it really started to come into its own and became something that one can do professionally.

When I started Gizmodo in 2002, it wasn't something I thought would ever really make money. I thought it would take off, but I never thought it would become as big as it did. But I was better able to work at it professionally and focus on it very intently.

When did blog advertising really get going?

It really was 2004. Google AdSense had a lot to do with it. Around the tail end of 2004, we started to see serious advertisers.

How did you go from Gizmodo to Engadget?

Well, I wasn't actually happy with the situation I had at Gizmodo. Nick's [Nick Denton, the founder and proprietor of Gawker Media, which owns Gizmodo] vision was for more of a casual site that would be done by one editor, part-time. At the time, this was the dominant mode of blogging.

I saw greater potential in blogging. I knew that if this was my full-time job, and I had other people working with me, I could do much more.

I decided to take the chance and partner with Weblogs, Inc. We really took off from there.

You have an extensive background in print media. Can you contrast blogging with editing or writing for a print magazine?

Blogging is a very differently structured media, in the same way that episodic television is very different from a film. Blogging is something that you do in real time—it's very fast, and it's much more intimate and conversational. A magazine has a slower editorial pace—a weekly is a little more hectic. And you can't update things in real time.

With a magazine, each week you have a certain number of boxes you have to fill, depending on how many pages you have, depending on how much advertising you have. Stories have to fit certain formats and have certain links, and there has to be a distribution of certain kinds of stories.

At Engadget, we don't have to worry about that. We do what needs to be done. We usually write between 30 and 50 posts a day, but we'll do fewer posts if there really isn't anything to write about. I don't really see that happening any time soon, given how intense the consumer electronic field is. I would love it if it slowed down to just 10 posts a day. But we do what makes sense.

> *"We're the audience, and our job is to be honest with the audience. Why would we lie to ourselves?"*

We don't have any sort of a target, and we don't have quotas. For example, the weekend after the iPhone release, we went overboard with the iPhone coverage because we have unlimited space. We could be as comprehensive as a 10,000-word review of the iPhone, and as casual as a photo of an iPhone with a Newton. Audiences really respond to that. And that's what's great about blogging and all niche media—you can really go in-depth. You go deep, not wide.

Is there more room to be personal in blogging?

Absolutely. When I started, Engadget wasn't about me, but it was my sort of perspective as an enthusiast. We are the audience that we're writing for. And I think that's sort of the critical difference between magazines and blogs. I come from a journalism background, and when I was at *Red Herring*, we weren't the audience. We were journalists who were never going to be venture capitalists.

So there was always this sort of idea that we were really different and set apart and that we were these arbiters. And with Engadget, it's like we're the audience, and our job is to be honest with the audience. Why would we lie to ourselves?

And this was a thing that I found very liberating about blogging. I am not an engineer, and I'm not a programmer. A lot of the technology sites before I started Gizmodo were very hard-core. On the other hand, you had these CNET [and] *New York Times* "Circuits" sections that were very broad market, for people who were just looking for information about what to buy. They weren't necessarily that interested in the market itself.

What I realized was that there was a market for people like me who are just really passionate about this stuff and want to be able to follow it. Engadget's not a good place to just drop in on once every six months because you want to buy something. It's a place to go because you're just kind of interested in following the gadget world, just like some people follow the sports world.

What do you do to bring in readers? Does Weblogs, Inc. or someone involved with Engadget work on SEO (search engine optimization)?

No. We don't do any SEO. I don't believe in SEO.

The blog world is very meritocratic. If you don't have consistently good posts, your blog is not going to go very far. There are tricks you can do to get some traffic here and there, but by and large, the cream rises to the top. The most successful blogs are generally the ones with the best writing, run by people with the most hustle.

You can see someone come out of nowhere and become a huge force in the industry. I was nobody, right? And now I'm a big voice in this world. And Mike Arrington [of TechCrunch]? I never even heard of this guy when I worked for *Red Herring* and covered venture capital in Silicon Valley. And he's been successful because his site is good. He works really hard.

You know, people talk about the A-list this, and the B-list that, and to be honest, it's a very fluid world. The people that work really hard and produce good work are successful, by and large.

You keep an eye on other blogs, then?

I read a couple hundred a day. At Engadget, we have a collaborative news-reader with about 700 sites. I personally read about 200 a day. I add some sites, and I delete some, but I'm still saturated. It's like having a second job, just keeping up with everything! It's worse than e-mail. People talk about e-mail bankruptcy? I'm on top of my e-mail. I don't have a backlog of e-mail to answer. It's the RSS feeds that overwhelm me. There's so much going on. It's exciting.

There's just so much activity in so many different fields. I'm interested in so much stuff—I don't just follow gadgets. I'm interested in a lot of stuff like online media, widgets, design, architecture, music, and film, so I read a lot of different blogs. And what I see over and over again, in every field, [is that] there's just so much going on. It's like an explosion of creativity, innovation, and ingenuity. It's totally different than Web 1.0, which I covered very closely. It's much more organic this time. It's really much more bottom-up and top-down.

When I decide I want to learn something about a field or an area, I just subscribe to blogs in that area, sometimes at random. For example, about a year ago I decided to learn about widgets. I literally Googled "widgets blog" and found a bunch of blogs. As I read and linked to more blogs, it became obvious what the best blogs in that field were.

I added those to my RSS feed, and deleted some of the other ones that weren't as good. And that gave me a pretty good sense of what was going on in the widget blogosphere.

It's a really good way to familiarize yourself with a field. Just start reading the blogs. You won't need to really spend a lot of time sweating over which is the best, because it will become apparent in a few weeks.

Do you comment on other blogs?

I do comment from time to time on other blogs. I don't tend to comment a lot. And I do have my own personal blog.

Because you don't have much time for personal blogging?

It's a time thing, and it's also a matter of: How much do I want to share my personal life on the Internet?

"NO PERSONAL ATTACKS" POLICY

I think there's a tendency in some other blogs to be harsh because that's their thing: they have to take people down. I don't feel that way at all. There is a no-personal-attacks rule at Engadget. You can't attack anyone personally—you can't take a cheap shot at anyone. It's one thing to make fun of Sony, but it's another thing to make fun of somebody who works at a Sony store. We try to look at products from a really fair and balanced view. We try to be very judicious about what we say and how we approach things.

Aside from time management, what is the most difficult part of blogging for you?

You have to get used to the fact that people are going to be very, very critical. Grow a thick skin and be prepared to accept legitimate criticism. When you're a very popular blogger, you have to be prepared to be treated as a public figure.

You also have to learn to chill out a little bit, and not take everything personally. People are jerks, and people are going to shoot their mouths off and say awful things. I've gotten death threats. You just have to realize that it's not the end of the world when someone e-mails you and says they're going to chop your head off. You have to be prepared to deal with a lot of that stuff—blogging can be a contact sport.

You see a lot of the same interpersonal interactions and dramas and miscommunications that you see over and over again in the real world. They can be dismaying sometimes, and the Internet is an accelerant for some things, but by and large, people are just as good or awful online as they are offline.

Another thing about blogging is that it is very, very competitive, and you have to constantly raise your game. And I think at Engadget, we've done a really great job of constantly raising our game, of consciously pushing ourselves to do better. We've never gotten complacent. We've never sort of leaned back and said, "Well, you know what? We're number one, and now we can sort of drift and hang out." We owe it to ourselves and [our] readers to constantly be doing a better job.

HIRE THE BEST

I've been really picky with the people we've hired and protective of making sure that our writers not only understand the field and can write in a conversational way, but also can uphold our high editorial standards. We don't cut corners, and we don't take junkets like some of our major competitors. In a way, that puts us at a disadvantage, because I don't get to tour the factory in Korea, but by the same token, could you trust our coverage if you knew that Samsung had paid for our trip? Yeah, disclosing it, that's fine. But on some level, it just doesn't seem right to me that you should be having that close a relationship with the company that you cover.

What do you find gratifying as a blogger?

One of the things I really love about blogging is that I've always been able to write up for the audience. I made this decision that the audience was very smart and wanted a lot of very in-depth, very thorough coverage. They didn't want just a cursory overview of things or watered-down coverage.

There are so many amazing things. Like the reader meet-ups we hosted, having 500 people show up for an event. Going outside and seeing the line stretched around the block. Honestly, that blew me away.

In some ways, blogging still feels like just this goofy thing that I do in my apartment. We don't have an office, so it's sometimes hard to get my head around the fact that this is something that millions of people read—millions of people love Engadget.

Things like interviewing Bill Gates are also good. But I think covering CES [the Consumer Electronics Show] in 2007 was one of my proudest moments, because I feel like I've really been able to transform the show.

When I started covering CES, it was a big show, but there was not a lot of awareness of it on the consumer level. But I think we've really helped turn CES into a really big event—something that not just the attendees care about, but something the rest of the world should pay attention to as well. I think we have, hands-down, the best coverage of CES that's ever been done anywhere by anyone.

I also think we've done a really good job with educating consumers, teaching them to expect more from their devices. That's why we're very picky at Engadget about stuff we like and stuff that we don't like; we don't play favorites.

As you read other blogs, do you get some feeling for the *gestalt* of the overall blogosphere?

You know, there isn't one. It's so big, and so much stuff is going on now that I find it hard to make sense of anything but the little corner that I'm a part of. I know other tech bloggers—like Dave Winer, Robert Scoble, Kevin Rose, and Steve Rubel—and this is kind of my little corner of the business.

But there are other universes out there where those names mean nothing. And I think that's actually good. I don't really know any of the people in the political blogosphere, of which there are many smaller political blogospheres. There is a celebrity gossip blogosphere, and many others. I have my little perspective on things and where things are going in my sphere, and I focus on that.

SOMETHING FOR EVERYONE

One of the things that gets lost when people tell the story of blogging is blogging means different things to a lot of different people. For some people, it's a way to update friends and family. For some people, it's a job. For others, it's a way to track something they're passionate about or a way to promote their name in a field. People aren't just blogging to make money or get their name on a list. People blog because it fills a need in their career or some other aspect of their life.

Any advice for somebody who's starting a blog?

My number-one piece of advice for someone [who's starting a blog] is find something to be passionate about. I know that sounds really obvious, but it is not obvious in some ways to a lot of people. And a lot of people think, "Oh well, I want to have a successful blog, so I should do a blog about something that's already successful." Like doing a blog about gossip because that seems to do really well.

But the thing about it is that what makes a blog really successful is the passion of the person or the people who are writing it. If you have that passion and you're blogging about something, it will be very, very obvious. The readers will pick up on that, and you will have a successful blog.

Another piece of advice is don't be afraid to start slowly. I wouldn't necessarily try to attract too much attention too quickly, because when you start blogging, you're going to make mistakes. You're going to do something that someone is not happy with. You might not link to someone properly or whatever. There's sort of a blog etiquette that you have to figure out.

You want to sort of give yourself a chance to acclimate to the pace and the writing style, to find your voice. And that can take a little while. It took me about six months at Gizmodo to find my voice. And really enjoy that time, because once you have an audience you cannot ever go back to posting anonymously. So don't necessarily feel pressured to have a successful blog right away. You're going to be doing stuff that's going to make your blog worse, like trying to write stories just to get on Digg or just to get a link from Engadget.

And that is really, ultimately what doesn't make it. There are blogs with everything like top ten this or top five that, and those blogs get traffic just because people link to them from Digg, Technorati, or a similar site. But they're not going to have an organic readership. No one actually thinks, "Oh, I love this blog!" It's more like this is a site that gets linked to on Digg every week.

> *"Enthusiasm makes a huge, huge difference. And readers can tell … When you really care, you actually start to ask the kinds of questions and do the kind of writing that creates something of value for the reader."*

That's not the kind of site you want to have. You want to have the kind of site where people say, "I am a part of this community. I am a passionate reader of this site. This site gives me something that I love, and I have to read it every day."

It's all about finding a subject. When I started Gizmodo and Engadget, gadgets seemed like such a narrow niche. I was thinking, "Okay, I'm not going to do a technology blog. I'm going to do a gadget blog. It's going to be *so* narrow."

But gadgets turned out to be this huge category. If I was going to start a blog now, I would go very, very, very niche—as niche as you can get.

The thing about it is, no matter how niche you go, there will always be too much to write about. But if you pick something specific and maybe that's not so heavily covered yet, you have a chance to really establish yourself as a voice in that area.

Enthusiasm makes a huge, huge difference. And readers can tell. When I read a blog, I can tell when someone really cares about the subject matter. And if you think about it, when you really care, you actually start to ask the kinds of questions and do the kind of writing that creates something of value for the reader. There's a difference between being an Apple fanboy and someone who really cares about the products they're buying from Apple. For example, the Apple blogs that I read that have a lot of value— the people say, "I care so much about this stuff that I am not going to shy away from criticism, or shy away from saying what I really feel, or being honest when I think Apple screwed up."

The unabashedly fanboy [sites that] never say a negative thing about Steve Jobs—those sites are not worth reading. You're not going to get anything of value, because they're just going to parrot what Apple wants them to say— nice things about Apple—which is not valuable for anybody.

It's the people who love Apple—who actually care enough about it to say what they really feel and to criticize—who are doing a great job. And that's the thing about Engadget that people like—I am not afraid to call it as I see it, to really level with the audience.

Finally, remember that the blogging entry barrier is so low that your credibility is the only thing you have to differentiate yourself from everyone else.

PASSION EQUALS SUCCESS

You have to be passionate about your subject and really love what you're doing. This is one of the big differences between bloggers and professional journalists.

For example, I worked at *Red Herring* but wasn't necessarily that interested in venture capital. I was just happy to have a job and work in a magazine and get paid. But I wasn't really that interested in the subject. And so I ended up trying to write stories that I was interested in. They were about technology, but they didn't necessarily fit in with what *Red Herring* was about. They wouldn't let me do a story about Napster, and I told them, "This is going to be a huge thing!" But they said, "There is no business model."

Points to Review

Few bloggers have as much experience as Peter Rojas, and obviously, you can learn a lot from his approach to blogging. Here are a few tips you can glean from his experiences:

- Blogging is a medium in its own right, and it's much more intimate and conversational than print media.
- SEO is not the ultimate answer to generating traffic.
- The blog world is meritocratic. Those who have the best writing and work hardest are usually the most successful.
- Blogs can be an excellent self-study tool.
- If you plan to become a well-known blogger, learn to accept criticism.
- Human interactions—in particular, those involving emotions—are often amplified and accelerated by the Internet.
- Choose as small a niche as possible; you'll never run out of things to write about.
- Don't try to jump to number one in your field immediately. A slow start allows you to make the inevitable mistakes when few people are looking.
- If you're enthusiastic about your blog subject, it will show; or if you're not enthusiastic, it will show.

John Neff
Autoblog

12

> *"You have to be passionate and interested in what you're blogging about. Otherwise, you're just not going to last."*
>
> —*John Neff*

Autoblog is the number-one Web destination for more than 5 million auto and truck owners, hobbyists, investors, and just about anyone else who has a personal or professional interest in automobiles. Founded in 2004, the blog is the single most popular site of its kind, and second only to Engadget in the Weblogs, Inc. blog network (which is owned by AOL).

www.autoblog.com

The site covers every imaginable aspect of the automotive field: cars, trucks, SUVs, racing, design, automakers, unions—everything. And Autoblog has spun off podcasts and several more popular blogs, including AutoblogGreen, Autoblog Spanish, and Autoblog Chinese.

Led by editor-in-chief John Neff, a dedicated team of more than a dozen bloggers around the world keep up with the automotive world 24 hours a day.

John Neff came to blogging in a roundabout way. After college, he moved from his native Cleveland to Detroit, to become the editor of *S3* (*Speed, Style & Sound*) magazine, a publication for custom-car owners. He had always been a car enthusiast (among his treasured possessions is a collection of more than 2,000 old car magazines in pristine condition), and notes that he has always had an interest in automotive journalism, "mostly because it's very entertaining yet at the same time packed with enormous amounts of factual information. It's a difficult balance to achieve in a piece, but when done well it is very satisfying to read."

Thus editing a car magazine was pretty much an ideal position for Neff. But after two years, he decided to return to Cleveland. There, he took a job with the Cleveland Apple Store. Around this time, his brother suggested that he have a look at several blogs hosted by Weblogs, Inc., among them The Unofficial Apple Weblog (www.tuaw.com), Joystiq (www.joystiq.com), and Engadget (www.engadget.com). These blogs led him to Autoblog, and he was soon a regular reader.

What happened next was almost natural. One day, Neff spotted an Autoblog post inviting new contributors. "I thought it would be a great thing to do to make some extra money," he explains. "So I wrote for a few months, and the guy who was the lead of the blog—which is what we call the editors—suggested that I and another guy take over responsibility for the blog. I happened to outlast the other guy and I'm running it on my own now."

Like most full-time bloggers in what is essentially a cottage industry, Neff works from his home. But this doesn't limit him. He travels to cover auto shows and get the scoop on big stories, and he is in touch with his bloggers via instant messaging (IM) throughout the day. "That's the beauty of the Internet—that you don't have to really be anywhere. You only have to be at a computer."

Obsessively Covering the Auto Industry

Neff has led Autoblog to more than 15 million page views per month, and he doesn't see the action letting up. "Every time I bring someone on, I tell them it's still the bottom floor. You're still getting on in the sweet spot and it's going up, and I don't know when it's going to level off or plateau. So it's still exciting two years later, and it's still growing at the pace it was two years ago. I hope it doesn't level off. I hope blogging entrenches itself as a traditional form of media."

How does blogging compare with editing or writing for a magazine?

At the magazine, I had a new issue to put together once a month. I do that on a daily basis now. At times, the stress can be a bit more intense, because we like to have posts going up all day long. I won't let an hour go by [during the day] where we don't have a post.

Also, in the car magazine business, they get letters and pick out the ones they want to respond to. Readers and advertisers have to wait a month or more to see those responses. But with the blog, we get comments instantly, and they're not edited. And I tell the automakers, "When you give us a car, and we do a review, watch it because you're going to get instant feedback that is very raw and very real."

> *"Probably the biggest challenge is coordinating our bloggers and encouraging them to make the blog better. But it's also more rewarding than just writing ten posts a day."*

And manufacturers take Autoblog seriously. Witness Dodge's participation in giving away a brand-new Dodge Nitro R/T on Autoblog in 2007.

Are there any other aspects of the job that are particularly difficult?

Just staying on top of the news can be a trial. There are lots of blogs and lots of automotive blogs, and we don't want to be the third or fourth blog or automotive news outlet to break a story. We're always trying to be the first on something.

Probably the biggest challenge is coordinating our bloggers and encouraging them to make the blog better. But it's also more rewarding than just writing ten posts a day.

With five million unique users, you seem to be doing well at it.

Yes, but sometimes it's tough. Nearly everyone who writes on the Autoblog team has a nine-to-five job. So a lot of these people are posting at night, or they have some arrangement where they're available at odd times during the day. So, when news breaks, hopefully somebody is in front of their computer. We have bloggers pretty much all over the world, so somebody's awake every second of the day.

Do you spend a lot of hours blogging every day?

Usually. Working from home, the hours are very flexible, which makes it easier to put in more time. I can start work at ten in the morning, and I'll usually work until about six. Later that evening, I usually do a couple more hours of work.

The idea of bloggers working at home seems as if it might clash with corporate culture.

Absolutely. This was something AOL had a problem with at first. All of us worked from home, but AOL was so used to handing out security badges and saying, "Here is your cubicle," and things like that, they didn't relate to having a small army of workers working from home.

Traditional work ethic seems to dictate that if you can't see someone, they may not be working.

I think that's definitely the case with the old type of labor structure. But with us, we're communicating via IM all day, and if I'm not around, eight people know it instantly.

But rather than keeping an eye on us every day, I think our bosses look at our performance. They don't have anything to complain about because Autoblog reached 15 million page views in mid-2007, and it's growing every month. I really must be doing something in my apartment to make this happen. As long as the results keep happening, and that's on my shoulders, I think that replaces the over-the-shoulder observation that happens in an office.

Before AOL, when we were just Weblogs, Inc., the business model was that we hired bloggers who worked from home. They contributed the computer, the electricity, and so on. There was no overhead. It was really just a perfect business model, and it still is.

How does it feel to have this huge audience? Some bloggers say it's difficult to comprehend.

I completely agree. On a blog like Engadget or Autoblog, you do have commenters, and you have people sending in e-mails all day long, so it's fun and it feels like you're carrying on a conversation.

But it's a relatively small conversation, even though it's happening in front of five million people. You almost get the sense that nobody's reading. You read the comments, maybe 500 or 600 a day, and you think, "Okay, there are 600 people out there reading this." But you can't wrap your head around five million unique visitors a month. It's mind-boggling.

But when you get out of the little cave that you work in, and you start to meet people, it's amazing. Again, at home it almost feels like there's nobody out there, like you're just writing because it's fun to write. But when I go to an auto show wearing a shirt with an Autoblog logo, people tap me on the shoulder and ask me, "Oh, are you with Autoblog?" Instant recognition.

You don't go into the office every day, but do you meet with other people from Weblogs, Inc.?

We meet about every three months, either in New York City at AOL headquarters in Rockefeller Square, or in Dulles, Virginia, where the main office is. Usually the meeting consists of the full-time bloggers who are hired by AOL, like me and Chris Grant [of `Joystiq.com`], along with AOL weblog producers.

I talk to these people on IM all day long. I hardly ever talk to them on the phone. And when we get together, we iron out a few things that can only be done in person and then go have fun. It's a great business model.

What special efforts do you make to bring readers to the blog?

While there are certainly a lot of strategies for promotion, the number-one thing that we do is just what we've always done: just put our heads down and keep our legs pumping, and keep posting.

Just having those posts going up every single day gets readers addicted to the site. They come back five times a day just to see what's new.

To bring in new readers, we work to find new stuff to write about. For example, if we write about car seats, maybe a parenting blog will link to it as well as other car blogs. That opens up whole new groups of people who've never seen us before.

Other Weblogs, Inc. blogs, like Engadget, link to our relevant posts, which helps a lot.

And we are in the very fortunate position that Weblogs, Inc. was bought by AOL in 2005. That works to our advantage in that when the people at AOL see something on our blog that they like, they put it on the AOL main page. That reaches the average Internet user, and we get to a lot of people who would have never seen our posts otherwise.

> *"In the past, we had this 'just don't talk to [our competitors]' attitude ... Now that we communicate with each other, it's really a great community ... Everybody has their own niche, and we all help out."*

For a long time, they seemed to leave us alone and didn't really take advantage of us. But I think AOL, knowing that its own image was very tarnished during the preceding decade, has really kind of come around to see that we're the one property they have where all the growth is completely organic. Readers look at us because they want to. I don't think AOL has had that type of viewership in a long time. People go to AOL because they have AOL and don't know how to get out of it, or they're comfortable with it.

So AOL has come to see the value in blogging and Weblogs, Inc., and [value] the people who are at Weblogs, Inc. because we've developed the skill to create concepts and content that people come to read of their own volition. They're not being tricked to come or held against their will.

And—giving credit to AOL—when they bought us, I don't think they knew what they were getting into. But there are a lot of visionaries on the AOL staff who see what we're doing, and see how valuable it is that Weblogs, Inc. generates original content 24 hours a day.

Here's something that most people wonder about: what kinds of perks do Autoblog bloggers enjoy? Obviously the manufacturers loan cars for review, and it must be fun to drive a new car for a few days, even if it's a lemon. What else is there?

We travel a lot for show coverage—probably more than Engadget bloggers, because there are so many auto shows in a year. Tokyo, Europe, America.

Show coverage has really become our bread and butter of traffic. We've gotten really good at it. It's something that happened that I didn't really expect.

And that's an aspect of the job that makes it even sweeter. What bloggers get paid is fourth or fifth on their list of things most important to them. Things like going to car shows, reviewing the vehicles themselves, and talking to designers—these are all perks that are way more important than pay, and make the job worth it.

Do you have much time to look at other blogs?

Part of my day is checking the RSS feeds of 150 to 200 other blogs that have to do with cars. Other blogs are very important because we can't cover everything. So when somebody takes the time to do a lot of work on a post or a story for a very small item on their blog, we do a post about their post, to let our readers know about it. Having those to refer to is a great service for us, and we hope our links introduce them to new readers.

What has been your most-gratifying experience with this blog?

There was a point at which we approached our competitors—the other blogs like Jalopnik, Winding Road, and several more. In the past, we had this "just don't talk to them" attitude. But we all got to talking, and now that we communicate with each other, it's really a great community. These are our competitors, but everybody has their own niche, and we all help out.

That was something we lacked at the print magazine, where it's really cutthroat. Because the overhead is way more at a magazine, you're always trying to do so much with so little. With the blogs, it's different. The auto manufacturers are just astounded that we're all friends and look out for each other.

But we all know that this is a very nascent industry, and that everybody is kind of watching us and they all think we're amateurs blogging in our pajamas. We're doing our best to confound that notion and show them that we're professional. We're not just people putting our diary online.

What about newer blogs, those that you aren't in touch with?

I haven't really been bothered by the new blogs coming along. Certainly there are some that show up with grand aspirations, but take less than ethical strategies to get ahead of their competition. But because we have this community—at least the larger blogs all merged together—the new blogs that do that are left out of the loop and that doesn't serve them. That pretty much puts a ceiling on their growth, because they don't want to play by the general rules we all have abided by.

We all depend on each other. The aggregation of letting our readers know what's out there, in addition to producing our original content, couldn't happen if there weren't a lot of smaller blogs very much keeping the spirit of blogging alive—that spirit being to focus on items that nobody else saw or noticed. Without that, we wouldn't have half the posts we do in a day.

What do you think of bloggers who accept payment for blogging on a particular product, in effect selling a positive review?

I think it's pretty bad. But at the same time, I'm not concerned about it because it's so blatant and obvious. Most readers are intelligent enough to spot that type of blogging a mile away. One of the founders of Weblogs Inc., Jason Calacanis, has written and argued extensively on how horrible pay-per-blog—which is what they call it—is.

> *"You have to [be passionate] every single day and not give up, and eventually ... [if] you're doing something interesting and original—you'll get noticed."*

At Weblogs, Inc., we are insulated from the business aspect. People ask me how much it costs to advertise on Autoblog, and I don't know. I've never seen that side of it, which hasn't been the case everywhere I've worked. As long as it has been around, pay-per-blog hasn't taken off. There is no real traffic involved in it. It's kind of sad, I think, that marketing people would think that it's a good idea.

What sort of advice can you offer bloggers?

You have to be passionate and interested in what you're blogging about. Otherwise, you're just not going to last. You have to do it every single day and not give up, and eventually—if you're doing it well, and you're doing something interesting and original—you'll get noticed.

And there is no way to make a lot of money in blogging unless you sit down and start a blog you're passionate about, and you do it for a year. Nothing happens very quickly. It's all about growing an audience and doing it organically in the right way. And the best way to make money—if that's what you want to do—is to sell ads.

Points to Review

Autoblog isn't the number-one Web destination for all things automotive by accident. It's successful because its bloggers are passionate about what they do. Here are some of the highlights of John Neff's interview:

- The editorial and business aspects of blogging must be separated as much as possible.
- Have passion for what you write about.
- Posting daily encourages readers to return.
- To bring in new readers, work up new subjects to write about.
- Don't neglect other blogs as news sources. Be sure to credit your sources.
- Growth does not happen quickly.

Ken Fisher
Ars Technica

13

> *"There's a lot to be said for having a personality that's obsessed with getting things right, digging to the bottom of things, really kind of being conversational with other people."*
>
> —*Ken Fisher*

A rs Technica (Latin for the art of technology) is both a blog and an online community. In its decade of existence, Ars Technica has developed a huge following by focusing not just on technical topics, but on the full range of human arts and sciences.

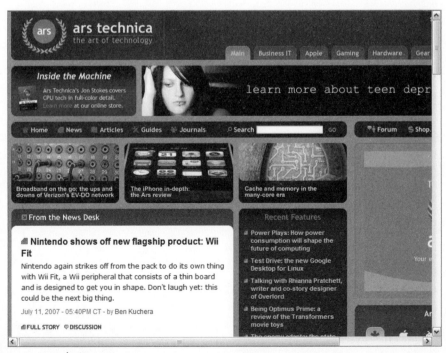

www.arstechnica.com

One of the most linked-to blogs on the Web, Ars Technica was founded in 1998 by Ken Fisher. Today the blog is essentially a full-time job for Fisher and several other bloggers.

Fisher is a doctoral student who studies Coptic texts. Interestingly, one of the other founders, Jon Stokes, who writes for the site, is also in a doctoral program, studying the New Testament. Plus, Fisher notes, "My managing editor has a graduate-level degree in theology. And I have an assistant editor who does not have any theological schooling but did graduate work in English and was a contributor to *Christianity Today*. It sounds like we're 'the priests of high technology.' But it's mostly coincidence."

In addition to its blog, Ars Technica offers journals, product guides, articles, and the Ars Technica OpenForum, a community database of technical tips and reference information.

Rumors: Distorted Reflections in a Mirror

If you talk with Fisher for any length of time, you'll probably come away feeling that battling rumor is a lot of what Ars Technica is about. From his viewpoint, the technology world is "dominated by rumor and speculation."

But he's never overwhelmed by it. As he says, "We absolutely thrive on trying to see through all the smoke and mirrors."

Were you a blogger before Ars Technica?

No. Ars was started in 1998, and what I was doing before 1998, I don't think anybody would call blogging. I don't believe that word was widely used back then, anyway.

I was an undergrad and I worked in IT [information technology], and I was quite often bored. So I decided I would have my own home page.

Back then, home pages were like a portrait, or a picture. They weren't constantly updated. They weren't meant to be logs, really. My home page was a web page with all kinds of blogging-like elements to it, but not really blogging.

What made you decide to start a blog?

I think it was part inspiration and part frustration. A handful of us were involved in starting Ars Technica, in getting it up and running. When I sent out the call to my friends to start it, I was thinking it would center on gaming and technology. I was thinking, "Gee, we all read these gaming news sites all the time. We just can't live without them."

But actually, even though some people would have said we were hard-core PC gamers, we didn't really consider ourselves PC gamers. We were mostly tech guys who couldn't wait until five o'clock to play Quake.

Our goal with Ars Technica was to bring the level of enthusiasm and technical accuracy we had for games to IT in general, and hardware in particular. That idea was born out of necessity—we felt that there were sites out there that were doing an okay job [of keeping up with tech news], but we felt we could do better.

And that's what Ars has really been trying to do since day one—to provide better coverage. And it's something that I really wish other tech publications would do, because it's frustrating to see the technology press sometimes stuck re-writing press releases.

And the emphasis was on original content?

Yes, we tried from the beginning to be original, and I think what enabled us to do that was the fact that we're all hard-core tinkerers. You just let us loose on a big pile of hardware, and we go crazy. If you're willing to play with stuff, build stuff, and test stuff—just put forth the effort—there is a lot of original work to be done.

We mixed that with just bouncing back and forth to other sites, and passing news along with our take on it. It was a real mix, but in the early days, we certainly earned our reputation and our name from original stuff.

> *"There were sites out there that were doing an okay job, but we felt like we could do better."*

Of course, it is still important to be original. I feel that anyone who wants to really stake a place in the conversation [of blogs] is going to have to do a significant amount of original work. Not only is it kind of boring to just rewrite other people's news, but these days, you run the risk of re-repeating errors.

Did Ars Technica carry advertising in those days?

We had no advertising for, I think, the first three months we were up. Really, what we thought at the time was that we were just going to start this website, and every year we would pitch in some money to pay the bills. At that time, I believe we estimated the cost of running the site to be $100 a year. We were thinking, "Oh, this will be nothing. It's just a hobby, really."

I think the first full month of publishing was September, and by December we were [at] over 100,000 page views. I looked around and said, "I guess maybe we should get some advertising," because by that point we had kind of climbed up our hosting plan, and costs were going up.

So we found advertisers. And as 1999 moved along, I started figuring that this is something we should take seriously, and we put more ads on the site.

But recently we've been trying to remove ads.

You're *reducing* the number of ads on your pages?

Yes. I'm pretty proud of this. If you go to Engadget or almost any site that competes with us, they will have seven, eight, nine, ten, or more ads on their pages. But on our front page, we have two.

> "*Anyone who wants to really stake a place in the conversation [of blogs] is going to have to do a significant amount of original work.*"

Slashdot beats us, I have to say. Slashdot only has one ad. And [large sites such as] CNET News.com and CNN.com also have small numbers of ads, but they get hundreds of thousands of dollars for their ads, and we don't.

In the hardware world, it's normal to have seven ads on a page, with blinking Christmas-tree effects. But we have tried to cut it back, and we're in the situation of probably having to replace one format with another. It's going to shake up the site a bit.

But we're really dedicated to keeping the advertising content low in the hopes that readers appreciate and respect our attempt to balance what they really want (content) with what they don't (ads).

Will you make up for the lost income in some way?

We're kind of unique in that we actually sell subscriptions to the site. And the site uses the revenue generated from that to fund our Forum, which is big and sprawling and consumes a lot of resources. One of the things that we're really hoping to do in the next six months or so is make it so subscribers don't see ads, and that all the ad spots just kind of collapse and fill with new information.

This is not an indication that you have anything against advertising on blogs in general, is it?

I feel that advertising is an absolutely fair tradeoff for free content. And I get very unhappy when I see people talking about blocking ads. My approach is if a website wants to inundate me with ads, that's a website I won't go to, rather than kill the ads.

I've gotten into many arguments with people about how that makes me a hypocrite because they know for a fact that when I watch television I don't sit and watch every ad.

> *"Advertising is an absolutely fair tradeoff for free content."*

But I insist that the two [television and blogs] are fundamentally different. And I think if I'm going to be such a fascist when it comes to ads, then I've got to be fair, too, and we have to keep the ad content down.

The other side of the advertising coin is that you just absolutely have to keep the advertisers at arm's length.

At Ars Technica, I handle all that stuff myself. No one else on the staff touches that, and I like it that way. We have third-party representation, so I'm not actually selling anything. At most I have to give a "thumbs up" or "thumbs down" to things and respond to requests. If you are the publisher and the guy writing it [the blog], you have to get your hands dirty with money. You cannot avoid it.

Many bloggers do not have third-party ad reps, and can't keep advertisers at a distance. This raises conflict-of-interest issues. What is your take on this?

There are issues involving whether bloggers keep products they review. So many of them say, "I never keep anything, and I don't get any special kickbacks." But I'm thinking there's a reason why certain people had their iPhones three weeks before everyone else. Access to hot hardware and new technologies is also a very real and quite capital benefit, at the end of the day. I'm not blaming them. I'm just saying that the debate is significantly more complex than who keeps things and who doesn't. We don't keep anything.

And then there are bloggers like the one who responded to my post about Microsoft giving laptops to bloggers with, "I don't know where Ken Fisher's coming from. I always keep everything I'm sent because it's the only way running this site becomes fiscally possible."

So there are conflicts of interest. But they don't just involve bloggers. Companies have been playing to journalists since companies were born. I can't stand this idea that there's this pristine "other side" where there are no issues.

> *"There's a bit of a double standard being applied to bloggers right now. Everybody wants to say, 'Well, bloggers aren't journalists … just idiots with computers.' Yet at the same time, they want to hold bloggers to 'journalistic ethics.'"*

Access is the most important issue of all, not whether some blogger gets to keep some $2,000 laptop.

I think this issue is more critical with the smaller sites. If you're a small guy and you want to be able to write about products, you need these companies to like you and to talk to you. You're not gonna necessarily rip 'em a new one because they told you, "Oh, don't worry about sending it back," or whatever.

There's also this whole spectrum of back-scratching going on. It happens in many different forms.

If there were more transparency in all this, the world would be a better place.

What about bloggers who solicit payment for writing positive reviews of products or other posts about products in exchange for cash or merchandise from advertisers or other manufacturers?

It's a trend. I think it makes certain sense to a certain kind of marketing mind. My reaction to things like that is that people are just way, way too smart to fall for that stuff.

And it's becoming easier to determine what content is authoritative and what is not. That still doesn't prevent somebody who has a marketing budget and who is really smart from sending the blogosphere into a frenzy for a day or two with a well-placed campaign.

Anyway, I think most readers are just too smart to fall for paid placement like this. It's a little like the best spam you get. You still kind of know it's spam, even before you get to the part where somebody's dying of cancer and desperately needs money. You just know from the first two lines that there's something not right.

For my part, I have a pretty refined crap-o-meter. Whenever I read something that's telling me about a product that I might be interested in, what I'm trying to sense is whether this guy actually uses this product. And does he really care about this product?

This points to another issue: a lack of regard for bloggers as journalists in a new medium.

Certainly there's a bit of a double standard being applied to bloggers right now. It seems like everybody wants to say, "Well, bloggers aren't journalists. Bloggers are just idiots with computers." Yet at the same time, they want to hold bloggers to "journalistic ethics."

Having had many, many stories lifted from our site by so-called "journalists with ethics," I'm not exactly sure that there's really such a black-and-white issue here. It seems like it's a very complicated spectrum of things.

> *"Even today there are bloggers out there who can't verify rumors, no matter how hard they try. Sometimes the companies mentioned in rumors won't even talk to some bloggers. That ends up spreading those rumors further."*

The fact that the Web is home to so many rumors does cast shadows of doubt on its reliability as a news source. How do you deal with rumors?

I have a couple of things to say about that. There are nasty people in the world who pull hoaxes on journalists and bloggers. We get hoax materials sent to us all the time. I'm fairly sure that we've never fallen for one.

You never know how that stuff gets started. And Apple seems to get the most rumors. It quite truly appears that there are people out there who spend hours making fake pictures—really compelling fake pictures—of Apple products. What could possibly make that fun? I don't know.

So, there is that angle, of people creating rumors for the sake of creating rumors. And there is the angle that some publications are just willing to put any wild idea up, saying, "This is not a rumor. This is speculation." They do this because of the potential for increasing traffic. It's frustrating to us at Ars because we definitely feel that you should at least try to get confirmation before you originate a rumor.

Getting confirmation can be a tough thing to do, though. While you're trying to do the upstanding, responsible thing and verify information, what sometimes happens is that you run into this corporate culture that's like, "Well, who *are* you? Why are you calling? We're not talking to you."

For Ars, that has pretty much vanished in the last couple of years. But we ran into it regularly when we first started. I think it was the site's design. We had a black background with white text and it looked…well, we always characterized our appearance at the time as like a pirate flag—a flag we were hoisting up like, "Ha ha ha!"

Not that we were stealing content. It was our way of saying, "Hey, we're different."

That burned a lot of bridges for us. People looked at that and thought, "These guys are psycho! Who in God's name would ever design their site to look like that?" We had problems.

But even today there are bloggers out there who can't verify rumors, no matter how hard they try. Sometimes the companies mentioned in rumors won't even talk to some bloggers. That ends up spreading those rumors further.

Speaking of rumors, I hear there are guaranteed ways to make big money blogging.

If you go into this [blogging] with that mindset, you are going to be an unhappy person because the landscape changes so fast. You can go in with your master plan and high expectations and the "Oh, we're going to be rich!" attitude. But then six months later, something will happen. The game always changes.

I definitely feel like I can say that because, of all the people you've talked to, not many of them have been doing this as long as we have. I think Mike

Masnick at Techdirt actually may be as old as we are, and Slashdot is certainly older. And they'll tell you how the landscape has changed.

Ars Technica alone has gone through at least three different revenue peaks, where the same amount of traffic can be worth a tenth of what it was worth just half a year later.

> *"I think it's impossible to live in any information stream these days without RSS."*

But if you're not like that, I think you're going to be unhappy, because it takes a long time before you make any money, and so much of it is out of your control.

And speaking of money, some people claim to have the "secret" to making big money blogging, and offer it for a price.

Those are the people that are ruining the Internet. Unfortunately the "secret" also includes stealing and repurposing everybody's RSS feeds and putting up blogs everywhere.

I thought that that was something that would not last very long, but it's still going on. Google has crusaded against these sites and apparently will pull them if it can find them.

Do you think Google is cutting down on gaming the system?

Well, that's what they claim, and certainly it's in their interest. Google has to look like they care about this kind of stuff. And they probably do—I don't mean to imply that they don't. But they have to look like they're pursuing these bad people in earnest. Advertisers have been a little surprised to find out, for example, that AdSense is matching up an ad for Microsoft Office against a blog post that's telling you that Office is horrible and that you should always use Open Office unless you're an idiot.

They've got to go after it. They say they're going after it, and I think that they might have had some success.

Switching to a more hands-on topic, are there any special blogging tools you like to use?

Probably nobody who is blogging can live without RSS. I think it's impossible to live in any information stream these days without RSS. It's indispensable.

We have a custom content-management system that we use, but I sometimes wish that we would use something like a WordPress because it is widely supported and there are all kinds of plug-ins and add-ons for it. We had to build ours because at the time we started the project, there wasn't any of the blogging software that's online now.

But beyond that, nothing really. We're a group of mainly PC users and Mac users. One guy is an Amiga addict and won't let it go. We have some Linux users. Everybody's got their own different things, but in terms of what keeps the site together, and our publishing efforts, it's all this system we built.

What advice can you offer other bloggers?

The number-one piece of advice I have is make your writing your own. If you have points of view that are yours, just share them. I think that the strength of blogging is that it's built for idiosyncrasies. If you embrace that, you'll have the most success in the long run, whether it's building a readership or finding people that are like-minded. Because if you embrace [what we at Ars call] your "inner geek," you're doing two things for yourself. The first is that you're not worrying about positioning your content so it appeals to certain kinds of people. You're just putting it out there and being honest with yourself, which is important. The second thing is, once you allow yourself to do that, that's when it's fun.

> *"The number-one piece of advice I have is make your writing your own."*

You've got to be personable. Whatever you do, don't try to write like you write for the Associated Press.

If you're wrong, admit you're wrong. If you feel like gloating, maybe gloat a little bit. There's nothing wrong with that.

Points to Review

As a blogging pioneer, Ken Fisher is as sensitive to what damages blogs as he is to what makes them succeed. The following tips address some of the more important of these issues:

- It is necessary to be original.
- Keeping advertising content low lets you balance content with ads, leading to happier readers.

- Content producers should not be involved with advertising, to avoid even the appearance of advertiser-influenced content.
- Try to confirm the truth of a rumor before publishing it.
- If you go into blogging with the idea that you are going to make a fortune, you'll most likely end up frustrated.
- The Internet landscape changes quickly, without notice, so don't count on continuing success.
- Write what you feel rather than trying to appeal to a certain group.
- Use a relaxed and personable style rather than trying to copy a news style.

Deborah Petersen
Life in the Fast Lane

14

> *"I eat, sleep, and breathe my blog."*
>
> —*Deborah Petersen*

There are people who start out to blog for one reason, but once they are involved, they find completely different motivations.

It was like that for Deborah Petersen. When she got into blogging, Petersen was already a Web veteran, having set up a professional site for Fast Lane Transport, a family-owned business. Fast Lane is a large freight company that serves Canada's four western provinces, as well as providing in-city industrial

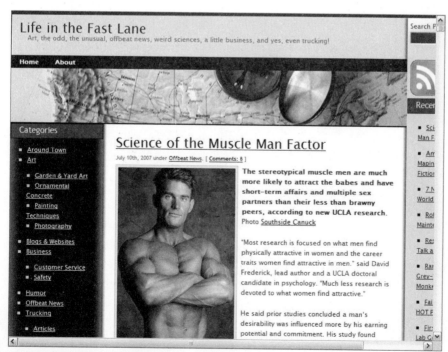

www.fastlanetransport.ca/blog

courier service in the Edmonton, Alberta area. Her husband, Layne Petersen, founded the company in 2000, and Deborah serves as business manager and dispatcher.

Petersen is a search engine optimization (SEO) enthusiast. In fact, it was SEO that got her into blogging. According to Petersen, the Fast Lane website was doing fairly well with search engines in 2006. But the idea that a blog could help get even better results was attractive. She decided to add a blog in support of the business.

Unlike many bloggers, she didn't just set up a blog and start typing. Petersen spent months researching blogs and blogging tools. She knew quite a bit about SEO from her research into that topic for the Fast Lane website and was aware that SEO for blogging was a subject that had much more to it. She also knew that there were many aspects of blogging that had nothing to do with SEO. So she looked at websites, asked questions, and read up on blogging.

On the Road to the Top

The Life in the Fast Lane blog, which includes several custom design features, went live in February 2007. By then, Peterson had decided that her blogging would not be confined to the freight business or even the trucking industry. She would cover a wide range of personal interests to maximize search-engine exposure and to fuel her enthusiasm for the tasks she was taking on.

As she said in her very first post, "You won't find me discussing business topics only—as important as this is to our company's success—rather, I will also share with you some of my other interests, including yard art, garden art, and details about what is going on in my home city, Edmonton."

And so it was. Petersen set up a number of categories for posts, covering art, ornamental concrete, photography, blogs and websites, offbeat news, and even trucking, among other subjects.

Supplemented by social networking and SEO, her interest-driven approach worked, bringing in thousands of readers. In just a few months, Life in the Fast Lane made the Technorati Top 100 and Digg's front page. Another few months, and the blog was the recipient of the Blog of the Day Award and the Making a Difference Award. Not bad for a blog that was less than a year old.

It's the sort of thing that bloggers who sell advertising dream of. But Petersen was pleased with the traffic not because she equated it with an increase in income, but for its own sake. She doesn't sell advertising on her blog—or anything else. Monetizing her blog doesn't interest her. Her primary motivation is enthusiasm, and she'd rather not have to worry about advertiser opinion.

Today, Petersen spends most of her time in the fast lane. Her home office makes it easy to switch between blogging and business—and sometimes it's difficult to say which keeps her busier.

For a blog that supports a freight and courier service, you have a wide-ranging mix of subjects.

When I first started, I had a vague idea of how I wanted to organize things. Then I started getting out and seeing things on the Internet and various sites I could get the information from. It grew as I went along. I just had a very basic plan and went from there.

Once I got into blogging, it became something more than just a means of SEO. It was a whole new ball game. Blogging itself became my new passion.

What I write about are all the things that interest me. When you enjoy what you're doing, you can go after your passions, and it's not so much like work.

So you went into blogging with the idea of using it to help with SEO?

After I started the website for our business, it seemed that everything I was reading said if you have a business website, you need to have a business blog.

My webmaster had been trying to talk me into doing a blog for some time. The writer [who did] some editing for the site is a blogger, and he told us it would be a great benefit for us in terms of search engine optimization. That was what convinced me; I already knew that SEO was the best way to keep our site high in search results listings.

> *"Once I got into blogging, it became something more than just a means of SEO. It was a whole new ball game. Blogging itself became my new passion."*

The website was already doing well with the search engines, and the blog was sort of an extension of it. It's built into the back end of our website.

Are you a programmer, or did you work with your webmaster to set up this blog?

We worked together, because I'm not an expert. It took a couple of months of going back and forth—now I need this changed or that changed, and move this here or move that there. I couldn't do it myself.

I'm very picky. If I could have done it myself, it would have been a whole lot easier, but I don't know a bloody thing about HTML. I'm so handicapped in that area that it's scary.

So it took some time to get it together the way I wanted it. I eventually found the layout format I wanted. My webmaster didn't like it, but we worked that out.

There are WordPress themes in my format, and there are other format themes. I scoured pages and pages of various themes. I found one and then altered it—we threw in coloring and all kinds of things, and moved things around.

Do you use any plug-ins or other tools?

Definitely. There are a few that are must-haves with blogs. One of the worst things blogging platforms do is create duplicate content. It took me only a week before I realized that this was creating a lot of different URLs. Search engines do not like duplicate content, and they'll penalize sites for it. You can be pushed way down in the ranks for having duplicate content.

> *"The truth is that the special-feature posts do take a lot of time to put together—to do a good job. It is worth it, going by the response I get."*

When I first realized that, I actually contacted Google's webmaster and ask them if this is going to be a problem.

They told me that it would be a problem, especially with a new site like mine. They wouldn't tell me how their algorithms work, of course. They just told me that it was not a desirable thing. And they couldn't really recommend anything because it could be taken as some kind of an endorsement.

So they couldn't provide me with any answers, but after a lot of searching, I found this plug-in called Duplicate Content Control. This one is for use with WordPress. So if you do a search for your platform and "duplicate content control" or something to that effect, you should find a similar tool.

SEO aside, how much time do you spend blogging, on a typical day?

I'm embarrassed to say how much I have my butt parked in the chair. I eat, sleep, and breathe my blog.

An average post takes me about four to twelve hours, depending on how much is involved, how much research. There are a few of my posts where I've gone really in-depth with things, where I've spent a few days putting one together. That's not the norm. But the truth is that the special-feature posts do take a lot of time to put together—to do a good job. It is worth it, going by the response I get.

Is it difficult to keep up with blogging and business?

I have certain days of the month—a couple of times a month—where the majority of my time is spent trying to run the company, because there are certain things that have to be done. I have to steal three or four days at those times, so trying to write the blog at the same time is a real challenge. I like to be able to have at least one post to leave every day so that my readers will come back every day. During those times, it's a challenge.

Fortunately, our office is our home, so I have everything around me. I'm just surrounded with equipment.

Aren't you able to save up posts for later?

No. I've tried to, but whatever my goals, there never seems to be enough time in the day. I wish I had a clone—seriously.

Do you use an RSS reader to read blogs, and do you comment on other blogs?

I don't use a reader—I just read the various blogs. I don't post comments on other blogs. I barely have time to keep up with mine. So I don't have any time to do guest blogging. I keep RSS available for my readers because I know there are a lot more readers these days who aren't bloggers. If you don't have RSS, they just aren't interested.

That locks you out of attracting readers with comments. So what do you do to get more readers, beyond SEO?

I link to blogs I read, and other blogs link to mine. Getting my blog "out there" has been through my efforts at social sites. I go to social sites like

MyBlogLog, spicypage, and Blog Catalog—there are quite a few of them. The more you get out there, the more attention you get from the other bloggers reading those sites. I get a lot of traffic from people talking about my blog.

You seem to be in a minority in not monetizing your site. Are you ever tempted to include ads?

> *"Without advertising, without monetizing, I don't have to worry about whether I'm posting something that's good or bad for an advertiser. I have no restrictions, whatsoever, so I've got total freedom to do as I feel."*

I've spoken to a few bloggers who have told me that I should be doing Ad-Sense, but I'm uncomfortable with it—for the time being, anyway.

For one thing, I'm new, and I don't want to be putting my readers off with my blog being plastered full of ads and whatnot. I think ads would clutter it up. You see them at the start of the post before you can see anything else, you know.

Without advertising, without monetizing, I don't have to worry about whether I'm posting something that's good or bad for an advertiser. I have no restrictions whatsoever, so I've got total freedom to do as I feel.

What is the return on blogging for you?

It has been wonderful to meet so many unique and interesting people. And I enjoy the interesting discoveries I make about events around the world during my daily search for news. Finally, my growing readership validates what I'm doing. Readers are the reason I continue blogging.

What is your least-favorite aspect of blogging?

Only a minute fraction of those who visit blogs leave comments. It's every blogger's complaint. They feel like they're talking to the walls. They appreciate every comment made on a post because it helps them to feel they're not talking to thin air. And the ones that do leave comments are almost always other bloggers.

None of my friends and family "get" blogging. I'm hearing much the same from other bloggers. Based on that, I think that the majority of people that read blogs are other bloggers. That's where the social sites come in, drawing bloggers to other blogs. But there are a lot of blogs that come up in search engine page results to attract non-bloggers, so it may only seem that way from a blogger's perspective.

What advice can you offer other bloggers?

Well, for those getting started: Do a lot of research before you start your blog, so you don't make mistakes like choosing the wrong platform or the wrong kind of format. There are things to learn for SEO—titles and whatnot, such as how to name your posts so the name of the post appears rather than an IT number, and so forth.

These things are all very important to know. They might be obvious to some people, but I've seen mistakes made on a lot of blogs where people haven't been aware of this.

I spent about five months [doing research] prior to starting my blog, because I was very nervous about it.

> *"Only a minute fraction of those who visit blogs leave comments. It's every blogger's complaint."*

So I put a lot of research into blogging, in order to find out what I was getting into before I went ahead and jumped in.

That's unusual. Seriously, most people just say, "Hey, I'll do a blog," and try to learn as they go along. They need to at least study a lot of other blogs first.

My inclination to research stems from doing the SEO research work on our website. In the beginning, I poured hundreds of hours into SEO for our website. I knew there would be other things involved in a blog, and there are variations and different aspects of SEO that are involved in blogging that don't really pertain to a website. So there were things to learn.

There will be things you will have to learn. I suggest that you take your time. Don't go jumping into anything until you've researched it.

Finally, if you don't have your heart in your blogging, you're not going to do well with it. You really have to enjoy what you're doing and have your heart in it.

Points to Review

In less than a year, Deborah Petersen has moved from running a medium-sized business website to running one of Technorati's 100 Most Favorited blogs. She credits her success to specific elements of her approach to blogging. Here's a summary of those elements:

- Blog from your heart.
- Learn more than the basics of SEO.
- It is important to post on a regular basis, to keep readers coming back.
- Avoid duplicate content. It can cause your site to be pushed down in search rankings.
- When it's appropriate, link to other sites to attract links back to your blog.
- Social search engines and social sites such as MyBlogLog and spicy-page provide opportunities to meet other bloggers as well as opportunities for networking to promote links.
- Only a fraction of a blog's visitors leave comments.
- If you don't have RSS available, you will lose readers.
- Research the formats and platforms used by other bloggers before you start blogging. This will help you avoid mistakes.

Joel Comm
JoelComm.com

15

"I'd like to think that I've always got something to say."

—*Joel Comm*

J oel Comm first went online at the beginning of the 1980s, when he discovered modems and computer-gaming bulletin boards. Over the next decade and a half, he would become involved with the online world in several roles, both personal and business.

When the Web came along, Comm was well-prepared to take advantage of the new opportunities it offered. In 1995 he launched WorldVillage.com, a family-friendly portal to the Web that still receives thousands of visitors each day.

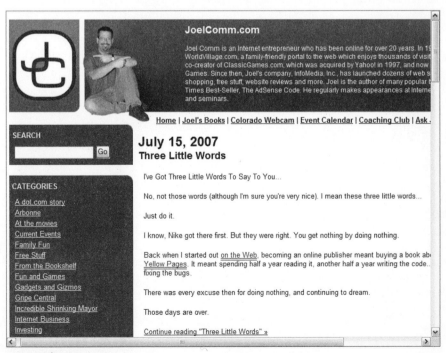

This site was supported entirely by advertising. In 1997 he cofounded ClassicGames.com, a multiplayer gaming site acquired by Yahoo! in 1998, and now called Yahoo! Games (http://games.yahoo.com). Since then, Comm has created dozens of websites that host online reviews, shopping, and more.

Comm is perhaps best-known for his book *The AdSense Code* (Morgan James Publishing, 2006), a hands-on guide for website owners and bloggers who want to maximize their returns from Google's AdSense advertising program. The cleverly titled volume became a bestseller almost immediately on its introduction in 2006 and remains a popular title today.

I Cracked the Code

An energetic entrepreneur, Comm hasn't rested on his laurels since *The AdSense Code* (which, interestingly, began as an e-book sold on his website). He continues to turn websites into moneymakers, and is constantly busy exploring new opportunities. He shares much of his experience and knowledge with readers of his blog, JoelComm.com (www.joelcomm.com).

He also consults and operates an AdSense coaching club. (He's tried every other advertising program out there, including Tribal Fusion, and says that AdSense is the best deal of all for publishers.) By the time you read this, Comm will have established himself as the producer of the first competitive Web reality show, "The Next Internet Millionaire."

As if that's not enough to keep him busy, Comm has moved into video blogging (vlogging) as a means of sharing his knowledge with a wider range of people. The vlog (which is at www.askjoelcomm.com) offered a means of managing reader communications. "People were sending me so many questions, I thought, I can't write about all these," he explains. "But I can shoot a few videos each week, and put up to three-minute clips of my answers." Which is what he started doing in 2007. He describes vlogging as a way to work on his brand and at the same time build a YouTube channel.

What prompted you to get online and become involved with the Web?

Technically, I've been online since 1980. At the time I owned a TRS-80 computer and modem, and subscribed to a BBS [Bulletin Board System] out of Chicago called the Game Master. After that, I went through lots of BBSs with my 300-baud modem, and was on Delphi, Prodigy, and the rest of the online services. I still have an AOL 1.0 disc.

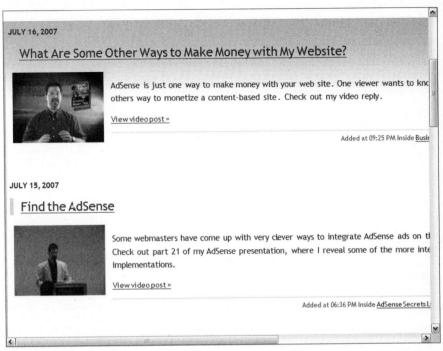

JULY 16, 2007

What Are Some Other Ways to Make Money with My Website?

AdSense is just one way to make money with your web site. One viewer wants to kno others way to monetize a content-based site. Check out my video reply.

View video post »

Added at 09:25 PM Inside Busir

JULY 15, 2007

Find the AdSense

Some webmasters have come up with very clever ways to integrate AdSense ads on th Check out part 21 of my AdSense presentation, where I reveal some of the more inte implementations.

View video post »

Added at 06:36 PM Inside AdSense Secrets Li

Vlogging on www.joelcomm.com

As you might guess from that, I'm a software collector—especially games. In my home, I have a room lined with five-high shelves filled with the old Sierra, LucasArts, MicroProse, and Infocom games. I've still got a couple of Infocom adventures in the original shrink wrap. I wish they still made the old, funky shaped boxes.

Which actually leads to the answer to your question about when I got into the Web. It had to do with games. In 1994, I was working for a syndicated radio ministry, editing their program on a Macintosh. I had done some sales, and I had my own mobile DJ business. I remember reading one of the computer magazines, thinking to myself, "I bet these guys get all the software they want for free."

So I formulated a small idea and wrote out a script, and started calling some of the software companies—MicroProse, Activision, Accolade, Sierra. "Hi," I would say. "My name is Joel Comm. I'm the editor of the *Dallas-Fort Worth Software Review*..."

Before I knew it, it was Christmas every day, with all sorts of packages arriving at my home. I remember one day, all five of the major delivery services dropped off packages.

So now I needed writers. I went onto BBSs and AOL and posted messages that said, "I can't pay you, but I'm publishing this magazine. I will give you the software if you write a review." Starving artists are happy to get anything, right?

I published one edition and distributed a thousand copies throughout the Dallas area. And then one of the writers that I brought on said, "You know, instead of publishing a print magazine, you ought to take your reviews and put them in HTML on the World Wide Web."

To which I replied, "What is this guy talking about?"

That was 1994. In January 1995, I went to the Consumer Electronics Show in Las Vegas, and the light went on. By the summer of 1995, I had worldvillage.com up, with Family-Friendly Software Reviews.

In fact, worldvillage.com is still online today. But we don't do reviews. It's more of a portal to the rest of my Web presence.

So you weren't blogging before JoelComm.com?

None of my sites were blogs. JoelComm.com was the first time I set up a blog. I believe we did that in the summer of 2003.

What gave you the idea?

I knew the technology was there, and other people were doing it, and eventually I decided that I could do this myself. I wanted to have my little corner, my little platform to talk about whatever I wanted.

I started just by sharing stuff about me, my family, my dog, my travels, politics, and movie reviews. It was just a mishmash of whatever came to mind. I still do a little bit of that, but I use the site more for my Internet marketing newsletter.

No matter what, I like to think that I've always got something to say. And these days, if I'm not writing directly about business, I seem to use my blog to rant. I don't know what it is. Just sometimes you gotta vent, and blogging is a great avenue to do it.

What do you rant about?

Well, there was a situation I had with a large regional furniture store chain where we had spent several thousand dollars, and then were treated shabbily by the company. I blogged about the problem, in detail, and soon after that, the corporate office contacted us and made things right. And of course, I reported on how they handled the situation. And the fact that they responded to the situation says something about the power of blogging on a local or regional level.

Another rant had to do with a business opportunity. I look at a lot of business opportunities, and I try a lot of different things. I am an entrepreneur. I am a risk-taker. If a few things work out but most of them fail, you're still having great success.

One particular opportunity involved promoting a website online—a website paid for by me and hosted by the company behind the business. I did my usual work promoting this site with SEO [search engine optimization], and traffic increased dramatically.

But the company didn't like this. They said it gave me an "unfair advantage" over their other agents. I thought this was unusual, maybe even a bit extreme. So their corporate people called, and told me that I couldn't promote my website, a website I paid for.

The company and I parted ways. But you can read about them at my website. Lots of people do—I used SEO to make sure that anyone who searches for that company finds my site before theirs.

What techniques did you use to build traffic for your blog in the beginning? SEO, obviously.

Well sure, but very organic SEO. I don't go out there and try to get my sites higher up on the search engine lists. Basically I know if you put keywords in your title tag, then that's going to help, especially with blogs.

If you script your page in such a way that whatever you put in your title tag also shows up in the meta tag—in the description—that's going to help. Google [in particular] pays a lot of attention to the title, and to the header of that article, which are the same thing in my case.

> *"If a few things work out but most of them fail, you're still having great success."*

I think it also pays to use best practices in terms of your title format. A lot of blog software will create a URL title like `whatever.com/June2007/5930256.html`. But it doesn't make any sense. So my title is `joelcomm.com/this_is_the_name_of_the_article.html`.

You must have had a lot of carryover traffic from your web sites when you started the blog.

We had been online eight years when we started the blog in 2004, so we had a bit of a foothold in the search engines when we started, and that certainly helped.

But today it is harder to get started. The barriers to entry are still pretty low, but I think you have to work much harder now to get inbound links. Or you have to hit on just the right topic to make your site go viral.

Moving back in time a bit, did you sign up with AdSense when it first started?

I did. I signed up the very month it came out, June of 2003, and I failed miserably at it. It was terrible.

> *"The barriers to entry are still pretty low, but I think you have to work much harder now to get inbound links."*

I wasn't making anything, so I tabled it for nine months, until April 2004, when I was at a conference. I happened to notice a guy next to me whose laptop was open. He was looking at what turned out to be his AdSense report, and he was making a couple hundred dollars a day. And I thought, *"Really!"*

After that I went back to the drawing board. I started testing the different colors for ad boxes, the different box sizes, and the page placement. And I started making more money that day.

I kind of cracked the code. That led to the book, which I originally sold online for $97.

How did you come up with the title?

That happened some months later. I was at a conference speaking with another entrepreneur, Mike Filsaime. I had been preparing the book for hardcopy publication, but I didn't have a title. I told Mike about my new book and how it was lacking a title.

He asked me, "So what happened that you started making all this money with AdSense?"

"I cracked the code," I shrugged.

To which he replied, "Well, that's it!"

"That's what?" I asked.

"That's the title of your book: *The AdSense Code.*"

And I said, "Oh, yeah! We can make it look like *da Vinci.*" So I went back to my hotel room and found *The Da Vinci Code* and a picture of me. Using my amateur Photoshop skills, I cut out the eyes from my photo and put them in the layout. [Then I] sent the image off to my publisher.

And he said, "I love it!"

I told him it was a joke, but he said, "No, no. Let's do it!" So we went with that title and cover.

As it turned out, we released the book the same week as *The Da Vinci Code* movie came out. We got some good PR out of that. In June, it hit *The New York Times* business paperback bestseller list.

But Oprah kind of kept us out of the top slot with "The Dog Whisperer," a.k.a. Cesar Millan. His book was on her shelf the day before, and number two was Tim Russert's *Wisdom of Our Fathers.* Russert spoke about his father on CNBC after Father's Day. We just didn't have a chance. It was like going up against Harry Potter.

But with me, the book is never about the sales. It's all about branding. It's a business card, and the credibility that that book has given me has just been absolutely phenomenal.

How much time do you spend blogging?

Not a lot. I write pretty quickly. Some people agonize over it, but I kind of zip through it. I usually am a first-draft kind of guy. I'll usually go back and proof it [to] make sure I'm not looking like a total idiot. But it takes me maybe ten minutes, maybe, to kick out a blog entry.

I like to post six days a week, but I do it less frequently these days, usually three to four days a week. When I travel, it's harder to post.

Do you travel quite a bit?

About five days a month, on average.

Last year, I spoke at so many gigs—I went 23 places during the year, and I told my wife I was going to scale back. I'm really blessed because I'm at a level right now that I can say "No" to most of them, and it doesn't hurt me. In fact, it makes for a scarcity factor.

Do you spend much time looking at other blogs, maybe commenting and attracting links that way?

No, not really—just because of time. I'm extremely crunched these days. We're doing so many things. We're getting ready to produce a Web reality show, writing two books, launching other products, and speaking. It's amazing that I haven't found a way to clone myself yet.

What sort of books do you have planned?

There is one I'm really excited about. There are a lot of books out there that tell the story of some of the bigger Internet companies, like Google, Amazon, eBay, and Yahoo! I'm part of an unintentionally underground niche—the whole Internet info-product marketing niche. Marketing seminars, e-books, and so forth.

There are some legends in this industry. So what I did was I interviewed 25 of those legends. I did over 45 hours of interviews, and I'm doing some research and compiling it all into a book that's called *Click Here to Order: The Stories of the World's Most Successful Internet Marketers*.

For the book, I spoke with people like Mark Joyner, who is known as the "Godfather of Internet Marketing" (he now lives in Auckland, New Zealand); Marlon Sanders, who has been leading the charge with *Amazing Ad Copy Secrets: Create Ad Copy That Sells* since 1995; John Reese, who was the first person to [make] $1 million in one day selling information products on the Web; and a lot of other people who are legends in this particular niche.

We're compiling a narrative. It's going to tell the story in an entertaining and an instructional way, so that people will walk away from it knowing the story, but also having learned a great deal about what works online.

What sort of advice can you offer other bloggers for getting more traffic and improving their blogs in general?

The one thing I get asked more than anything is how I decide what to write about. In response, I go back to an answer that maybe a lot of people say, but it's still the main thing. And that is to write about something you really care about. Write about your passion, [your] area of knowledge, or that special skill or training you have, and really focus your blog on that particular niche so that you're building an authority site.

This goes along with the assumption that you want to make money with your blog. If you don't care about making money with your blog, then I say write whatever [you] think you want to write and let it be a mishmash. My blog, when I started it, wasn't about making money. It was just about whatever I wanted to do.

So, depending which avenue you're going to go, there are tips that can be critical. For example, you should use short URLs and place the title and your keywords in the URL meta tags and titles that show up on your page for SEO. Most people miss these things. I actually shouldn't talk about it and make it public, because the more people you have [using these tips], the less effect [the tips] will have. But it's going to get out there anyway.

Overall, I encourage people to just go ahead and [create a blog]. Get used to creating content, because you really can build a business on it.

Points to Review

Joel Comm's experiences demonstrate that discussing ideas with other people can often be the tipping point that turns a good idea into a winning idea—as happened with the evolution of Comm's software reviews and the title for *The AdSense Code*.

Comm's business experience has resulted in his creating, or causing to be created, quite a bit of original content. Some of that content originated offline, and some has moved from the Web into books and seminars. Our conversation with Comm yielded these tips:

- Blogging's effects are not limited to the Web or technology—it can also affect local or regional events.
- Put keywords in your title tag and meta tag (description).
- Make sure that URLs are in the form of `/this_is_the_title.html`, rather than `5930256.html`.
- One element of AdSense success is finding exactly the right combination of colors and ad box designs. This requires experimenting.
- Blog about something you really care about.
- A business can be built on original content. Get started, and get used to creating content.

Brian Lam
Gizmodo

16

> "If you keep the editorial quality up, people show up and they stay."
>
> —Brian Lam

I t's 1989, and an American kid roams the streets of Hong Kong in search of gadgets. In shop after shop, he finds an amazing array of high-quality electronics, things that will never make it to the Western world. It's an endless treasure hunt in an alternate universe, where vast stockpiles of advanced technological gems are constantly replenished....

Sound like a tech geek's dream? This was Brian Lam's childhood during the late 1980s and early 1990s. From the age of 11 or 12 on, his summers were spent with his grandparents in Hong Kong—an epicenter for technology shoppers. He hit the streets almost daily in search of the latest high-tech wizardry from Japan and other sources of the gadgets of the future. And he was rewarded with unbelievably low prices and high quality. "Everything was a lot smaller, cheaper, and better," Lam notes. "It became really hard to justify buying anything during the school year [in the United States]."

It was a perfect situation for someone with as much interest in gadgets and electronics as Lam—an interest he came by naturally. His father, a Hewlett-Packard engineer, was obsessed with gadgets, and this heavily influenced the younger Lam.

All of this turned out to be the ideal foundation for Lam's future as a technology journalist. After studying journalism at Boston University, Lam "bumped into" an internship with *Wired* magazine. He then made a series of career jumps and rose to assistant editor at *Wired*.

So Much in Love with Shiny New Toys, It's Unnatural

After a couple of years at *Wired*, Lam was invited to take on the job of editor-in-chief at Gizmodo. It is a position that might have been custom-made for him. His wealth of experience as a technology journalist and his enthusiasm for gadgets were exactly what the position called for. In the 12 months following Lam's signing on with Gizmodo in July 2006, the site's page views increased from 11 million to 42 million—proof of what a dedicated journalist turned loose on his favorite subject matter can do. It's also proof that enthusiasm and high editorial quality make a difference when it comes to bringing in blog readers.

How did you come to move from *Wired* to Gizmodo?

As you can imagine, *Wired* was a great learning environment. But the problem for me was that there was nowhere really to go. *Wired* had a very top-heavy staff—a lot of senior editors, maybe two junior editors, and more than ten senior editors.

I didn't want to go to *MacAddict* or *PC World*, or CNET. So I soaked up knowledge for a couple of years, and then happened to talk to Joel Johnston, the former editor and managing editor of Gizmodo, who said he was looking for someone to run the site, and we began talking about it. I had always loved reading Gizmodo, but I thought that maybe it wasn't reaching its potential. I knew I wanted to contribute to it.

But I really hedged once I got the offer. I was terrified to leave my comfortable magazine job—going from an established magazine to something that was really not that established was kind of scary. But it's been the best job I've ever had.

Had you done any blogging before you started with Gizmodo?

No. I never really got too involved with user-generated content. When I worked at *Wired* magazine, I didn't really feel like I had any energy to do stuff online that wasn't part of my job. I was reading what I had to read for work, as far as research went.

What were the biggest changes in switching from magazine work to blogging?

When I worked at *Wired*, there were multiple editorial steps. I could potentially work on a thousand words for a whole month, dragging it through 11 editorial steps—multiple copy-desk and fact-checking [steps], and then top-editing [and adding] art. That was really draining in a way. I don't like working in a situation with diminishing returns. You lose some of the spirit when it takes that long to do something.

When I do stuff online, there's immediate gratification. It's so free and unencumbered by the system. That makes it even more rewarding. I'm not really organized, and at Gizmodo, I surround myself with more-organized people. I have a very organized staff of writers who help me keep track of things. It's nice, because I couldn't do that as a junior editor. As a junior editor, you pretty much have to fill in the blanks for your bosses. But now that I'm in charge, I can find people who help me stay on track with things.

At the same time, you have to work on shorter deadlines. That must make for some pressure.

It's a lot of pressure, but I love it. It's really fun to dedicate yourself to something, and this is the thing for me. I love it, so I do it.

I know that some people are doing minute-by-minute news blogs, like when they're covering meetings or other events. They take notes by writing them in the blog post in Movable Type. So they're actually taking notes in

Movable Type, and publishing them as they type. I don't typically do that. I don't know if it matters that much, but posting that way is the most intense.

What is the most challenging aspect of the job?

Two things. As the company [Gawker Media] grows, it's easy to find people who are good, but not great. It's getting harder to find great people who aren't too egotistical to work here.

> *"Editorial quality speaks for itself."*

A lot of writers are somewhat egotistical. There's a lot of limelight. It's self-involved, and a lot of the best writers have a good sense of showmanship. Certainly there is a little bit more style than there should be in some of the posts, and that's something that's been changing in the past year. We're just hoping it doesn't eclipse the content as well.

And the other part is that, besides being fast and being where you have to be, you can't be ahead of the news all the time. Sometimes you have to follow other people's stories, so that takes someone spotting the news almost 24 hours a day. And that's kind of what I'm trying to set up here—hiring internationally to get writers in every time zone that I can.

Right now I don't have someone in Asia, and I'm trying to, but that forces me to work from late at night until my people in Spain wake up. The problem is that people who are in the right location and good with English are expensive and rare to come by. People I have tested just get by on being slightly bilingual and in the right place.

I think that, at this point, I could just go fill in the blanks with people, but I really want the right people. I think that's key in this case. It's hard to find all these different factors. It takes a long time to find someone like that.

What changes have you made since you started with Gizmodo?

I conduct Gizmodo as more of a news-breaking blog, as opposed to a service blog like Lifehacker. It's more newsy than it used to be, and I think that's why we're so successful. We really put the time into being fast.

By its very nature, a blog like Gizmodo can break news faster. Because we don't have fact-checkers, copy editors, and other processes to hold up publishing, we have the potential to be the fastest. I don't think bloggers who don't have a traditional journalism background can see how it really fits together.

And it's highly audio-visual. One of the things we've done in the last year is gotten really good with photos, and I think that other sites have followed suit. We've started doing stuff like live video—me with a camera on my head. So there are several kinds of media in this blog right now, and it all takes a lot of energy and time. [I do this] partially because I think it's better for the site and partially because I don't want to get bored.

And I don't get bored. As long as I've been working in the gadget world, this is by far the most demanding and exciting position, because we have to catch the news as it comes.

Do you work closely with your bloggers?

Yes. I try to be a controller for this team. But I'll spend some days doing a lot of fact-checking. And of course, we correct errors. It's interesting that magazines with the whole copy-editing and fact-checking structure can have as many errors as they do.

Are you achieving what you set out to do with Gizmodo?

I have a very, very specific task that I've been put to, which is to pace Engadget. There's a long history of rivalry between the two blogs that I think is beneficial and makes us strive to be faster.

We're not trying to do the same thing as Engadget any more. Sure, a lot of our content overlaps, but not as much as it used to. And it's fun to have someone to spar with.

> *"When you work on a website, you have all the stats on every story on the site— you can see how many people click on your story."*

What do you do to bring in new readers?

It's just been happening. If you keep the editorial quality up, people show up and they stay. I think that's something that Engadget would agree on and that Lifehacker is definitely proof of. Editorial quality speaks for itself.

The fact that the Web is growing right now helps. We're seeing magazines and newspapers being shut down because of circulation issues and advertising issues. But it's quite the opposite with blogs, where everything is still in its infancy and there's a lot of growth to be had. As long as you just keep writing, editing, and doing surprising, interesting things, people just come.

How much time do you put into blogging in a day?

I'm on about 14 to 15 hours per day, sometimes 17 or 18. Some days I'll go for 20 hours, and the next day for 12. That's just my style.

Do you have much time for reading blogs outside your field, following other interests?

To be honest, my consumption of media has dropped, outside of my own work, because there's so much to read. I'm reading more long pieces because I don't want to lose perspective. After a year of doing this, believe me, I've lost some of it, and I'm deep within the machine.

We play a lot with the models of how we scan the news. I've got about 400 blogs in my RSS feed. I should probably cut some of those out, and probably will.

I would imagine there's little time to leave comments.

Yeah. But I do sometimes. I'm at the point where I'm working on a lot of features and announcements, so I don't often have time.

What do you find most rewarding about this job?

This job feels like a sport to me, because I really do enjoy the rivalry with the other tech blogs like Engadget. I really like those guys. I really respect them, and I think scooping is a great feeling. Working at a magazine with a three-month lead time, it was almost impossible to get a scoop. So that's really fun, to be first on stories.

And when you're working on a magazine, you don't know how many people like your story. When you work on a website, you have all the stats on every story on the site—you can see how many people click on your story. So it's really good, and it teaches you a lot about what works and what doesn't. You learn quickly from stats.

What's your advice to other bloggers?

The beauty of a blog is that it's an independent art, just like the free press. And I don't think it's that different. You just have to think and move the conversation forward, like any good story.

If you want to and you're really up to it, try to break news by reporting. But you have to check your facts. It's just like basic journalism. Because I was an editor at *Wired*, I

> *"The beauty of a blog is that it's an independent art."*

didn't get to learn all this firsthand, and whenever I'd broke this rule, I would get burned by many, many readers—and I learned. Writers these days don't get that because they are shielded from it by editors. But I hear about it from a hundred readers if I don't check my facts.

Points to Review

Brian Lam's evolution into blogging is one of the more unusual stories in this book, but you'll find that his advice for successful blogging is not very different from the advice that other top bloggers offer. Here's a summary of his tips:

- Providing up-to-the-minute news can contribute greatly to a blog's success.
- You cannot stay ahead of the news all the time.
- Competition among blogs can be a positive motivator.
- High-quality writing and editing will attract and keep readers, as will surprising them.
- Blog statistics can tell you what works and what doesn't.
- Check your facts before you publish.

Kristin Darguzas
ParentDish

17

"The Internet has opened up possibilities for entrepreneurial, career-oriented women who also want to be hands-on Mommies."

—Kristin Darguzas

Kristin Darguzas has what is probably the ideal job for a working mother with a young child: working from home—she runs ParentDish, one of the world's most popular family blogs. The blog addresses all aspects of parenting, covering newborns through teenagers. The blog's categories also encompass pregnancy, birth, celebrity parenting, family, and family law.

www.parentdish.com

ParentDish enjoys more than two million page views per month, and some two dozen bloggers share news, opinions, and other information several times daily. It is consistently among the top blogs in the Weblogs, Inc. network.

Before getting into blogging fulltime, Darguzas worked in sales for large technical companies such as IBM and Bell, and then switched to radio media sales for several years. Early on as a parent, she realized she wanted more flexibility and time for her son, and started looking for new career options. Opportunities for blogging popped up around that time. Actually, she created the opportunities for herself. She was already a blogger, and found the idea of blogging for money—from home—extremely appealing. So she approached ParentDish and another company, BlogHer, about working for them. Together the jobs generate a full-time income equal to her corporate earnings.

Darguzas has also done some magazine writing on the subject of parenting, for publications such as *Alberta Parent Magazine*, *Literary Mama*, and *Mom Writers Literary Magazine*. Her earlier personal blog (now offline) received a Canadian Blog Award for Best Family Blog.

It's Better to Be Accurate than Cute

When you talk with Darguzas, you know you're talking to someone who has made her own path to where she wants to be. She certainly did this when she decided to make the transition from the corporate world to working at home. She sought out one position and literally created another—both to great success. If she ever decides to get back into the corporate world, she's likely to do it by creating a brand-new position for herself at the company of her choice.

How long have you been with ParentDish?

I've been at ParentDish for a year and a half, which is actually six months longer than the normal burnout time on this blog. I've been at it as lead since October of last year.

The normal burnout time is a year?

It seems to be around that time in general. Blogging like this looks like it's easy, and it is—it's really fun. But you're writing about the same topic, and there's only so much you can say about parenting sometimes. You're also opening yourself up to a lot of rabid commenters, and that can be a little draining.

Were you a blogger before starting with ParentDish?

I started a personal blog back in 2004. When I found out that I was pregnant with my son, I was a career woman. I was a snowboarder. I was a world traveler. I had no idea what to do with a baby. I didn't even know if I liked them. (I learned that I do like them.) But I've always been a writer. I've always really enjoyed it, even just writing in my head. So I just started writing this stream-of-consciousness thing. I didn't know much about blogging, but people started coming and leaving comments and linking from other places.

I soon became immersed in this community of people who were visiting my blog, and I discovered some really great writers at other blogs, through the links they left.

> *"People seem to like the weird and wacky stuff in general."*

When I had my baby in August of 2005, there was a virtual shower arranged by several readers of my blog. They got in touch with a friend of mine, and arranged it all behind the scenes. They sent my son gifts from all around the world. It was amazing.

How did it happen that you started working for ParentDish?

I first learned about ParentDish because they linked to my personal blog. They were called Blogging Baby then, and one night they featured my blog in a post. When you're a blogger you always check to see who links back to you. I combed through [Blogging Baby] and thought it was an interesting site, and I started reading it.

Then they linked to me again. It was Sarah Gilbert who linked to me. She's a producer, and I knew she was one of the bosses at Blogging Baby. And I thought, "Well, she said she likes my writing and my personal blog—I wonder if she'll pay me to write for them there?"

So I got in touch with her via e-mail, and she messaged back right away and said, "Yes, definitely—we'd love to have you." And five months later, they offered me the lead position. The lead before me, Karen Walrond, burned out and was going to quit. But they offered her a full-time associate producer position, which is a great work-from-home job. She took that and recommended me as lead. And the pay increased accordingly.

Do you get much time to look at other blogs now?

> *"If you highlight a popular blogger with a post, they'll usually reciprocate and link to you, and it becomes all viral."*

I make time. It's a part of my job. I comb through POPURLS [http://popurls.com/] every day to see if there are any stories relevant to parenting. It's a conglomeration or aggregation of all the top-traffic blogs and websites. If a post is on their lists, it's inevitably going to be a big draw. It's not quite as big as Technorati or Digg, but it's getting there.

I'm also connected with the lives of a lot of bloggers I read. I read mostly family blogs. I think I have maybe 120 blogs on my personal blog line that I use.

That sounds manageable.

Really? A hundred and twenty?

The average number of RSS feeds that bloggers follow seems to be 200.

Well, I think all bloggers obsessively read other blogs. I don't linger and comment as much as I used to, but I make sure I read them all pretty much every night.

Do you make any special efforts to bring readers in?

I do. I submit stories to Netscape to bring people in. I go to other blogs and make comments from ParentDish. We also solicit feedback from our readers and ask what they want to see.

And we highlight other bloggers. That's a great way to bring people in. If you highlight a popular blogger with a post, they'll usually reciprocate and link to you, and it becomes all viral. I know that all bloggers—I shouldn't say all, that's a commonality—but I think 99.9 percent of bloggers enjoy recognition. Otherwise, they wouldn't be writing on the Internet. If they are linked to by someone, they're going to go back and check it out. Even if they say they don't, they will.

How much time do you put in on ParentDish each week?

I'd say I put in about 20 hours a week, sometimes 30. If our traffic is low, or if there is a really interesting celebrity baby boom or something like that, I may spend more time.

During the week, I'm with my son from four until seven [in the evening]— he's in daycare during the day. On the weekend, I try to spend as much time as possible with him. And to make up for that flexibility, I work every night, too.

I also work fulltime for a company called BlogHer (www.blogher.com).

What is BlogHer?

It's a community for women who blog. It's about three years old, and it was founded by three women out of San Francisco. It is very popular. A BlogHer conference in 2005 attracted female bloggers of every stripe from all around North America, and I think they had a blogger from every continent. There were a couple hundred attendees, but in 2006, it grew to nearly 700. This year they're expecting 1,000 bloggers.

As I did with ParentDish, I actually approached them [BlogHer]. I told them about my media sales background, and that I was a blogger myself. They had a limited advertising program but had no dedicated sales organization, or a plan to tackle agencies and big-brand clients. I saw a huge opportunity for ads on blogs and thought with my background in radio sales and my knowledge of blogs, it would be a no-brainer. They offered me a decent salary, and they allowed me to keep my position with Weblogs, Inc., because being a blogger at such a well-known parenting website lent credibility to my title.

> *"You come to the understanding that you've somehow personally impacted the lives of other women who might not have an outlet."*

You appear to have made a successful transition from a sales-oriented, ladder-climbing corporate world to working at home. Are there any special problems associated with that?

Oh, yeah. People ask you to do things because you're at home, or they invite you to go for extended lunches because you "don't really work."

Working from home is almost harder than working in the corporate world, because you never turn it off. You are always "at work." There's never really a day off.

Technical and personal-interest blogs are really big on news. ParentDish seems more service-oriented.

It depends. We try and do a little bit of everything. Like when I stopped writing up my personal blog, I had a lot of my personal posts appear at Blogging Baby—things about parenthood not always being totally rosy.

> "Link and make mention of celebrity stories, particularly slightly snarky stuff."

We do product reviews, but we only cover items that we think are really cool. We get requests all the time from companies that want us to profile them, but we won't do it unless we like their products. And sometimes we'll cover the products, too.

We'll do our own spin on news stuff that's happening in the blogosphere. We do a lot of linking and a lot of articles [about] really cool stuff that we found in the blogosphere.

What is the most popular subject matter at ParentDish?

Ironically, our celebrity section. People say they don't want to read about celebrities, and yet the topic continually gets the top page views. They always say, "Don't write about them … we are sick of hearing about Britney [Spears]"—but Britney is always a top search item on our blog.

People seem to like the weird and wacky stuff in general. We can tell by the stats. In addition to how many read a given post, the back-end of the blog also shows how many times it's forwarded.

What do you find to be the most difficult part of blogging?

The daily criticism. It's immediate and close, and there are no checks and balances. People can write anonymously, and they say things online that they would never say to someone's face.

I have pretty thin skin, and when some random person who I will never meet tells me that I'm a bad mom because of this or that, or that I wrote something that made them angry or made them think I am stupid, insecure, or whatever—those comments stick with me. And they shouldn't, especially at a site like ParentDish where you get so many random people.

The verbal attacks don't happen as much as they used to, but I'm also a lot more careful. I censor myself a lot more than I used to.

What have been some of the gratifying things in blogging for you?

You come to the understanding that you've somehow personally impacted the lives of other women who might not have an outlet. I get a lot of e-mail, even still, from my old personal blog, from women who say thanks for being honest about parenting, relationships, and everything else that goes along with parenting.

You get a great deal of positive feedback on your writing, and other moms say, "I've been through this! Thank you for expressing this in a way that I thought but haven't articulated." And that's gratifying. I have made some really serious connections with women I would never have otherwise met.

The connections are amazing. I have gotten two full-time jobs from it, and the ability to support myself, and those two things are both pretty cool.

What is your advice for those thinking about blogging for money?

I think that you really have to ask. I went out and said to Weblogs, Inc, "Do you want to hire me?" I didn't go through the normal application process. I reached out individually. I think you have to get to know who the players are and ask them.

That stuff works for me, and I know there is a Work it, Mom! [blog] that's come on board, and a Club Mom [blog], so there are opportunities. For people who are good writers, especially for parenting bloggers who are good writers, I think there are many opportunities. Parenting blogs are becoming a hotbed of marketing opportunities. This is reflected by marketers creating names for online moms—like "mom bloggers," "mom-fluential," and "mom-osphere." I think the Internet has opened up possibilities for entrepreneurial, career-oriented women who also want to be hands-on Mommies.

> *"If you don't have your heart in your blogging, you're not going to do well with it."*

What other tips can you share?

I think the most important thing about being a successful blogger is being a decent writer—if you want to have any kind of an audience, although I have seen mediocre bloggers who get tons of traffic because they're empathetic with others. They'll comment a lot on other people's blogs, and make sure they respond to comments on their blogs. That can build an audience because of the give-and-take in the comments.

Link and make mention of celebrity stories, particularly slightly snarky stuff. When ParentDish posts celebrity stuff, we get dozens of readers groaning, "Enough of Britney, enough of Paris!" But the celeb parenting stuff is invariably hugely popular and receives a lot of Google juice.

Comment on the blogs of high-profile bloggers in your niche area. If you can make an impression, you may get link love, which from a big-name parenting blogger, means thousands of visitors a day.

If you don't have your heart in your blogging, you're not going to do well with it. You really have to enjoy what you're doing and have your heart in it.

Points to Review

In addition to writing ability, success for Kristin Darguzas means having a can-do attitude, a willingness to experiment, and a passion for her subject. Here's a blog-specific list of how you might apply these attributes:

- Posting in public means opening yourself up to criticism, so you may want to be cautious in your posts.
- Submit stories to Netscape and other venues to attract readers.
- Soliciting reader feedback can generate new ideas for posts.
- Comment on blogs of high-profile bloggers in your niche area to draw traffic.
- Working at home can be difficult because you are always "at work."
- Good writing is important to blogging success.
- Celebrity subjects often get top page views, and can increase search engine rankings.
- Celebrity topics are always a big draw. If you can make a link between one of your blogging topics and a celebrity, however strange, do so.
- Write about what you enjoy.

Chris Grant
Joystiq

18

> *"The secret to success is consistency and quality."*
>
> *—Chris Grant*

O ne would expect the editor of the Web's most linked-to gaming blog to have a long history as a gamer. This is certainly true of Joystiq's Chris Grant, who began playing games like *King's Quest* and *Zork* around the age of six. Making notes as he experimented with moves and playing some segments by rote, the young Grant undoubtedly accelerated the development of his reading and writing skills.

Some years later, thoroughly enthralled with video games on consoles like the NES and Genesis, he returned to *Zork* via Activision's CD-ROM *Return to Zork* game. "Following that experience," he says, "I went back to the original *Zork*—equipped with slightly better reading comprehension, of course." He found it every bit as engaging and baffling as he did when he was a child.

Grant's interest in games did nothing but grow as new generations of video game consoles came and went throughout the 1990s. After college and a move to Philadelphia, he began writing a gaming column for *Philadelphia Weekly* in 2005 while holding down a day job as a carpenter.

Meanwhile, January 2004 saw the debut of Engadget. Game-console fanatics crowded into the blog, right along with wireless, CD, DVD, communications, and other kinds of gadget enthusiasts. Concurrently, a generation of gaming consoles was coming to an end, and there was increasing talk about the new equipment on Engadget. It quickly reached the point where the site just had too much gaming news, and a lot of Engadget-loyal readers got frustrated.

Winning the Blog Game

At this point Engadget editor Peter Rojas decided that a new blog should be spun off for dedicated gamers—a blog that not only covered gaming hardware, but also the software side of the games, the latter not being one of Engadget's topics.

Joystiq launched on June 16, 2004, and before long was spinning off sister gaming sites of its own—among them DS Fanboy, Nintendo Wii Fanboy, Second Life Insider, and Xbox 360 Fanboy. Less than a year after Joystiq started, a fortuitous set of circumstances resulted in Grant becoming a Joystiq contributor.

How did you get started as a contributor to Joystiq?

I learned about Joystiq as I imagine most other people did: from the post on Engadget that announced it. I remember being really thrilled when they spun off Joystiq. I was a loyal reader for quite a while before I started writing for it. I was already writing a column for the *Philadelphia Weekly*, just writing about games—reviews, news about game companies, etc. And I had a small blog that I had just started keeping up where I wrote about new technology, games, and whatever else I was interested in.

One day in the fall of 2005, Joystiq's lead, Vlad Cole, left a post asking about something in Philly. I forget what the post was exactly—maybe asking if there were any arcades in the city. I left a comment, and he followed the link attached to my name to my blog. As it happened, he lived in Philly and was a reader of my *Philadelphia Weekly* column. He was attending Wharton [the business school of University of Pennsylvania] to get his MBA. We got together and played some games, and Vlad let me know Joystiq was hiring. So I applied and began working [at Joystiq] in October or November of 2005.

You were working as a carpenter when you started blogging for Joystiq. What skills did you bring to the job?

I originally went to college for film production and quickly realized that it was a fool's errand. I wound up getting two degrees, in English and history, so I did a considerable amount of reading and writing in those disciplines. As a history major, I always enjoyed research, which turns out to be an asset in blogging.

When I was in college, I worked as an assistant editor for a production company that did work for The History Channel. But I always had hopes of writing a novel. Nonfiction writing had always appealed to me, too, though not necessarily journalistic the way that I think blogs are.

While I was a carpenter, I didn't do much writing. But I'm really a voracious reader—reading books. blogs, and all kinds of stuff. My professional or academic interest in video games developed during that time, when I was looking for more things learn about.

So when you started blogging for Joystiq, you were still working as a carpenter?

Yes. But it was one of those situations where, when you first come on board, there are a million things that need to be done and there's no one to do them. This meant a plethora of opportunities for me.

Even though the pay wasn't very high, I started posting enough that, coupled with the relatively meager pay the *Philadelphia Weekly* dished out, I was making enough to work for Joystiq full time—even though I was making less than I had as a carpenter. It was almost as if all these things had come together so I could do this job and do it well. Before long, I was writing maybe 250 posts a month and doing a lot of managerial stuff on the site.

It looks as if you were pointed right at the lead position. When did you get the job?

By late 2005, it became obvious that Vlad had less and less time to devote to the site. So I became *de facto* editor of Joystiq, from around January of 2006 on. Vlad left that summer to work an internship with Microsoft, at which point I took over full-time—officially.

I had to be hired through AOL, and they requested my resume. I thought it was kind of funny, as I'd been running their site for months. But being an AOL employee is awesome, especially the benefits.

From college, to carpentry, to blogging. Did you ever imagine you'd be doing anything like this?

I certainly never had any ambition for any kind of journalistic career. And I say that with some trepidation, lest I get caught up in the giant debate over whether blogs are journalism.

What do you find to be the most challenging part of this job?

There are several difficult aspects. I think it's pretty hard for blog writers to maintain a consistent level of interest. Writing can be so hyperkinetic, so hyperactive, especially when you're running a blog that does 30 to 50 posts a day.

> *"My job is to really know my subject and really care about it. I like to think of it as being professionally passionate or curious."*

Keeping everything to do with the blog in your head—keeping it indexed and organized—is difficult. As the editor, I have 10 writers, but Joystiq has a bunch of sister sites that I also manage, so I supervise 40-something writers. We keep in touch via instant messaging, and I have people sending me IMs all day. They query me on minutiae that I always seem to be able to remember—things like, "Two weeks ago somebody said that one thing about that one game…what was that again?"

Fortunately I've gotten good at remembering that sort of thing. I wouldn't quite call it an eidetic memory—it's not that accurate. But I have a very good sense of what's going on with the blogs at any time. I suppose a lot of people aren't able to do that.

Keeping writers can be difficult. We're constantly looking for people because the burnout rate is so high. A writer starts out saying, "I love video games and I want to write about them," and they're really into the task. Then, after a certain amount of time, they'll just stop or slow down drastically.

But you do manage to maintain the necessary level of interest.

Yes. My job is to really know my subject and really care about it. I like to think of it as being professionally passionate or curious. In some respects, I'd say I'm kind of an autodidact. I pick up hobbies and teach myself about them, and then move on.

For any given post I write, I have to educate myself on the subject in five minutes. I have a really quick and easy sequence of events that I use to edify myself on a given subject. Quick Wikipedia searches, Google searches, searches across different blogs, searches at Technorati. In a few minutes, you can really find what the conversation is and what people are

> *"If you want to bring in readers and keep them coming back, you have to produce good content, and be consistent, reliable, and trustworthy."*

talking about, then quickly step in line as if you had been there the whole time.

It's one of those things that I probably have always been good at. Blogging has certainly honed it, certainly sharpened it.

And there's a certain amount of mimicry that you do to sound as if you know what you're talking about. It's pretty much impossible to have played every game and know everything about everything. Yet the job is to know everything. So, you focus on your research abilities—developing the ability to tell whether a Wikipedia entry is erroneous, for example. And you take everything with a grain of salt, and double-check with two sources.

It's like any writing job, where you have to be diligent, and give yourself time and concentrate. But there are so many things pulling my attention that sometimes it's just really difficult to do that.

Does the workload ever get overwhelming?

Computer work flow is an element that I think distracts a lot of people, and in some cases deters them. I'm certainly not the best. I remember when I first started, because Vlad was local, I went to his house and watched him do some blogging. (You know, a lot of the writers that we have I never meet unless we go to a big event.) Vlad was a Type-A, business-suit kind of guy. He strictly avoided using the trackpad on his computer. He would only use keyboard shortcuts. I could see him jumping between his e-mail and web browser, opening up tabs and composing things in the notepad, pasting them in here and there, and searching the RSS reader—all just with keyboard commands. He was wickedly fast. I couldn't see what he was doing.

Perhaps that is a legacy of playing arcade games.

Well, seeing that inculcated in me the necessity to improve my speed. I'm still not at that level yet.

Which reminds me of something I think a lot of people really underestimate: the crushing, grueling schedule that a successful blog demands. You look at a blog post and think it's simple, but the time required is often more than you might imagine. Often when you're blogging, you end up thinking too hard, which costs time.

Other times, you're on a roll and just going, and you're hammering out these little nuggets that are just hysterical. But there's no way to tell when those times will be.

By the way, stupid puns are really a blogger's best friend. They say puns are lazy writing, but I can't tell you how many hours I've worked over a stupid pun. They're really rewarding.

Do you do anything actively to bring in readers?

Not really. Every once in a while, people at Weblogs, Inc.—leads, editors, or writers—get ideas that we should advertise. But the company, as far as I know, has never done any advertising, ever. We've never run a print ad anywhere. We don't have banner ads on other sites.

If I'm on an RSS reader at a website that I know links to other sites a lot, I'll ask for a link on their blogroll. But that's about the extent of our evangelism.

The basic mantra is produce good content, and people will find you. If you're timely, and if you're smart and really involved and integral to what's going on, people will eventually come to your site.

If you keep that up, and if you're different, they'll keep coming back. That methodology has worked really well for Joystiq, Engadget, and Autoblog.

Those things aside, there's not a lot you can do. There are certain things that other blogs do. They make redesigns that are really intended to inflate page views by forcing people to open more pages or follow additional links to finish reading articles. But if you do that, I don't want to go to your site because it's no longer as usable and friendly as it was.

So on the one hand, it increases your traffic, and on the other hand, you're going to lose readers. And then your traffic's back down. There's a kind of karma to all of it, I think, as cheesy as that sounds.

It's as if there's a democratization to it. There aren't a lot of ways (short of being straight-up unethical) that you can manipulate your traffic. If you want to bring in readers and keep them coming back, you have to produce good content, and be consistent, reliable, and trustworthy.

It helps to be funny. But that's the icing on the cake.

So you see content as what really rules the blogosphere?

Yes. Think back to when the iPhone was released. Even now, if you do a search for iPhone, Engadget comes up in the top two results, right after Apple. It has a little to do with inbound links—that's how Google works after all—but Engadget produces a quality product, and the way Engadget achieved that was by writing a post about the iPhone right away. Just by virtue of being quick, and by having a lot of eyeballs on them [iPhones], they [Engadget] got that result up there. It had nothing to do with SEO [search engine optimization] or the kind of sleazy manipulation a lot of people advocate. It's just good content, period.

Do you have much time to look around at other blogs? You mentioned using RSS feeds.

Oh, yes, we use RSS. We try to keep our eyes open to everything and look at specific blogs. I have friends' blogs that I read, and sites that I like to read on my own—BoingBoing, for example. Every once in a while, it has video-game content, but I'll read the whole thing anyway because I enjoy reading it.

> *"Part of the appeal of this job is doing something different every day."*

To be honest, I don't have as much time as I used to. Before writing for Joystiq, when I used to come home from a hard day building something or digging a ditch or doing whatever I was doing that day, I would usually grab a beer, sit on the chair in front of the computer, and spend two hours basically "info-dumping." I mean just reading, reading, reading, and absorbing. I kept my brain well-stocked. I don't have that luxury anymore. My reading is distributed throughout the day, so it's not quite the same. But I'm sure I get more than enough information into my head.

Still, I feel like somebody who works out one side of their body. I have a completely overdeveloped video game side.

What's the most gratifying part of blogging for you?

I don't know. I could talk about the freedom of working at home, but the reality is that the freedom doesn't really affect me that much. I don't leave the house often. I could work from anywhere in the world, but I work from my third-floor office and don't get outside a lot. As nice as it is to know I have that luxury, I certainly don't take advantage of it.

Part of the appeal of this job is doing something different every day. I really enjoy that, the same way I enjoyed it when I was a carpenter. What routines there are are so unique and so fascinating that I really enjoy them. There's enough going on that's challenging, entertaining, or just different that every day is something new.

And being able to follow a space like video games in 2007 is a real blessing. There are so many phenomenal and fascinating things happening in this space, accelerating at a breakneck pace, that you can't keep track of it, really. We can do 30-plus posts per day, and we're still missing things.

Just being a part of that, being a part of blogging in 2007, I think is a real privilege. I think blogging is bigger and more important than a lot of people realize.

What about getting all those games for free? Any gamer who reads this interview will think, "Oh, if only *I* had that job!"

Well, in a kind of twisted irony, I don't have as much time to play video games as I used to. I know so much more about all the games coming out, but I don't have time to pick up even half of them. They are sent to me for free, and they go right into my giveaway box. In addition to that, Weblogs, Inc. has a policy of bloggers not accepting junkets or free games. That is probably unique—less so for some than others.

So you really are serious about keeping editorial and advertising separate?

Yes. We've been contacted by publishers of video games who didn't like our coverage of their title. One of them was a company that is so successful, they don't talk to the press—they don't really have to. They invited us to see two new games, and our writer said one had some good ideas and the other was formulaic.

The company didn't like it. They wrote Jason Calacanis [Weblogs, Inc. co-founder] and said, in effect, "Your writers were given this great opportunity, and they're squandering it." Jason more or less told them to bug off. So this policy comes from the top down.

The result of our no-free-stuff policy is that my backlog of games to give away is so high that we're trying to get some other prizes to give away with them. If I just handed out games, I'd be giving unbalanced prizes, like 40 Xbox games. We're hoping to maybe have a TV to give away along with some games, or maybe an Xbox with games.

How much time do you spend blogging and managing?

It's much more than I want to admit to. I'm up at 8:00 [in the morning], and usually on the computer by 8:15. I take breaks throughout the day for the dog park and eating and stuff, but I'm probably on the computer until nine or ten at night—sometimes a little later, sometimes a little earlier.

What is your advice for somebody who's starting a blog or who wants to improve their blog?

We've seen gaming blogs, and blogs of all sorts, start up and disappear, start up and disappear. The secret to success is consistency and quality. It sounds almost profane to simplify it that much, but that's the reality.

Think about this: If BoingBoing every once in a while stopped updating for four days, and then came back and said, "Sorry about that, folks—we're back," and then updated with really bad posts for a couple days, and didn't update again for a while, their readership would be gone within a month. But

> *"Most of us are much more autonomous than the typical blogger for a blogging network ... I'm my own boss."*

BoingBoing is consistent, and they have quality postings, so they are always near the top in any list.

Another thing would be to consider blogging in a niche. Actually, BoingBoing is an excellent example of a blog that specializes in niches and has a wide appeal at the same time. It's unique because a lot of their content is so esoteric. If, for example, you're searching for *mimikaki* (Japanese ear cleaners), you'll find BoingBoing pretty high up in the search results list. This is partly because of the size of their readership and the number of inbound links they've got, and partially because there aren't a lot of people writing about that stuff.

Or you can spread wide—create a larger net and go after several niches that way. We've done that with Joystiq's spinoff blogs. *World of Warcraft* is a good example—it's our most successful spinoff site. The growth has been phenomenal, even though it's so niche and such a targeted market.

All of that points to the difference between us and Gawker. Gawker has a kind of boutique model, where they have a handful of blogs that are really cultivated by Gawker on high. Weblogs, Inc. is kind of the exact opposite model, where we have a ton of blogs, and a ton of writers.

Most of us are much more autonomous than the typical blogger for a blogging network. John Neff [of Autoblog] is his own boss. I'm my own boss. There are people above me, but they don't know what I do every day. They don't know much about video games. But if the BBC calls me to talk about a game or a company, I figure I'm doing something right. We're allowed a lot of freedom.

Points to Review

From carpenter to blogger, Chris Grant's route to blogging underscores the fact that successful bloggers can come from any sort of background. Grant's experience in writing a magazine column was helpful to him as a blogger, but it was largely his enthusiasm for and knowledge of gaming that guided him on the road to blogging success. And he shares certain attitudes and techniques with other successful bloggers profiled in this book. Here are some highlights:

- Being able to rapidly educate yourself on a subject is an asset for a blogger, as is a memory that allows you to retain even the most trivial of details.

- Take information that you find on the Internet with a grain of salt, and check everything against multiple sources.
- You must post consistently, no matter how inconvenient it is to your schedule. Readers expect to see the same volume of posts every day.
- Consider blogging in a niche. If you blog about things that no one else blogs about, you'll always be high on search lists. Working in several niches at once can have a similar effect.
- Delivering timely information will keep readers coming back.

Scott McNulty
The Unofficial
Apple Weblog

19

"Don't write anything in a blog that you wouldn't say to someone face-to-face."

—*Scott McNulty*

The typical blogger has been a computer enthusiast for at least a decade or two. Some were hobbyists before they could legally drive, and more than a few trace their roots back to the days of the first TRS-80, IBM, and Apple computers—when they were called *personal* computers and their owners "home computerists."

From that perspective, Scott McNulty is a somewhat atypical blogger. For that matter, he is an atypical computer owner. He didn't buy his first computer

until six months *after* he graduated from college in 1999. And, despite not having owned any sort of personal computer, he ended up working as a systems administrator for Windows computers.

Blogging at TUAW

The computer McNulty selected as his first happened to be an iMac, and it was the first step on his journey to becoming a professional blogger and editor at The Unofficial Apple Weblog (TUAW, pronounced too-ow, with an emphasis on the first syllable).

How long have you been the lead editor at TUAW, and how did you come to the position?

I've been the lead for about a year and a half. I was a regular reader, and one day I found an advertisement—a blog posting, actually—on the Weblogs, Inc. blog, looking for Apple bloggers. I applied, and completely forgot about it. Then a couple months later, I got an e-mail asking, "Do you want to blog for us?" I replied, "Sure!"

Had you done any blogging—or writing—before that?

I have an undergraduate degree in English. And I've been writing all my life—short stories, fiction. That kind of fit with blogging. I've been blogging since 2000, when I started with a personal blog that I still maintain. Since then I've contributed to a number of other blogs.

Is blogging a part-time proposition for you?

Yes. My full-time job is as systems administrator for Windows machines. In my personal life it's all Apple, of course.

Do you anticipate going full time with blogging?

It is a thought. But I work for a university and the environment is nice—really laid back, [with] great benefits. I get paid well, so it makes it hard to want to leave that. And a freelancer's life is not as stable. It's nice to get that regular paycheck.

Some full-time bloggers I've talked with put astounding amounts of time on their blogs. How about you?

It takes a lot of time to manage TUAW. Fortunately I have a good team behind me who are passionate about Apple. Looking for material to write about, and then writing and editing, I spend probably 30 to 35 hours a week.

I don't have to spend a lot of time telling people what to write, because they are passionate. I write less than I used to, and nowadays I edit more than I write. I read and edit every post, including our longer posts, which we call features. If I were editing and still blogging as much as I used to, well, I wouldn't have time.

What's editing for a blog like? Are most bloggers writing at a publishable level?

There is little bit of tweaking to be done, but not too much. A lot of it is just making sure they're following our tone. We try to have, not necessarily a definitive artificial Weblogs, Inc. voice, but more of a tone. Bloggers have their own voice, but as long as that meshes with the overall tone of the blog, that's fine.

> *"I don't have to spend a lot of time telling people what to write, because they are passionate."*

How would you define that tone?

The tone we're going for is that of a kind of friendly, slightly sarcastic friend who knows probably way too much about Apple.

Do you do anything actively to bring in readers?

No, we don't advertise. In all my years of blogging, I must say I've learned that consistency is the best way to grow an audience, so we try to post 20 quality posts every weekday. That way, people know that we always have something new waiting for them. And this really has drawn some traffic.

We have a few competitors out there, but most people who are interested in Apple do not get their news from just one site. We know they like to subscribe to a number of Mac-related sites. So we link to other blogs that cover the same stuff we do. We cross-link and promote everyone, and everybody wins. Also, there's an unspoken agreement that if someone is first with a news item, everyone else attributes it to them.

There are other ways, of course, to bring in readers. There is the sensationalistic way to do it, where you try to manufacture or find juicy rumors that will attract lots of readers. But it's far more effective and simpler to just consistently deliver solid content. It may not be sexy, but it is what people really want.

What do you find difficult about running a blog?

Well, I think it's assuring the quality. When you're paying per-post, there is a temptation for some writers to try to get two or three posts out of one. And as lead, you kind of have to say, "No, we're looking for quality over quantity. We're paying you per post, and we want each post to be good." We have to maintain a level of content that brings people back.

So I try to say no to people as little as possible. But you do have to rein them in from time to time, and say, "No, we can't call Bill Gates a jackass in the title of this post. It would be fun, but we just can't do it."

Making the decision and telling somebody who's very excited about their post that it can't go on our site is difficult.

Looking at the other end of things, what do you find rewarding?

The pattern of immediate gratification when you write something. You write something, and it's immediately available for people to see and comment on.

> *"We have to maintain a level of content that brings people back."*

I meet a lot of really great people through blogging, and that's really what makes me do it day in and day out—all the great people I blog with, people on the other Mac websites, developers, and such. There's an amazing community around Apple and blogging in general.

Do you take vacations from blogging?

At my job, we get a fair amount of vacation time—one of the great benefits of working for a university. But every vacation I have taken for the last two years has been so that I can go cover something for the blog. I've taken time off from my real job, but only to do my other job.

Blogging has become part of my life. It's my everyday routine to read through all the blogs that I read, and line up some posts. Then I go in and clear out all the waiting posts from the other bloggers. And so it goes. I haven't really had any desire to take any time off.

I could take time off of the Apple blog, but I can never stop blogging completely. It's just such a big part of my life—both professionally and socially. And creatively—it's my creative outlet. Being assistant systems administrator doesn't give too much room for creativity. I would be blogging about Apple stuff even if they didn't pay me.

Although there are days when I just don't even want to read anything about Apple, let alone write anything about them.

With TUAW being so successful, have you thought about spinning off any topical blogs?

There has always been talk of spinning off an iPod blog, or an iPhone blog. But I resist that because I think covering Apple is a good strategy for us, because the whole Apple experience is what readers want. And that's what we are covering—that's where we add our value.

If we were to splinter TUAW into an iPhone-only blog, we would end up just linking to each other all the time. So why not just keep doing the same thing? That's my feeling.

I don't know if the higher-ups have given any thought to it. We have Engadget to do that kind of gadgety coverage. We're much more focused, and we're not afraid to admit right up front that, yes, we all use Mac, we love Apple, we're fanboys, and we love it. So this is our perspective on the news. And underneath all our criticism, we're hoping to make Apple a better company.

I would say 95 percent of the people who read TUAW are not as interested in the doings of Apple as we are. So we have to keep that in mind. We're avoiding the whole snarky, computer-guy attitude. We go for a nicer tone.

So I spend most of the time making sure that we're getting that talent right, and that whatever is being written about is understandable in context. When you're writing about your passion, it's easy to just assume people know X, Y, and Z. But they may not know these things. We [TUAW bloggers] just know these things because we read about Apple 24 hours a day, and it's too easy to assume, "Oh, yeah—of course the readers will know this!"

But our readers constantly remind us they're out there. So a while ago, we started a series called Mac 101. We realize a lot of people new to the Mac are reading our blog, so we just slip them some very simple tips and tricks in Mac 101.

Someone who's had a Mac for over a year will know about these things, but a large percentage of our readers have not had a Mac for a year. They maybe bought an iPod and liked it so much that they say, "Let me get a Mac and see what that's all about," or, "I'm thinking about getting a Mac." These people come to TUAW.

So we put some very simple tips and tricks out there for these readers. Get a few comments that are like, "Well, anyone who's ever used computers should know this!" and we have to explain that not everyone knows.

Negative comments can discourage other bloggers from commenting.

You are certainly not lacking in passion for Apple, Scott.

> *"If you're as interested as I am in any particular subject, you'll just do it for the love of the subject; the success will usually follow."*

The nice thing about the Apple culture is that there are a lot of small third-party developers out there who are building great applications. I cover them, and I want to help support their efforts. The best way to do that is to buy what they're making—to which, as Weblogs Inc. bloggers, we are beholden.

It takes away your credibility to have free stuff given to you. Even if we love a product, we still pay for it. I pay for all my software and all my hardware.

We review things, and if the manufacturer says, "Give them away to a reader or give it back," we do that. If it's something I'm going to use on a daily basis, and I want it myself, I pay for it.

Are you are happy working with Weblogs, Inc. under AOL?

I do like AOL and Weblogs, Inc. The upper levels have never told us what to write about. They are very hands-off, and that's very nice. They let me guide the editorial direction of the site. Of course, I talk with my writers about what we want, and what we think the blog should be covering. But at the end of the day, the blog's goal is my goal, and I get a lot of support from AOL.

What's your advice to other bloggers?

A lot of people put up a few posts and wonder, "Why isn't anyone commenting on my blog? Why am I not on the front page of Digg? Why is not everyone in the world recognizing my brilliance?" It's just not going to happen overnight. It's the same as everything else: If you work hard and stick to it, eventually you'll grow your audience. People will start commenting, a little community will grow, and from there, [you] just keep it going.

Of course, if you are as interested as I am in any particular subject, you'll just do it for the love of the subject, and success will usually follow.

It's also good to remember that blogging is a public discourse, and that it is Google-able. Apropos of that, here's my golden rule for blogging: Don't write anything that you wouldn't say to someone face-to-face.

So, take accountability for your actions and never be ashamed of anything you write. The best way to accomplish that is to think about it before you write.

Points to Review

Scott McNulty's approach to blogging is a carefully balanced blend of enthusiasm and honesty. There are several ways he achieves that balance. Here are a few pointers to help you do the same:

- If you do something for the love of a subject, success usually follows.
- Success doesn't happen overnight.
- Don't assume all readers will understand everything you post. Write so that subject-specific terminology can be understood in context, or post a primer about your subject.
- Create a tone for your blog, and be consistent in using it.
- Consistency is important in growing an audience.
- You must be passionate about your blog's subject.
- Cross-linking and reciprocal promotion with competing blogs can be positive.
- Produce a large amount of quality content, and readers will come.
- Don't write anything in a blog that you wouldn't say to someone face-to-face.

Philipp Lenssen
Google Blogoscoped

20

> *"You have to work on your blog for some time and maintain your passion before it turns into anything."*
>
> —*Philipp Lenssen*

Philipp Lenssen created Google Blogoscoped for what is probably the best reason anyone can create a blog: because it didn't exist. This is the reason many authors write books—because the authors feel the books ought to exist. There was certainly a need for Lenssen's Google blog. Google and search engines in general are such a huge topic that few are willing to take on the

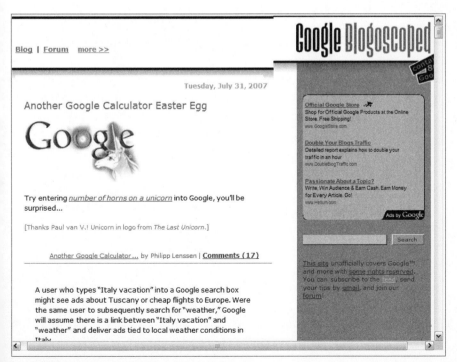

http://blogoscoped.com

subject—and few among those are able to maintain consistency and quality in their blogs.

Lenssen has experimented with a variety of blogs since 2003, including a contemporary telling of Goethe's 1774 volume, *The Sorrows of Young Werther*. In much the same manner that American author Jane Smiley created her best-seller *A Thousand Acres* out of *King Lear*, Lenssen took the Goethe tale and set it in a contemporary city, with contemporary characters and language.

That, of course, had limited readership, as did Lenssen's ChoiceBlogger (http://choiceblogger.com), in which he allowed readers to tell him what to blog about for one-month periods. A blog about bad customer service in shops and restaurants did somewhat better.

Blog *for* Readers, Not to *Get* Readers

Google Blogoscoped has been Lenssen's most successful foray into blogging, reaching the Technorati Top 100 Most Favorited list.

If you have any interest at all in Google, the controversies surrounding it, and the uses to which it is put—not to mention the other important search engines on the Web—Google Blogoscoped should be on your list.

How long have you been blogging or commenting on blogs?

Since around 2003. I came across the concept earlier, around 2000 or 2001, but I dismissed it as something technical. I was programming a Content Management System [CMS] at the time [and] I figured, "What's so new about blogs? CMSs have been around forever." But I didn't get it that the technical aspect was just one small part of it. More important is the way a blog can be a simple, working communication channel.

I guess it's like in the "old days" when people first heard of the invention of the telephone. Maybe you'd dismiss it and say, "Why? I can already take my bike, ride down to my friend's house, shout something across the street, and they'll hear it through their window!"

How long has Google Blogoscoped been up?

Google Blogoscoped has been running more or less daily since May 2003 (plus a couple of posts in April of that year). During the first few years, it was a spare-time project, but since late 2005, I've worked on it as a full-time freelancer, though not every day. And I'm also switching to other projects in between.

What prompted you to start the blog?

I was living in Kuching, Malaysia at the time, on an extended holiday, but I was also looking for a job. Getting a job permit without a university degree is a bit harder in a foreign country. In the meantime, I was hanging out in Internet cafes

> *"If there wasn't feedback, I'd probably have stopped it some time ago."*

and working on some websites. I've been working as a programmer and designer since 1997, and around 2003, I got heavily interested in Google and search engines.

However, I couldn't find a daily blog on this topic. Two blogs—one by Aaron Swartz (Google Weblog) and one by Elwyn Jenkins (Google Village)—were on my reading list, but they weren't updated often enough for my taste.

So then, around the time Google bought Blogger.com, I figured it would be a good time for me to just start writing the blog I wanted to read.

So I started a Blogger.com blog. I had been creating HTML files, time-stamping them manually, linking to them from the homepage, and so on—all things a blog does for you automatically. My blog started as `blog.outer-court.com` and was an "extension" of my regular homepage, but earlier this year I moved the blog to its own domain at `blogoscoped.com`.

Are you achieving what you set out to do with Blogoscoped?

That's a question I'll probably keep asking myself for as long as the blog runs. What I can say is that it's not me that's achieving it, but the whole community. I couldn't go back to writing this alone like in 2003. Now there's a lot of participation from a lot of people who send tips, participate in the forum, or provide articles. I really, really enjoy doing the blog—editing, writing, programming it, and so on—and from the feedback, there are people out there who enjoy reading it. If there wasn't feedback, I'd probably have stopped it some time ago.

Have you had other blogs?

I'm running a German-language "bad service" blog [`www.schlechtbedient .de`], but it's intended not to carry my writing, but stories people send in. Every German can tell so many funny stories about how they've been verbally attacked or rudely treated in a shop by an employee. Some weeks ago,

I received a polite letter from a lawyer urging me to take down some content from the quote "block." Otherwise, this blog's turned out to be rather quiet—not many people send in stories, so it's not on my daily to-do list.

I had another blog around 2003 that was what I called a "palimpsest" of Goethe's book *The Sorrows of Young Werther*. What I did was to take this great, great book from 1774—which I found to be completely valid in regards to its story even today—and not only translate the German (my mother tongue) to English, but also translate the setting into modern times. Instead of a diary, the protagonist now writes a blog; instead of a horse, he'd be riding a car; a barn where people danced the waltz might now be a big-city rave club; and so on. I'd transpose the whole setting, but it still carried the magic of Goethe's writing, so I actually didn't have to do all that much.

And then, a while ago I tried out an idea I had, which I put up at `http://choiceblogger.com`. Basically, every month I gave the readers five topics to choose from, and I'd then blog about the winning topic for one month. This would continue every month. After a while, however, I wasn't able to find time to do two daily blogs. But it was fun to blog about [things like] cats, conspiracy theories, or Napoleon Dynamite for one month.

What do you find to be the more difficult aspects of blogging?

> "You can draw on many other people helping out, and you can draw from the knowledge you acquired if you've been writing about something for so long."

There are different types of challenges, depending on which "phase" you're in with a blog. In the beginning, you have to find an audience—you have to get the word out. You might be writing what you think is a terrific article, but maybe not many people will read it. So you have to work on [your blog] for some time and maintain your passion before it turns into anything.

When the blog does develop a lively community after some time, then there might be the second phase or challenge of maintaining a fresh view on things. I guess that is a challenge particularly for single-topic blogs like Google Blogoscoped, which focuses mainly on Google, other search engines, and search technology, with 20 percent [comprising] everything else.

If you write about a topic for four years, how do you make sure your "filter" isn't set up to a point where nothing gets through? How do you add perspective, outlook, and crucial opinion, and avoid being lost in echoing the hot news of the day? You can draw on many other people helping out, and you can draw from the knowledge you acquired if you've been writing about something for so long.

There's a third phase that you may or may not want to enter, and that's when you move up to a multi-author, business level. A blog can have its own ad department and its own staff, and you have expenses for traveling to events and so on. This is also the peak point where a blog risks being "sold out" or—to put it differently—growing too large for its own good.

I guess the three phases are analogous to being a writer, and then an editor, and finally, a publisher. But these roles are not clearly separated—you need to be a bit of all to do a blog. You may also decide you don't want to enter a particular phase, and there's nothing wrong with [that]. A blog can be very valuable even if it's just a one-personal-essay-over-the-weekend thing.

What do you find gratifying about blogging?

So many things! You get to meet the most interesting people through a blog. You can learn immensely by writing about something, or listening to feedback you get. You can connect with the world, or at least the segment of people all over the world who are interested in the blog's topic. You can provide a place for a community to connect, and to have discussions, like a bar [tender], which I often find is one of the best analogies to being a blogger.

You may work to change things for the better by being a watchdog on some topic or other. Or you can try to cause some sort of progress by providing analysis for others on some topic. It's just great when you can help others with something you write. I guess it's like any other job in that regard: you want do be good at your craft and do something

> *"I write what I think of as interesting, what's on my mind, what's sent in, or what might help people or shed some light on something."*

worthwhile for a community. In that regard, it's neither more nor less heroic than being, say, a carpenter who's taking pride in their work.

Do you do anything specific to increase your readership?

> *"It can be counter-productive to think about promotion or search engine optimization first."*

I write what I think of as interesting, what's on my mind, what's sent in, or what might help people or shed some light on something. Getting the word out on the story then comes as an afterthought if I think the story deserves it. This means I send out pointers when I think a person or blog might be interested in a story that's running on Google Blogoscoped.

Another way to help get the word out is to have an accessible website. This includes HTML that relies on the World Wide Web Consortium [W3C] guidelines, and clear titles that allow you to glance over them before deciding whether or not to read the full article. An illustration, too, can help make an article more accessible, because it can convey information to those who quickly scan a page.

Some of these aspects are also beneficial in search engines, but it can be counterproductive to think about promotion or search engine optimization first, I think. The whole term "search engine optimization" is a bit off in the wrong direction—search engines change their algorithms, and in the end, their algorithms must follow good common sense anyway; in the long run, search rankings must acknowledge what people like to read.

What's your advice to other bloggers?

Don't think about increasing traffic. If that's your main goal, you've already lost sight of what's important. Rather, think about what things in life are interesting to you and others, what things deserve coverage, which areas you want to see progress, and so on. You should watch your traffic stats every once in a while because it's a form of feedback, but you shouldn't start your morning by brainstorming, "What content might really take off today?" If you do that, you'll be hunting the latest trends, and even if your posts take off, where's the long-term merit in that?

As for improving the blog in general, I think the best way to do that is to (a) listen closely to the feedback you get, and even if you disagree with certain feedback, analyze why this feedback came about (maybe it's hinting at another problem that you actually might agree with); and (b) think about the different people reading your blog, and try to understand how they will see it. When you want to get an idea across, you need to have certain readers in your mind, as if they'd be watching over your shoulder. It's good to consider diverse readers.

For instance, you can imagine the reader who sits in the office glancing over your blog for 15 minutes every morning. You need to wrap up the story, because this reader may not follow all of your posts; you need to give a precise title, because this person might be cherry-picking your blog posts, and only read what they decide interests them; you need to make sure not to put up nudity, because their boss might walk by their screen; and so on.

> *"When you want to get an idea across, you need to have certain readers in your mind, as if they'd be watching over your shoulder. It's good to consider diverse readers."*

Or take another reader, who sits at home and who's new to a certain technology, and they arrived at your blog post from a search engine, researching this technology. They don't know who you are, and they may not yet know about this technology—this might actually turn out to be a loyal reader, but for now, this is the first post on your blog they've ever seen. How do you make the article accessible to them? How do you give context? Where should you avoid abbreviations (even seemingly obvious abbreviations [such]as SEO or CSS)? How do you make sure your blog doesn't turn into a closed, elite club?

And take yet another reader, who's reading many blogs in your niche, who's a complete expert on a topic, who's also a programming guru, and who has half an hour to spend reading some blogs. This person might be bored if your articles are too easy, if they don't get anything advanced out of it, or if they feel like you're repeating old issues.

Or if it's a controversial topic, imagine the reader from either side of the discussion. How do you write the article so it's fair to both?

Is it even possible to combine all these different needs into a single article? I think sometimes it is, sometimes it isn't—but it's always worthwhile to at least try. For instance, a CSS [Cascading Style Sheets] guru won't be offended when you call something a "stylesheet" instead of CSS. Then you managed to offer a word that is okay with both a beginner and a guru. You could also use the abbreviations tag in HTML [`<abbr>`]. You can also turn a word into a link when you're in doubt that the topic is known to all—the one who knows it doesn't have to click it, but the person trying to find out more about this gets the chance to delve deeper into the topic before continuing your article.

Points to Review

For Philipp Lenssen, blogging is a means of communicating ideas and sharing information. Focusing on increasing readership, he feels, distracts from the blogger's primary mission of communicating and sometimes even collaborating with the reader. Hence, much of what can be extracted from his interview involves concentrating on your readers. Here are the highlights:

- If you can't find a blog that covers a given subject, or the subject is not covered enough by existing blogs, create your own blog on that subject.
- Make your website and blog accessible by using only standard HTML.
- Clear, sensible titles make it easier for readers to scan your content—and more likely to return to scan (and read) again.
- Illustrations in posts increase the appeal of a blog's page, while conveying lots of information in an instant.
- Experimenting with blogs on various subjects can provide a positive learning experience.
- Blogging with a narrow focus is accompanied by challenges in finding new perspectives and new things to write about. The challenges can be overcome by bringing in other bloggers to help.
- Rather than focusing on increasing traffic, let content guide your blog. Think about what's interesting to you and others, what topics deserve coverage, and areas you want to see progress.
- The best way to improve your blog is to listen to your readers, and think about them before and as you write.

Brad Hill
Weblogs, Inc.

21

"The golden rule in blogging is to be authentic in every aspect of your operation."

—Brad Hill

Brad Hill is Director of Weblogs, Inc., the largest network of blogs in the world. Some might expect one of the founders to be in that position, but the founders—Jason Calacanis and Brian Alvey—have moved on to other things.

Hill, who's also written several computer books, started out at the bottom in blogging. As he recalls, "It was early in 2004 when I heard about Weblogs,

www.weblogsinc.com

Inc. as a startup. I began e-mailing Jason Calacanis right away, saying, 'First of all, you should have a digital music blog, and, secondly, I should be writing it.' And that's how it all got started."

The Power of Passion

Weblogs, Inc. has never stopped growing. It has dozens of blogs. The network's blogs cover hobbies, health, personal interests, gaming, stocks, and more, and at present, there appears to be no limit to growth for Weblogs or blogging in general.

Fueled by advertising, the network employs scores of writers and knowledge workers as bloggers. It's an occupation that didn't exist just a few years ago, but which now supports thousands of people as they indulge their passions.

How far back do you go with blogging?

I started blogging in 2002. I wasn't one of the real pioneers in blogging, but I had a couple of personal blogs that were like many people's personal blogs: they were self-indulgent and enjoyable to do, and not many people read them.

Then in 2003, I wrote a book called *The Digital Songstream*, about digital music. I decided to put up a blog for it because digital music is a very fast-changing topic, and a book can't really keep up with it, due to book-publishing lead times. The idea was that the blog would be promoted in the book and would keep readers up-to-date. So I did that, and it became a daily read for people who were very interested in that sort of thing.

And not long after that, you started with Weblogs, Inc.?

Yes. When I started with Weblogs, Inc., there was no money in the picture. But it started off being respectable and high-profile right out of the gate, which is because of Jason Calacanis, who knows how to make a lot of noise about projects. He was already a well-known entrepreneur, so there were a lot of eyes on it.

Weblogs, Inc. also gained high visibility because it was one of the first blog networks—and high search results in Google because of all the cross-promotion from one blog to another. All that inherent "linkiness" helps give you a high page rank. We also practiced basic SEO [search engine optimization] practices from the start.

All of us who were involved in those early days stayed involved for a few crucial reasons, I think. One was that blogging is so intensely gratifying, especially when you've got a good platform and you know you've got readers. And second was that Jason kept promising money would come down the pike soon, and those of us who believed him stuck it out. But for months, I was churning out blog posts every day for several different blogs on the network for no money whatsoever.

That certainly underscores the importance and gratification of knowing that you have readers. And it sounds like the network literally pulled itself up by its bootstraps, building readership by cross-linking.

You're exactly right. And knowing you have readers really is key, because then you feel you have a little bit of an influence over how people are thinking about something. I remember in those early days, we were all traffic-report addicts. Our publishing tool right from the start had good traffic reporting, so we were always looking in there, seeing who posted the most entries, and seeing which blog was doing well. So even without the money, it was a gratifying experience.

Even today, some of my motivation comes from the urge to publish my own account of current events, and from the impulse to feed the readers who make us what we are.

Was SEO a part of blog development in the beginning?

Jason has a good understanding of SEO—a very good understanding—and it was always part of our early discussions just to do basic, white-hat SEO. To do it well and responsibly—for success. It was about making sure your post titles were descriptive—not so clever that the search engine couldn't figure out what the hell you were talking about. But we have never done anything like keyword spamming or any of that.

No gaming the system, then, like some bloggers?

There was never anything like that with us. Jason has many different reputations in the larger world, but I know the man. I worked with him and spent a fair amount of time with him, and I can say confidently that he is one of the cleanest operators around. When it comes to SEO, relations with his employees, the determination to pay people fairly—all that—he's a very cool guy.

The mandate you had to keep editorial separate from advertising was established at that time—the rule that bloggers could not keep merchandise they're given to evaluate, and so on?

Yes that's right. Those rules were established very early, and collaboratively too. We've gotten so big now that it's not the small family-type group that it was before. But in the early days, we would hash these things out in a group—what our best practices would be. And Jason was always the leader, no question about it—what he said became policy. But setting that policy was collaborative. And that was part of the fun, too.

That's a switch from the many people out there trying to game the system to make money. They might as well be spammers.

Exactly. There is very little difference between the two.

What advice can you offer other bloggers?

Well, I think the golden rule in blogging is to be authentic in every aspect of your operation. That means addressing topics that you have genuine feelings about, that you are genuinely passionate about. And adding background, so that you know what you're talking about.

> *"If you've got a lot to say and you enjoy talking about yourself or about your blog topic, then you will find blogging intensely gratifying."*

Be authentic in how you present things—just as you've been saying, don't try to game the system. The blogosphere operates on a principle of transparency, and that should be, in my opinion, everybody's guiding principle. If you make a mistake, you should correct it transparently, so the people can see the mistake and the correction. Don't try to cover your tracks, don't try to fool the search engines, and don't try to be inauthentic in any way, because the underlying transparency of the community and of the technology will out you eventually. You'll be revealed.

It's gotten so competitive in the blog marketplace now that if you don't know your stuff, and aren't approaching your subject from a position of genuineness, you are easily and quickly uncovered. That really doesn't work. But if you've got a lot to say and you enjoy talking about yourself or about your blog topic, then you will find blogging intensely gratifying. I do know that for most people who start up a blog on a whim, the most difficult thing is keeping it going. And just finding something to say every day or every couple days or whenever can be difficult—though I don't have a problem with that.

Going back to what you were saying earlier, about being passionate as a blogger, I hear much the same from other Weblogs, Inc. bloggers. Do you hire people who are already equipped with this philosophy, or do you teach it to everyone?

That *is* kind of a company philosophy, I would say. It goes back to the founding days when Jason Calacanis started up Weblogs, Inc. Not meaning to speak for him, but his guiding philosophy was to find knowledgeable and passionate people, and then turn them loose on the blogs. That's pretty much how it operated back then, and it hasn't changed all that much since we were acquired by AOL. It's still the basic operating principle.

I think when it comes to signing on new bloggers, one of the best and most appealing parts for the gig is that you have editorial freedom. We do some assignments of feature writing, and we do some editing in some cases—minor editing of blog entries. But for the most part, it's that principle: find the people who know how do it right already, and then set them loose to choose their own editorial agendas and go for it.

> *"Now, as in those pre-Web and early-Web days, there is the sense that every morning can bring something new, wonderful, and unforeseen."*

The writers here have always been given an insane amount of editorial control. In that regard, the writer isn't even a partner—the writer is the boss. Blogging here reminds me, in an oblique way, of my old CompuServe days of 1991 to 1995, when I owned and managed community forums in that service. The type of work is different, but the hurtling pace is similar. Now, as in those pre-Web and early-Web days, there is the sense that every morning can bring something new, wonderful, and unforeseen.

Some Weblogs, Inc. bloggers say they really enjoy the autonomy, and they feared this might be changed with the AOL acquisition, but it hasn't.

We were all a little bit nervous just before we were acquired, because we knew we were going to be acquired. I have a pretty long history in online content management, and I used to be a content manager for CompuServe, which, as you probably know, was also acquired by AOL.

I've watched AOL do other acquisitions as well. The company has a good track record, in many cases, of allowing its acquisitions to continue operating in the way they did to become successful. So I had optimism that that would be the case with Weblogs, Inc.

Points to Review

Brad Hill's experience encompasses the entire blogging experience—from concept through startup and execution and on to writing, editing, and management. Among the most important lessons woven into Hill's experiences is the fact that autonomy—letting bloggers pursue their agendas—is one of the underpinnings of success. Here are some other lessons to keep in mind:

- It is still possible for a dedicated individual to take an idea from concept through implementation.
- A blog can support and extend the life of a book.
- Knowing that you have readers can substitute for material rewards.
- Setting up titles that appeal to both search engines and humans is all the SEO that most blogs need.
- Be authentic as a blogger by addressing issues and interests for which you have a genuine passion.
- Don't try to cover a mistake. Correct it in a way that shows you're not hiding anything.

Steve Rubel
Micro Persuasion

22

"Today you have to be different, because it's harder to get noticed than it used to be."

—Steve Rubel

Steve Rubel is a marketing strategist and senior vice president at Edelman, the world's largest independent public relations (PR) firm. He has spent most of his professional career—15 years—in PR. Rubel's first new computer was an Atari 800, which he bought when he was 12. He learned to program on the Atari and soon upgraded to an Atari 800 XL. It was around this time that he discovered the online world and its communications potential. In

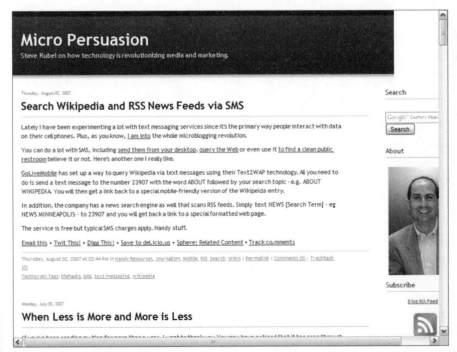

www.micropersuasion.com

addition to setting up a bulletin board system (BBS) on his home computer, Rubel spent time on several of the pre-Web online services—CompuServe, GEnie, and even the PLATO network for Atari owners. He was, of course, an early adopter of the Web.

Rubel became interested in blogs in 2003 and soon had several on his RSS feed. (He cites bloggers Robert Scoble and David Winer as his favorites.) He realized that blogging was going to have a strong effect on the business world, so he began thinking about how to get on top of the blogging phenomenon.

At the time, Rubel was working at a small PR agency, and there he found an opportunity to get two of his clients to start blogs early in 2004. The move was highly successful, increasing the companies' media coverage. "From there," Rubel says, "I was hooked."

Blogging Persuasion

Rubel increased his consulting on blogging as a business strategy, and in February 2006, he moved to Edelman to advise the company and its clients on effective blogging. The subtitle of his blog, Micro Persuasion, is "Steve Rubel on how technology is revolutionizing media and marketing." He uses the blog to explore conversational marketing and how blogging and other social networking experiences affect marketing and public relations. In addition to his roles as a consultant and blogger, Rubel writes a biweekly column for AdAge Digital. Rubel has been named on several important lists, including MEDIA magazine's 100 People to Know in Media, the AlwaysOn/Technorati Open Media 100, and the CNET News.com Blog 100.

When did you set up Micro Persuasion, and how long did it take you to get on the Technorati Most Linked To list?

I just stumbled into this. I've been a geek my whole life. It's been about 25 years since I bought my first computer, an Atari 800, and I've been playing with computers ever since.

> *"Feedback helps me learn, which is primarily why I blog."*

In 2004, I started thinking about what I could do with social media, and I began to try things with clients that ended up being successful. Then I decided to have my own blog and be a part of this giant conversation that I'd been missing. So I launched the site and called it Micro Persuasion. I figured it was a good place for me to go and really advance the profession.

I had no ambitions for it, no idea of where it might go. I figured I'd just see where it went. And it took off. I discovered blogging was my calling—something I love to do. I really enjoy putting out valuable information and getting responses back—even when they're negative. Feedback helps me learn, which is primarily why I blog.

You have 45,000 readers via RSS. How long did it take you from a cold start to build this audience?

Oh, things moved quickly. It just kind of happened organically, in less than six months. But it was a different time then. What I did in 2004 is very difficult now—the niche I covered was largely unmet back then. I think you could do that in some online communities, but I don't think you could do that on a blog.

To do that today on a blog, you need a smaller area that is not fulfilled—a really good niche. Becoming the most influential food or mommy blogger will be very hard to do. All of those popular subjects are taken, filled.

You've been on the Technorati Top 100 lists for about two years. Do you spend a lot of time blogging?

I have cut down a lot. I used to blog 10 to 15 hours a week. Now I'm probably down to about four to five hours a week. But I am engaged with other social networking activities, and when I do blog, I put more into it. It's my brand, and it's my laboratory to try out new ideas.

I spend much more time exploring, learning about, and working with the social networking revolution. I help Edelman and our clients benefit from it.

Is there anything you find particularly difficult about keeping a blog up?

One is that… it's really hard when you have a day job to do news—it's just really hard to do news. There are many sites that already do this. If blogging is your sole profession, you can do it. Otherwise, you're really competing with too many people.

Two, I now work with a big company with a lot of stakeholders, and I can't blog about companies or products as often as I used to. It's too risky. I could alienate my coworkers, or I could alienate my clients. Or I could alienate my competitors' clients—companies that could one day become clients. It's just too difficult.

And so I went to a longer format, and it became much more work. It now takes about two hours to do a post, most of the time. Occasionally I do one in about 10 minutes. But for the most part, a post takes me an hour or two. And I have a pretty hectic schedule, so it becomes harder now to find the time. And I have to be a lot more thoughtful about it.

> "*[Blogging] is a great relationship builder, just like social networks.*"

At the same time, all these social sites—Facebook, Twitter, and so on—have arisen. They allow you to blog anywhere in a short format. I'm getting a lot more mail through Twitter, Facebook, and other channels. People who I normally would not think would be [blogging] are using them—maybe there's some sort of big shift happening. Maybe people are just spending so much time on these sites that it's easier just to send e-mail from them—I don't know.

I became very attracted to those because I'm on the go a lot. I can fire off an SMS [Short Message Service or text message] and still be in touch with people. I think it's where a lot of people are going. It's a lot of work just to build an audience, just to get people to come to your site. If you can go where people are, it's easier.

What do you find gratifying about blogging?

A lot of things. First of all, it is a great leadership tool for me and the agency. It's a great way to put out ideas and express yourself, and to take the temperature of the public—to listen. It's a great way to connect with people I've met offline and online. [Blogging is] a great relationship builder, just like social networks.

Social networks make communications a little bit more closed and a little bit more controlled than blogs. But in one respect, everything is a social network. Community is going to run through everything online—I think that sites will interconnect and people will kind of scoop up community from many different sources.

What advice can you offer bloggers who want to increase their readership or do a better job?

Today you have to be different, because it's harder to get noticed than it used to be. And you've got to fill a void, by providing something that people need. You've got to add value. And you have to be a salesman and a sales promoter.

Quality is important. And you have to be active—to post in volume—although I don't think you have to go crazy with it. But if you're just getting started, you have to be much more active.

One of the best things you can do is become a part of the daily themes on which conversation and news are based by linking your product or service to one of those themes. And it is in your power to do this through social media like blogging.

Don't be afraid to explore new technology. It's our future. Most of it may not pan out, but the small portion that does can pay off.

And of course, you should have a passion for what you are doing.

Points to Review

Steve Rubel was one of the early adopters of blogging as a PR tool, and he has proven that blogs can be a channel for mainstream media attention. He harnesses the power of online conversation by following these basic guidelines:

- If you want people to come to your blog, you must offer them something of value.
- Bloggers just starting out must post in high volume to build an audience.
- Sometimes it's easier to go where people are than to get them to come to you.
- With competition among news bloggers being so strong, and bloggers filling every available subject, the best option for new bloggers is to find a niche.

Rebecca Lieb
ClickZ

23

"I don't decide to blog and then look for something. I find something, and then I blog it."

—Rebecca Lieb

Rebecca Lieb is editor-in-chief of the ClickZ Network. Self-tagged as "the largest resource of interactive marketing news, information, commentary, advice, opinion, research, and reference in the world, online or off-," ClickZ is arguably the most search-engine-obsessed site on the Web.

Before working for ClickZ Network, Lieb held executive marketing and communications positions at several e-consultancies, and for global entertainment and media companies in the United States and Europe.

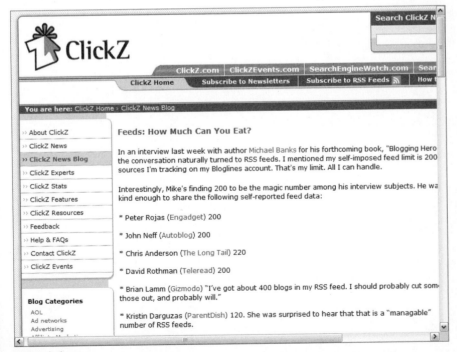

www.clickz.com

As a journalist, Lieb has covered media for several publications, including *The New York Times* and *The Wall Street Journal*. She spent five years in Berlin as *Variety's* German/Eastern European bureau chief. A member of the graduate faculty at New York University's Center for Publishing, Lieb also serves on the university's Electronic Publishing Advisory Group.

In addition to fulfilling her editing and administrative duties at ClickZ, Lieb writes for both of ClickZ's blogs: SearchEngineWatch (http://blog.searchenginewatch.com/) and the ClickZ news blog (http://blog.clickz.com/).

Watching the Search World

Lieb tells an interesting story that highlights one of the many differences between blogging and writing for other media. When ClickZ was acquired by Incisive Media, she and her staff were being greeted by the Incisive Media staff of one of the company's monthly magazines when an editor asked her, "So, when's your deadline?"

As Lieb relates, "I drew a deep breath and said, 'Now. Now. Now...'"

> *"Anyone on the staff can go in and blog anything."*

It was her way of saying that the deadline was and is constant. "There's no beginning," says Lieb, "and there's no end to this. It never stops, not even for a minute."

How long have you been working with ClickZ?

Just less than seven years. I started at the beginning of 2001.

Do you own the place yet?

I don't. We were acquired about two years ago by a British company called Incisive Media. Incisive is becoming a fairly significant-size [company] on this side of the pond, having recently acquired American Law Media and [hired] 1,000 people.

Did you do any blogging before coming to ClickZ?

There wasn't much blogging before I got this job. I don't think the term existed then. But once blogging came into being, ClickZ was very much in the forefront of it. In fact, about four years ago, we ran the first conference ever on blogging as a marketing strategy [ClickZ Weblog Business Strategies, June, 2003.]. It was a conference at which most of the A-list bloggers met one another in person for the very first time—which was kind of a wonderful you-had-to-have-been-there experience; a "Dave Weinberger, meet Doc Searls" moment.

As both editor of the site and a blogger, do you do much hands-on editing of the blogs?

The blogs are the only sections of our websites—and this is a very conscious decision—that are not copyedited, proofread, or fact-checked. There's no editorial control on the blogs. Anyone on the staff can go in and blog anything.

The blogs are good places for us to go on record about something, without having to throw full editorial resources at it. This allows the news to get out there much faster, and it lets us put up more news stories than we're able to dedicate editorial resources to.

Blogs are also where the news editors can get a little more opinionated.

So the other parts of the site do get edited?

Yes. All the other editorial content on every section of our site adheres to rather strict editorial standards, some of the strictest in our particular vertical. We never, for example, will write an article strictly from a press release, but we will write a blog post from a press release, if we find that it's necessary or appropriate. And content is never posted on our websites by the person who actually wrote the story.

> "The blogs are good places for us to go on record about something, without having to throw full editorial resources at it."

Because we have these policies in place—because all our articles are sourced, proofed, fact-checked, and copyedited—we produce a quality site. But that's not the world's most scalable model when it comes to blogging. With a blog, you're not creating a publication the size of *The New York Times* or *The Wall Street Journal*. But our people are getting paid to blog, and are therefore motivated to blog appropriately.

How much time do you devote to looking at other blogs?

I personally track over 200 blogs. I have a cap at 200, but sometimes I exceed it. I sort of have a one in/one out policy on my RSS feeds. On the other hand, I'm paid to be glutted with information. Bloglines is my home page, and that window is always open, as is my e-mail client. If I'm stuck in an airport, I'm more likely to be reading my blog posts than my e-mail. My job is to stay on top of news and opinion in this industry.

Do you find it difficult to decide what to blog?

I don't decide to blog and then look for something. I find something, and then I blog it. So I might blog three things in half an hour and then blog nothing in a week.

> *"We're blogging with a mission and an audience and an understanding of what that mission is and who comprises that audience."*

But I don't want to make stuff up or blog stuff because you're supposed to be blogging. That would be as irresponsible as writing a news story because you have paper to fill. We don't have paper to fill. We want to be relevant, and we want to be interesting. We are blogging for a wider business audience—we aren't blogging for our friends or our family. We're blogging with a mission and an audience and an understanding of what that mission is and who comprises that audience.

The staff bloggers and Search Engine Watch [also known as SEW] don't have established quotas for that very reason. I tell them, "We're paying you to blog on the site. I therefore expect you to blog more than once a week. Less than once a day is fine, and if you're not productive enough we'll talk."

What do you find gratifying about blogging?

The immediacy—the ability to get a story out there and be on the record about something that we wouldn't really have the resources to cover otherwise. Blogging is also a terrific way to expand on a story when more information comes out. We can add another point of view or anything else that expands the story.

We can blog, link to the story, and have the story link back to the blog posts—I think that helps expand themes our readers might be interested in. Plus it's good for the site. We cover search. We know it's good for search visibility. That's a bonus.

We can also use the blog as a place to run stories that wouldn't be appropriate for regular features. For example, a certain publisher claimed they had an exclusive story—that they had gotten access to an internal Microsoft document that said Microsoft was going to serve ads into desktop applications.

Because we cover online advertising and marketing, it was a very good opportunity for us on the blog—we never would have done this editorially—to point back to an article we wrote earlier about Microsoft publicly announcing they were going to serve ads into desktop applications. This was not an internal document—I was actually at the conference where Microsoft announced this.

So we could say, "This isn't the story that they're saying it is. We were there and did the story two and a half years ago." But that never could have been a news article.

I notice a trend among some of the larger blogs to spread posts across two or more pages. Yours stay on one page, which makes for easier reading.

Well that's a strategic position on commercial, ad-supported blogs, like Gizmodo. They want you to click through the pages to see the ads. That is much the same as many Web publishers who continue an article after a jump, so to speak—or whatever the Web equivalent of a jump is. It's because they're trying to generate page views. The jury is out on whether that's best practice or not, but with a very popular blog like Gizmodo, it works.

> *"If you have to hire the people who have the passion, let them [blog]. This isn't an area for control freaks."*

A sort of extension of that is how much of a blog post do you put into an RSS feed? At what point do you make people click through to the site and see your more lucrative advertising?

What is your advice to bloggers?

Have passionate interests and expertise. But I think bloggers, like anybody who sits down to write anything, should have to have an idea of what that something is going to be. You see this again and again with companies that want to start newsletters. They blow their wad on the first issue, and they don't have anything to say the second time. Some bloggers are like this. [If you] really have only one thing to say, even if you say it in different ways— if that's all you have, and you just want to write one thing—you're not blogging.

For business blogging, I think the long-term strategy is pretty critical. My thinking behind the long-term strategy is woe to the business that hires outside bloggers and then abandons the project. Then you get these derelict blogs that live on in perpetuity.

And business blogging really should be an inside job. You don't need the consultants as much as you need the passion. It's more of a "just do it."

But if you have to hire the people who have the passion, let them [blog]. This isn't an area for control freaks. You don't run a blog post by [your] legal [department], just like we don't run it by editorial, and we're a professional news organization.

"Have passionate interests" echoes the advice of most veteran bloggers. Of course, some subjects are too crowded with blogs, so the advice is to find niches to blog in.

Well, yes, but you still have to have a sustainable niche, meaning you have to have new things to say. I go through this all the time when people tell me they want to write a column for ClickZ or SEW. Many of them don't want to write a column. They want to say something, and once they've said that, they don't have anything else to say.

Blogging is to a large extent about accessibility. It's not like being a famous columnist for a big-city newsletter or national magazine [who] is not going to personally respond to feedback or a note or a comment that you leave. But bloggers are really there, or should be responding.

So one of the things I say to my prospective writers is send me six or eight ideas of what you would write about. And I think that would be a very good exercise for bloggers as well. Prove to yourself that you have more than one thing to say on this topic, and maybe you can blog about it.

Points to Review

Rebecca Lieb is member of a distinct minority: professional bloggers who come from a journalistic background. She brings a different perspective to blogging. But even though her roots are not those of the traditional blogger, her practices underscore the importance of many of the same points other successful professional bloggers emphasize:

- The fact that blogs aren't heavily edited and fact-checked allows news to get out faster, but it requires bloggers to be more responsible with facts.
- Blogging allows the writer to inject opinions.
- You should not write just to fill space or meet a deadline. Readers expect you to post something on a regular basis, but they will not accept fabricated or meaningless material.
- A critical advantage of blogs over magazines is being able to expand a news story as new facts become available.
- Before starting a blog, be sure you have more than one thing to say; create a list of a half-dozen or more ideas.

Deidre Woollard
Luxist

24

"People want fresh content—every time they come, they want to see something different!"

—Deidre Woollard

L uxist is one of an elite group of blogs that cover luxury items for those who can afford the best (or just really expensive) stuff, and for those who like to window-shop. A Weblogs, Inc. property, it covers everything in luxury, from apparel, art, and auctions to holidays, pets, wings, and writing instruments. No category is left unexplored. There's even a weekly high-end real

www.luxist.com

estate feature, focusing on the estates of the wealthy and famous, like singer Stevie Nicks.

As the blog's editor, Deidre Woollard works with several other writers to produce a constant stream of information about merchandise, events, experiences, and other things that you just won't see anywhere else.

Woollard's worked with Luxist since its opening in December, 2004. Concurrently, she was the lead of Luxist's sister blog, Slashfood (www.slashfood.com). The blog has consistently served up an amazing array of luxury ever since.

Woollard started blogging late in 2003, while living in a tiny town in a remote area of Northern California. In the beginning, she blogged to keep herself entertained and involved with the outside world. The town, with a population of 300, offered few opportunities for either.

She was not new to the Web. She had set up her own websites before, but blogging had a special attraction for her. She saw it as a way to share her interests with the world at large, as well as communicate her enthusiasms to friends without having to send repeated e-mails.

Blogging also gave her a chance to relax. "I was writing a novel at that point, and it was a good break to jolt myself back into the short form." It also served as a break from working on her MFA.

Blogging in the Lap of Luxury

When Woollard talked to me about blogging in general, she immediately stated both why she is enthusiastic and what her focus is: "I think the thing that keeps me into blogging is that I am constantly finding new things I want to talk about or show to someone else. Blogs and the Web in general have led me to so many of the things that I am fascinated by—whether it's new authors, foods I haven't tried yet, or places I long to visit." Here, then, is the rest of her interesting interview:

Do you still keep up your personal blog?

I have two personal blogs now, and I also write for *Consumer Reports'* blog.

You obviously aren't in a time crunch. Do you have any problems coming up with material to write about?

I don't usually have a problem with that. Sometimes the comments can get you down, as they're not always kind.

I find story ideas through news alerts and other material on the Web. When I find a story—an exclusive—I want to get to it before everybody else covers it. It doesn't matter what time of day or night it is, I'll write about it.

How do you feel about having such a huge audience?

It always feels very intimate to me, because you have the regular commenters among the readers. So you really feel that you're talking to them, but you're actually talking to the larger group, too.

What is the most rewarding element of blogging for you?

It's a great chance to write whatever I want to write about, and not have to pass it through an editor—which is so nice! And you develop relationships with the readers—you learn what they like, so it becomes a cooperative effort in some way.

And that's the good thing about the comments: you can tell what readers like, what they don't like, and when you've pushed it too far. Blogging is such a flexible medium that we can work with our audience and each other to constantly create a better and more entertaining product. It's a bit like cooking—you can tinker and test until you get it right.

> *"Blogging is such a flexible medium that we can work with our audience and each other to constantly create a better and more entertaining product."*

One of the things I have enjoyed most about working on Luxist is finding small companies that are making amazing products, and highlighting them. The Web makes everyone and everything accessible. Someone who is making unique jewelry in a tiny town in Oregon can have a worldwide following.

There's also the feedback. It can be the most frustrating and the most gratifying part, because mean commenters will hurt your feelings. It's the same way when you're writing, if you workshop a piece and people tear it up. But from that, you grow. It's the same kind of thing.

> *"And that's the fun thing about blogging: you get to become an expert in a certain area, where you consistently cover one thing."*

I think people have to learn to handle feedback as part of the process. I think a lot of people, when they get into any kind of writing, are not prepared for that sometimes. Certainly when I was in grad school I noticed that some people who hadn't done a lot of submitting stories and things like that weren't prepared for people to ever say anything back to them. And so I think for beginning bloggers, too, that can be sort of startling.

If you put yourself out there in a blog and think you've written a nice piece, and someone rips it up, I can understand the reaction.

I think it makes you a better writer. It makes you a better blogger.

Do you think through the possible reactions of readers?

It's such a fast process that I don't usually think that way, but I usually know what people are going to say when they read this!

Do you work at home like other Weblogs, Inc. bloggers?

I live in Los Angeles now. I used to go to the Writers' Room in Boston [a company that provides work space for writers in downtown Boston], and I'm really thinking Los Angeles needs a good writers' room. We don't have one.

People are using such spaces now because a lot of them work from home, and the idea of cooperative office space is attractive.

You pretty much run your own schedule. Do you work business hours or are you a night person?

I tend to work out in the mornings, so I tend to start late and work later into the night.

How much time do you spend blogging in a week?

I don't know—I'm pretty much on queue [online] all the time, so it's hard to really say.

You have five other writers working on Luxist. Do you have specialty areas?

I've done this beat for a long time. I do estates, I do wine, and I do some décor (but not a lot of it). And that's the fun thing about blogging: you get to become an expert in a certain area, where you consistently cover one thing.

The estate postings are fascinating.

That's definitely been one of my favorite things. Those take longer than other posts because finding subjects is sort of a hunt-and-peck thing of looking through all the different real estate listings—but finding a great one is a lot of fun. And the commenters love an interesting story.

Some of the estates belong to celebrities, which must be a good draw.

It's the same kind of thing that draws people to celebrities—it's the gawk factor.

Had you been published before you started blogging?

I've written some articles, and I've been published as a short story writer. Paid blogging is great for me because when I got out of grad school, I didn't know exactly what I was going to do. I wasn't sure I wanted to teach. For an MFA student, it's pretty much a dream to be able to write and get paid. Freelancing is hard. To have a place where you can write basically as much as you want to is pretty amazing.

> *"It's pretty much a dream to be able to write and get paid."*

Are you involved in any writers' organizations?

I don't belong to a writer's group right now, but I need to get back into it so I can inspire myself to write more fiction.

Do you get merchandise to review?

Not too much. Sometimes. Sometimes I'll go to events, but I don't usually get things here.

When you do receive merchandise, you return it after you check it out?

Oh, absolutely. Ever since Weblogs, Inc. started back in 2004, they have always been very careful about that—which I think is good. I think some people think that if you start a blog, then people will send you free stuff—but that's no reason to start a blog!

What kind of advice can you offer bloggers? Either people who want to start a blog or bloggers who want to get more readers?

The most important thing is to be passionate about what you write. Be passionate, and be consistent. These are the two most important things.

People want fresh content—every time they come, they want to see something different!

So it's the quality that makes a successful blog; not search engine tricks and driving traffic to it?

You have to respect your reader. You can drive someone to your blog, but you're not going to keep them there if what you've got isn't compelling.

Points to Review

Luxist is a unique blog, but as Deidre Woollard's experiences illustrate, even the most exotic subject matter requires quality writing and research. Here are some of Woollard's tips to keep in mind:

- Experience with a personal blog can prepare you for blogging for pay.
- The regular commenters among a blog's readership can keep writers in touch with the overall audience.
- New bloggers should be prepared to take criticism, and understand that it can make them better bloggers.
- Readers expect fresh content every time they visit a blog.
- A successful blogger must respect readers.

Gary Lee
An Internet Marketing Web Site

25

"A quality article to me is something that plants a seed in the mind of the reader."

—*Gary Lee*

Gary Lee takes a decidedly different approach to blogging. He created Mr. Gary Lee (www.mrgarylee.com) as a forum for his observations on things he finds on the Web, and to provide Internet marketing tips. Still learning, Lee shares the learning process as he goes, creating an ever-evolving tyro's guide to search engine optimization (SEO) and networking.

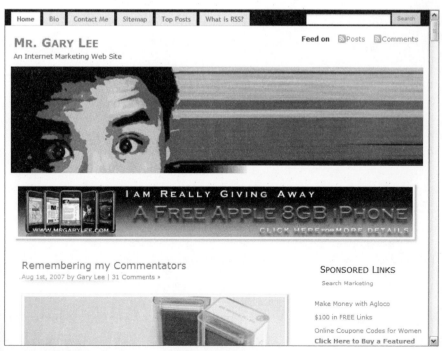

www.mrgarylee.com

The blog has been a venue for some highly successful experiments in driving traffic. Although they are somewhat manipulative of the system, Lee's experiments have lifted Mr. Gary Lee into Technorati's list of the Top 100 Most Favorited blogs. Although some of his traffic-building techniques are frowned on by mainstream bloggers, Lee sees the process as an experiment in networking and helping others.

Lee's most notable accomplishment in building traffic was with what is called a "link train," aimed specifically at getting into the Technorati list of the Top 100 Most Favorited blogs—which ranks a blog by the number of Technorati members who have added it to their Favorites list. Unlike Technorati's Top 100 Most Linked To blogs, the Most Favorited list is fairly easy to break into. It relies largely on social networking, and involves a system of trading links. If you know enough people who are interested in placing you on their Favorites list, you can probably make the list. And making the list can result in a tremendous increase in a blog's traffic.

My Name's My Domain

Lee made the Technorati list about six months after starting Mr. Gary Lee, which is an unusually short period of time, especially considering the thousands of competitors trying to make that list. Lee will eventually get knocked off the list, but as far as he is concerned, making the list was a successful experiment.

Lee lives in Southern California, and has a degree in economics. He currently works for himself as an Internet marketing and business development consultant. After several years of working at established companies, Lee now helps businesses bring traffic to their site and teaches them how to monetize that traffic.

A dyed-in-the-wool Apple fan, Lee celebrated that fact by giving away an Apple iPhone through his blog. The giveaway was of course designed to increase traffic, but the selection of an iPhone as a prize was something of a tribute to Apple.

You've made the Technorati Top 100 Most Linked To blogs list. When did you set up your blog, Mr. Gary Lee, and why that name?

January of this year (2007). The domain name is part of a "my name in my domain" link train that I originated. It has to do with getting noticed by search engines and other bloggers. It helped me rank in Google when someone searched for "Gary Lee."

Did you have a blog before this?

Not really. My only blogging-related activity was a personal blog at Xanga. I was never into blogging every day or blogging about anything specifically—just random thoughts.

Plus, Xanga was really good for keeping in touch with what my friends were up to. I couldn't talk to everybody every day, so I just read their blogs, and I knew what was going on in their lives.

How did you climb to the Top 100 so quickly?

I'm not going to lie and say, "I did this on purpose." I really attribute it to my network of blogger friends. The people I started blogging with all pretty much started to blog at the same time as I did. We met one another on John Chow's blog [www.johnchow.com] and commented on John Chow's blog because we were trying to get noticed. And we linked to each other. We would start dialogues in the comments sections.

You monetize your site with advertising, and you have high traffic. Do you make more money from blogging or consulting?

Consulting, for right now. Honestly, my blog is more like a flagship site or a business card. The purpose of it was never to make money. That would be nice, like a cherry on top. But I just use it to learn and to build up my name. It's also a good way to meet new people.

What kind of consulting do you do?

I mainly do Internet marketing consulting, for an Asian website and for various clients throughout Los Angeles. I help people out with their SEO and their PC programs, and also guerilla marketing and viral marketing. We consult on the layout of the website to make sure that the flow of the website is optimized as well as possible, for look as well as functionality.

It sounds like you covered all the angles.

Well, I had to. There weren't that many people into the Internet when I started, so at most jobs I was the only person. I had to be a jack-of-all-trades.

How much do you work with SEO on your blog?

I test out a lot of SEO stuff on my blogs. I try to learn as much as I can by talking to other bloggers. I read forums and tips, and see what new things are out there. Then I test them on my site to see what works. I also have other sites for testing. I'm just trying to keep as much of my hands around SEO as I can.

I optimize the blog as best possible, the goal being to increase my effective CPM [cost per thousand impressions] so I make as much money per thousand impressions as I can.

I'm surprised that you moved up so quickly.

When I started the link train, everybody was very thankful that I included them in the train. I did not pick just anybody, though. I looked at all the blogs I favorited. I saw what kind of demographic they were going after. I wanted a selection of demographics across the entire social spectrum, not just one demographic.

> *"If you look at a link train as a tool to get backlinks, then you won't succeed. But if you think about it as an opportunity to discover new blogs and get some link love, then I think you'll be happy."*

The reason I got so much support for the link train right off the bat is because each person who is supporting me has their own spheres of influence, and it just took off from there. So, meeting the right people and having the right people to help you is kind of one of the main purposes of the blog. Looking back, I don't like to say that I manipulated this. I just wanted to help each blogger as much as possible. I didn't know how or if they would pay me back. If nothing else, it was a way to meet people and make friends.

If you look at a link train as a tool to get backlinks, then you won't succeed. But if you think about it as an opportunity to discover new blogs and get some link love, then I think you'll be happy.

You put a lot of effort into SEO and the link train. What about the quality of your blog's posts?

I'm not the greatest writer. I wish I had been a better writer in high school. I'm still learning. I feel more natural when I just try to write the way I talk.

That's my style. After years of just maturing, you know how to talk to people. Of course, I can write better than I speak—because when you speak, you don't have a delete button.

The thing is, I wouldn't say quality is always what's right. A quality article to me is something that plants a seed in the mind of the reader. It's not necessarily something that's authoritative. I don't like authoritative. I like writing posts that make people think and comment. A blog is a community, and you need to get people to talk on your blog or your blog gets boring.

Do you have much time to read other blogs?

These days, I'm trying to carve out more time to read more blogs. Recently, one of my clients had me do a total site redesign, so I haven't been able to keep up with other blogs for about a month and a half. I feel so out of the loop. And now, especially with my iPhone contest, it's getting crazy because so many people ask me to read their blogs. They send me their RSS feeds. But it's hard. I try to keep up with my main blogs, the ones I talk to and keep in contact with. And the important blogs—I try to read Dosh Dosh [www.doshdosh.com], Blue Hat SEO [www.bluehatseo.com], and Digital Point [www.digitalpoint.com] as much as possible. I spend more time reading those than my RSS feeds. I would say I have a hundred-something RSS feeds, and I'm not a fast reader.

What is the most difficult aspect of blogging for you?

Probably the most difficult part is trying to create original content—or even trying to find a new angle. It's so hard because SEO is so big. SEO is a fundamental principle, and you can just twist it any way you want. So many bloggers out there right now try to make money online like other bloggers, but they go about it the wrong way—by writing the same stuff as successful bloggers write, which doesn't work. You have to be able to create your own content, and it's really hard to come up with original content.

> "I look at the whole blog thing as a big party, and everybody is trying to meet each other—trying to build their cliques, as with any social function."

When I put together content, I try to write three to five good quality articles per promotional article. I don't want the site to look too self-serving. I know people can see right through that.

What do you find gratifying about blogging?

Networking. The fun has been meeting people from around the world. There is nothing more gratifying than that, and knowing you've been able to help people—just increase their rankings, or plant a seed in their mind to help them be more creative and do things. Meeting people and watching them grow—that's been the most satisfying part.

I look at the whole blog thing as a big party, and everybody is trying to meet each other—trying to build their cliques, as with any social function. There are always cliques. And there's always that one person who is just trying to meet people, and right now that's what I am.

You certainly have a different perspective on gaming the system.

When I saw the potential for gaming the system, I thought, "I can use this and make it my own." I used it to make friends, and to show people that I can help them.

> *"My advice on getting more traffic is to participate in other blogs."*

Of course, it's not all about getting links. I still try to write good stuff—stuff people will *want* to read and link to. I don't want to step on too many toes by gaming the system, because I know there are bloggers out there who have put in their work and use the system in the true way that it was meant to be used. I don't want to disgrace that by gaming it too much.

Do you have advice to offer new bloggers?

My advice on getting more traffic is to participate in other blogs. You need to participate by commenting and supporting other bloggers.

Meet people who share some of your interests—even if the interest is just reading a particular blog. If you can do that and produce quality content, you're going to develop a rapport with just about everyone you approach. Your reputation will precede you.

It's also important to concentrate on what you're doing, rather than whether you're getting to a goal. I learned this from the president of a large bank who said he made it to his position by just working and not worrying about those ahead of him, because he knew quality work would always count.

So, do your work, participate, let people know about you, and don't be shy. People will come to recognize you, and people will talk about you.

I would not recommend gaming the system, even though I did it and that's how I got top ranking. It's hypocritical, but I tried to do it the way I wanted to begin with. And it worked to a point, and I got support to where, when I tried a link train, it did well.

Points to Review

Gary Lee was one of the early adopters of blogging as a PR tool, and he has proven that blogs can be a channel for mainstream media attention. He harnesses the power of online conversation by following these tenets:

- Blogging is a learning process.
- The system can be gained on some levels, but gaming the system successfully doesn't necessarily mean making a lot of money.
- Blog posts should inspire readers to comment. Without that, your blog can become boring.
- Producing quality posts—material that people will want to read and link to—is as important as networking with other bloggers.
- Participating in (commenting on and linking to) other blogs is a vital part of getting more readers. When you can, connect with people who share your interests.

Richard MacManus
Read/WriteWeb

26

"The really popular blogs are the ones where readers can tell the author is passionate about the topic."

—*Richard MacManus*

Like so many bloggers, Richard MacManus started blogging as a hobby, a means of sharing his thoughts on technology—Web 2.0 in particular. He was a corporate web manager until August 2005, when he quit the day job and went to work for himself—his first venture into business.

Since its launch in 2003, Read/WriteWeb has evolved into a lineup of offerings that includes web technology news, reviews, and analysis, with some

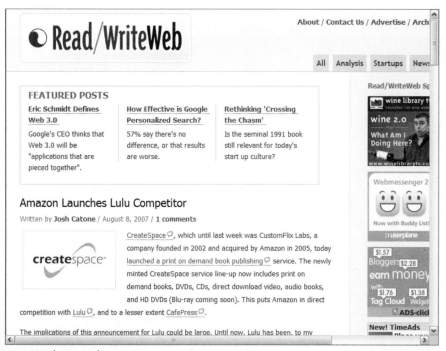

emphasis on startups and beta products. It is the first blog in MacManus's Read/WriteWeb Network, a group of web technology blogs. His other sites are last100 (www.last100.com/), which is a blog about the digital lifestyle, and AltSearchEngines (www.altsearchengines.com/), which is a source of news and commentary on search engines and content aggregators. Additional blogs for the network are planned.

Running the network is a full-time proposition for MacManus, who lives in Wellington, New Zealand but often runs on Silicon Valley time. But as with other blogs, location is almost irrelevant—Read/WriteWeb is a blog with a global perspective and a global audience. Fifty percent of its readership is in the United States, and the next biggest source of readers is the U.K., with Canada close behind. Racking up more than 30,000 page views per day, the blog enjoys high rankings on Technorati's lists. In 2007, Read/WriteWeb was included in *PC Magazine's* list of 100 Blogs We Love, a notable distinction at a time when 120,000 new blogs were popping up every day.

From his home office, MacManus coordinates a team of writers who write from several locations around the world. He uses a combination of Skype and a San Francisco phone number to stay in touch with the United States.

MacManus encourages would-be bloggers to "just start writing." According to MacManus, "It will take a while to find your voice, but in the end what attracts readers is being knowledgeable about your topic and contributing original and thoughtful commentary."

Read/Write/Blog

> *"As soon as I get up in the morning, I'm straight into blogging. And I can often go until quite late in the night, as well. So, it's a huge time commitment."*

MacManus lives a life that is probably the goal of millions of bloggers. He earns a good income working from home at something he enjoys—blogging. But he is the first to say that his is not an overnight success story. Read/WriteWeb was online for almost three years before it reached the point where he was making significant money. Now MacManus is indeed his own boss, but he starts early and works late—proof that making it requires a lot of time and energy. And writing.

How far back do you go in computing?

I guess I started playing around with computers like the Commodore 64. I wouldn't class myself as a programmer. I've never been that technical. I've worked at web design and website management, as well as product design and analysis. I've also done consulting for some companies.

> *"There are thousands of articles on the website, so there's a lot of content available to turn up in search results."*

When did you first start blogging?

I first tried it out early in 2002. But Read/WriteWeb itself did not start until April 2003.

What was your intent in starting a blog? Was it personal?

When I started it, the intention was mostly to get down all the thoughts I was having about technology and just connect with people with similar interests.

Do you follow other blogs?

Yes, absolutely. I still follow blogs on Google Reader and on their own pages. Google Reader is my main RSS reader.

What kind of time do you put into blogging and management?

As soon as I get up in the morning, I'm straight into blogging. And I can often go until quite late in the night, as well. So, it's a huge time commitment. It's hard sometimes because I'm working from home, and it's sometimes difficult to juggle work life and home life.

What's the most difficult part of running a blog?

My challenge right now is building the business, creating unique new blogs, and several other sorts of things. It's just time management at the moment. I've got other writers to help me with the blog, so I just need to attend to all the business-end details nowadays.

Do you handle all the advertising business yourself?

I handle all of the sponsors on the sidebar, but I use FM Publishing to handle other advertisements on this site, mostly CPM [cost per thousand impressions]. It's kind of half-and-half.

Do you put much time into SEO (search engine optimization)?

> *"I'm actually building up something that comes from my creativity and that of my writers."*

Funny you should ask. I am currently trying to find out how to track my search results. Google is my number-one traffic driver, but I think there's still room for improvement. There are a couple of blogs that I can point to that always rank higher on Goggle than I do, so this is something I want to improve.

How much of your blog's growth can you credit to Google?

It's hard to say. I think because the blog's been around for about four years now, it has a good page rank. And there are thousands of articles on the website, so there's a lot of content available to turn up in search results. I do believe the blog's rank at Google has provided more search traffic.

In addition to SEO, have you made other efforts to bring in readers—like commenting on other blogs or linking to other blogs?

Yes. Especially in the early days, I commented on other blogs to drive traffic to my blog. At this point in time, I still comment on other blogs, but I'm just so busy with other things that I don't have as much time as I used to. And also I look at the blog kind of like as a media property. It's more about reporting on the news and analyzing the news. There is the more personal kind of commentary as well.

What do you find gratifying about blogging?

There are a couple of things. One is the fact that I'm creating something. I'm actually building up something that comes from my creativity and that of my writers. The other part of it is that I'm constantly in touch with other people all over the world who are interested in the same thing as me—all the new technology.

What tips in general can you offer bloggers?

It's important to be passionate about your topic, and focused. Pick a niche topic that you are interested in and know about. And you need to blog pretty much daily.

Another thing that I encourage new bloggers to do is to reach out to others in the community who are experts and know their topics. Link to them and comment on their blogs, and get into conversations with those people.

They're usually part of a whole new world going on. And they bring their own opinions and experiences. That's what I found when I started four years ago. I didn't know there was this whole other world with people talking about this kind of stuff.

Points to Review

Like many bloggers interviewed in this book, Richard MacManus is an example of what can happen when you dig in and work at something for which you have passion. The rest of the recipe follows that of most successful bloggers:

- Choose a niche topic you are passionate about and know about.
- Focus on your topic.
- Raise your profile by posting to other, related blogs.
- Connect with other bloggers in the community who share your areas of interest.
- Be prepared to commit a lot of time and energy to blogging.
- Don't count on making lots of money right away.

Eric T.
Internet Duct Tape

27

"If you can make other people interested in what you're writing about, then search engines will follow."

—Eric T.

As described by Eric T, the semi-anonymous Canadian engineer who runs it, Internet Duct Tape is a blog about making technology work for you instead of making you work for technology. Eric also enjoys making things work that were never intended to work.

Internet Duct Tape (sometimes referred to as IDT) is part philisophy, part how-to, and all about sharing knowledge and helping other people. It has

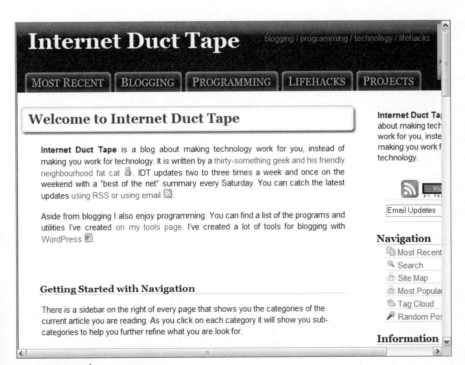

www.internetducttape.com

made the Technorati Top 100 Most Favorited list more than once, and has been linked to every major blog and technical website—including Download Squad, Digg, Slashdot, Fark, del.icio.us, and so on. At its peak in February 2007, Internet Duct Tape was getting more than 120,000 page views per month. Things have slacked off since Eric T. demoted blogging from his primary activity to the status of a secondary hobby. But it's still visited by thousands daily.

If People Are Interested, Search Engines Will Follow

In addition to blogging, Eric T. connects with other Internet users through a variety of free software tools for bloggers, presented under the aegis of IDT Labs. His applications (many of them designed for Firefox) include tools to use with Flickr, del.icio.us, Digg, Facebook, Google Reader, Technorati, and WordPress (his blog's platform). All are available for download.

How long have you been blogging?

I started playing around with blogging in 2003. I was just doing the usual—starting a blog, sending a couple of friends the link, and talking about what I was doing that week or on the weekend. I never really reached any kind of mainstream, but friends checked it out.

> "The best way to learn something is to share the information with other people."

Then in April of 2006, I was laid off for the first time. I decided I was going to try this reputation management thing, and try to build an online presence. So I started a blog with more of a technological bent, and it started getting pretty popular. That's when I found myself enjoying blogging for the sake of blogging. So, my taking it seriously started around April 2006.

You have good traffic, but you're not monetizing this. You don't have ads.

Not yet. I may do that in the future, but now I'm doing it for the sake of learning, enjoying connecting to other people, seeing comments come in, seeing how people link to me, and so forth. I find it's a very good tool for learning about things. The best way to learn something is to share the information with other people.

Writing is one of my favorite things. When I get hit with a problem now, instead of being really frustrated by it, in the back of my head I think, "Wow, this will be a great post!"

Do you have much time to look at other blogs?

I do make time for it. I find that when you first start blogging, there are two paths you can take. One is a very clear path, where all you really concern yourself with is writing for yourself.

The other path is one where you're more outgoing, where you've connected with a lot of other bloggers, and you start getting involved in communities and connecting with other people.

And you start reading lots of blogs. I find there's like a cycle, where it kind of goes through a bell curve. As you go through that, you reach the high point where you're reading lots of blogs and you're almost never posting to your own blog. But then you realize you're reading a lot of the same things over and over again. Then it becomes more insular again, where you pick the best of the blogs you're reading, cut back the rest, and you start focusing on your own [blog].

How much time do you think you spend blogging?

When I first started, I'd spend lots of time at it. I think everyone gets heavily interested in blogging, and they spend a lot of time on it. Now I've cut back on it, to where I'll only do a couple posts a week. It used to be that I felt like I had to read every post on every blog that I followed.

Now if I miss posts, I know it's not that big of a deal. I do it more at my leisure, when I have time available. But it's still a significant hobby—it's probably still 10 to 20 hours a week.

That *is* a significant amount of time for a hobby. Do you comment on other blogs?

I do, when I have time for it. I definitely have my order of preference in commenting. It depends on how well I feel I know the other blogger. If I've been commenting on someone's blog for a year, I'm more likely to comment on that blog again than I am a blog I discovered just last week.

I've recently hit a problem with the spam software that everyone uses. For whatever reasons, it's identifying my comments as spam. That led to an involuntary cutback, because it's just not worth the effort commenting and then having to send an e-mail saying, "Can you make sure that didn't get marked as spam?" So that's one way to cut back, but I don't really recommend it.

Do you practice search engine optimization (SEO)?

I do to some extent. I find it pretty amazing that it does work. Around Valentine's Day last year, I wrote a post about romantic Valentine's Day movies just because I thought, "Hey, it's Valentine's Day—this will probably be really popular." Six months later, it's still within the top five search results on Google for "romantic movies." Sometimes it's number two! Which is pretty crazy when you think that ["romantic movies"] ought to be a very-highly valued search term and that someone hasn't bought it from Google.

Valued by marketing people, you mean?

Yes. I followed the rules of SEO when I wrote that post. I was doing things like adding text to my images with keywords and making sure my title was "friendly" so people would want to click on the title. It does work.

> *"The sad thing about all this frantic activity is that it's not really adding value to the conversation or making a positive impact on people's lives."*

I find you can call SEO something else completely: "Socially Engineering Others." It's a more appropriate name because it's logical. If you can make other people interested in what you're writing about, then search engines will follow.

I think a lot of people don't realize that when they're starting out. The problem is that there is so much misinformation [about] blogging out there, and there are so many people telling you what to do. If you actually really looked at things, you might see that they're not as knowledgeable as you think they are. The number of search engine optimization [SEO] blogs that are written by someone under the age of 25 who are telling you, "I'm an SEO expert!" Well, you know, you read the same websites I read! [laughs]

And they're going to make $1 million at it.

Yes. Because I was so interested in blogging, I hit a point where most of the blogs I was reading were blogs about blogging and making money online—stuff like that. You reach this point where it's kind of its own little subculture of all these people who want to sell you each other's self-help things. And that's how they make money online: by talking about making money online!

The sad thing about all this frantic activity is that it's not really adding value to the conversation or making a positive impact on people's lives.

And of course, it is possible to have a positive impact through blogging. When I look at the communities where I've written posts about "I had this problem with my computer, and this is how I fixed it"—when I look back on it, 200,000 people have read that, and there are hundreds of comments saying, "You saved me. I thought my baby (or my cat) had broken the computer, and that fixed it!" It's nice to have that impact—more so than, "I made a hundred extra bucks this month."

I find that when you dig into the numbers, there are people who actually make money from blogging, but they are very few and far between. You basically kind of bastardize your hobby—[you] devalue your hobby and make some change on the side.

Have you ever tried to make money with your blog?

I tried out that ReviewMe thing. That's one of those brokerage sites where they'll broker people who have products with people who want to write about products. I tried that out, and I did a couple of them—it's not worth the effort, if you look at writing a good review of something and what you're actually getting paid for it.

There's one called PayPerPost [PPP], where people are paying bloggers [about] $5 to write about their product. You have to look at how inane of a post you have to write to make it worth $5! I understand that some people could be drawn to it, depending on what's going on in your life. There's a very big culture of stay-at-home mothers—mommy bloggers—and for them, if you're staying at home with the kids anyway, and you're not working full time, I could see some of those motivation options. They might actually make a really huge difference in their lives. For other people, instead of chasing this, you should change your career to something you're really passionate about.

Instead of chasing money, finding things that you'll be very successful at and very interested in naturally is healthier.

Something you said earlier, when you were talking about "Social Engineering Others"—a great term!—if you attract people, search engines will follow. Do you mean search engines will pick it up because people are linking to you?

Yes, that's what I meant by that. People are linking to you because you have good quality. There's search engine optimization, and the other term that's being thrown around these days: social media optimization [SMO]. So many websites created in the last two or three years have been about sharing content between each other, right? There are sites like del.icio.us, where [it's just] people who have put their bookmarks on the Internet. The intent is to find someone with similar interests or who is an expert in a certain subject matter, and a subscriber can just search through the bookmarks and find all sorts of interesting things that could have taken you hours to find with search engines—if you even could have. So that's an entirely new factor. But you have to know that search engines take sites like that into account with special algorithms.

You have sites where you can pay for people to vote for you. That's not worth it. There are also people who submit everything they ever write to these sites. Again, is it actually worth your time to do that? In general, chasing traffic must be balanced. What I like to think of as one of the greatest lies is the old "Write good content, and everything else will follow." It's a mixture—you need to find the happy medium between promotion and writing good content.

By promotion, do you mean actually going out and being active?

[It's] being active in communities, buying advertising somewhere, or asking people to link to you. One very common thing for promotion was (it's starting to die down a bit now) creating blog themes, like blog templates. You would release a template for Blogger or for WordPress that included a link to your site. That was a great way to promote [your blog]—some search engines would count that as if the person using your template had linked to you.

Promotion has the end goal of writing something other than for yourself so people link or come to you.

There was a great blog that shut down a while ago called Creating Passionate Users. On almost any page, you could find a great quote, just to remind you that the question you should be asking yourself is, "What am I doing to help someone kick ass that day?" A lot of people forget that. I forget that.

You've made it to Technorati's Most Favorited list, and then lost the listing, started all over, and made it again.

I came up in Top 100 Favorited sites with a different site. The Top 100 Most Linked To—I never reached that list. I think I got close to the top 1,000, and I was pretty proud of myself for that. Then I changed my domain name, which broke Technorati, and I had to start all over again.

> *"I find the one thing that almost always works is helping people."*

Did your existing readers find you?

I went from zero to however many pretty fast—from nothing to pretty high pretty fast. Again, the thing is, once you're established, it's very easy to stay on the top. It's getting there that's the hard part.

A lot people are trying different things to get there, things that don't work.

I find the one thing that almost always works is helping people. If you help people with something they need help with, or if you give them something they weren't looking for, that's always going to work for reaching out.

You mean in terms of what you're providing in your posts?

Yes, in terms of giving them information that actually helps them do something better, helps them learn something they wanted to learn, or even lets them know something they didn't know about at all—that's very useful and helpful.

Whether you're working your way up the rankings or at the top, what do you find difficult about blogging?

The hamster-wheel effect, in that you're never done with it. "Okay, I've finished blogging," you tell yourself, but there's always more to do. Even if you've written a post every day of the week, you have to go moderate your comments, and your comment spam is the most horrible thing in the world to deal with.

And once you're done doing that, there are more feeds to read, and there are always more sites to read. And now that you're reading more sites, you're inspired to do new things.

Or you want to go out and write comments on these, your favorite sites. I have some friends who are just running something like a "four friends group blog," where they just write what they want to write and they don't care about traffic readership—much more of a relaxing atmosphere to blogging.

I think probably the worst thing that was ever invented was Blogstats, because you can just get so caught up in these arbitrary numbers that don't actually mean anything. If you're monetizing it—if you're trying to make money from blogging—then at least it is a dollar amount in a bank account. It's easier to justify paying attention to it.

It's so easy to check the stats. That's the problem. You can get them on your cell phone. They're everywhere.

What do you find gratifying about running a blog?

That's a good question. When I look back over the time I've been blogging, every now and then I'll go back and catch something I wrote a long time ago—and I'll look at it and think, "I like what I did there." Also, in terms of diversifying, I've developed skills I wouldn't have developed otherwise.

Just this past month, I participated in a web design competition. I didn't place anywhere—it was just something that inspired me to learn. I've been finding it very creative and very interesting to do.

My personality: I'm very much a generalist, a breadth person more than a depth person, so I find that blogging has been very good because it is so diverse. Blogging isn't cultural in general. It's very diverse—there's always something new to learn—and I find that very interesting. Actually applying everything I've ever learned is much harder!

When you're a generalist, there's not enough time for everything, and you're always busy learning something new.

The joy is actually in the learning something new, not in your becoming an expert in something you already kind of knew. Doing web design for the past month—spending time doing some web designs that weren't going to become really popular and weren't going to set the world ablaze—it was something I was learning, something I wanted to do. But, yeah—it took time away from other things I was already good at.

If you look at blogging in terms of site promotion and how to become a popular blogger and all, there's one thing the experts don't mention (actually, some of them do mention it). And that is to pick one thing and do that well, instead of always changing your mind and trying something new—which is what I like to do.

I have a thought about blogging I'd like to interject. This is probably the worst thing in the world about blogs, and the number-one reason why they won't be mainstreamed: they are horribly self-referential. Blogging is a culture all to itself. It's a culture that talks about itself and writes about itself—and again, I say this as a person who does that all the time.

How do you feel about gaming the system—bloggers trying to trick or force their way in?

I think gaming is a bit of—I used the term "socially engineering others"—I think there's a line there between gaming and "socially engineering others." On one side, you're applying techniques like copywriting, and doing very effective writing that has a clear message—like convincing someone to take an action based on what you're writing. On the gaming side, it's doing things like literally creating multiple accounts to vote up a story—creating a voting bloc to kind of keep the algorithms on your side.

> *"If you know what you want to do with blogging—what your goals are and what you want to get out of it—it's a lot easier to catch yourself when you're getting caught up in all the other areas."*

And there are people who solicit others for that, who claim to teach it and so forth.

There's this website called SEO Black Hat, and it's all about methods to affect the search engines in a way that you want to—stuff like that. And I think that they sell forum memberships for several hundreds, if not thousands, of dollars per year—just to access their forums that have all these hidden things—so their blog is just a way for people to come in and click through the forums. They get members that way. It falls under the same heading as the selling-making-money-secrets thing.

You've made the Technorati list twice. You've helped hundreds, if not thousands, of people. You've learned a lot and had some fun. Based on your experiences, what advice can you offer?

Know what you want to get out of it. That sounds very glib and simple, but knowing what you want to get out of it is actually the hardest question, and something you should ask yourself repeatedly every few months or so. Is this what I want to get out of it? It's a huge time sink. What are you doing it for? Are you doing it to build an online entity? Are you doing it to create opportunities and connections with other things? Are you doing it to make money online? Purely for fun?

There are a lot of different ways to blog, and a lot of different things to do with it. If you know what you want to do with blogging—what your goals are and what you want to get out of it—it's a lot easier to catch yourself when you're getting caught up in all the other areas.

In one word: focus. Have a focus and stick with it. If your focus changes, that's fine too.

Points to Review

Much of Internet Duct Tape's success seems rooted in simplicity. In Eric T.'s approach to blogging, there are no complex rules to follow, no mantras to chant, and no search engines to optimize. Instead, he emphasizes helping people, learning, and staying focused. Here are a few things to keep in mind:

- Know what you want from blogging when you start, and focus on that aspect.
- Pick one thing you know how to do well, and do it.
- The best way to learn about a subject is to share what you learn as you learn it.
- If you have a problem, consider making it a blog post.
- If your readers have the opportunity to get to know you, they will comment more.
- If what you write interests other people, search engines will naturally follow, leading more people to you.

> *"To blog successfully you have to be passionate about something and stay true to it."*
>
> —*Victor Agreda, Jr.*

Are you puzzled by projects such as making new plants from cuttings? Or do you need to know what to do to get rid of the stench of a defrosted freezer or smelly sink drain? Do you know whether you should use coffee grounds as fertilizer, and with which plants? Can you really paint your car for

$300? Answers to these and related questions—as well as lots more completely unrelated questions—are free for the reading at DIY Life, a blog that delivers a steady stream of tips, ideas, do-it-yourself projects, how-tos, and pragmatic info such as product reviews and safety recalls.

The blog's categories include Home & Family, Home Improvement, Hobbies & Crafts, and Tech—with coverage of everything from crafting and power tools to home interior and mechanics.

DIY Life's editor, Victor Agreda, Jr., has an interesting mix of education and experience that is probably ideal for blogging on a mix of subjects. He has a degree in English, and went to journalism school and film school. He has worked for a cable television company and in a music library, where he was first exposed to things like Mosaic, HTML, Archie, and Gopher. Today Agreda teaches college-level English, as well as hands-on multimedia subjects.

Working primarily in an administrative capacity, Agreda doesn't get to blog nearly as much as he'd like, but he finds working with over a dozen bloggers mostly agreeable.

Do-It-Yourself Blogging

Agreda enjoys the current work environment, largely because, while the end result is in essence an online magazine, he and his staff are not encumbered with the structure that usually goes with a magazine. "We don't have a dedicated editorial staff that goes through and assigns stories, reads them, and changes them," he explains. "It's still very much a blogging medium, and we haven't gone over to the magazine tradition."

EDUCATORS TURNED BLOGGERS

Something I find very interesting, at least at Weblogs, Inc., is that a lot of the bloggers come from an educational background—that is, they were working in education. That was especially true when I was starting out, when blogging was new. I don't know if this is because schools have an always-on broadband connection, which is probably part of it. I don't know if it's because there are long periods when you're waiting for other people to get done with things, or maybe it's just easier to multitask in education.

How long have you been blogging?

I would say this is my third or fourth year of blogging. Going on four years, actually. I started blogging a sort of a little mini tech blog. It was a server tech blog, called Solution Spheres. I have it archived now. It was all Mac tips. TUAW [The Unofficial Apple Weblog, www.tuaw.com] didn't exist when I first started.

How did you get into working for Weblogs, Inc.?

The way I got into this is probably different than most. I may be only one of two people at Weblogs, Inc. that started as a commenter. I got involved partly because of my comments on Engadget, and partly from my Solution Spheres blog. As soon as the Mac mini came out, I had a little piece on how to turn it into a media center. Barb Dybwad at Engadget did a full write-up about it on Engadget, with pictures and everything.

I also made a little iPod case from a milk jug. That sort of got me on their radar, and I was already commenting quite a bit on Engadget, so I think that's how they got to know me. At the same time, I became a top-rated commenter on TUAW, back when Weblogs, Inc. used to give stars to top commenters. So it only made sense that when I applied, they said, "Okay, he's a known quantity," and hired me.

So that's how I got in with Weblogs, Inc. I blogged at TUAW for about a year, and during that period we were acquired by AOL. I was making four bucks a post when I first started. One of my posts was a feature-length article, but I didn't know they paid more for features. It got on Digg's front page pretty quickly, so I had bragging rights. [Payment for posts and for features has, of course, increased since Agreda started with Weblogs, Inc.]

I was one of the launch bloggers at Download Squad [www.downloadsquad.com]. That was one of Jason Calacanis's (co-founder of Weblogs, Inc.) pet projects— he wanted it to be the software counterpart of Engadget. We rolled up a lot of people who ran Weblog, Inc.'s retired blogs and brought them to Download Squad.

Of course, that's a really competitive space right now, with blogs like TechCrunch. We didn't have anybody at Silicon Valley, and I think we lost a little traction on that. And then C.K. Sample asked me to come over to TUAW, because that's really where my heart is—in Apple stuff.

Then when my current position came open, I applied for it, and here I am.

Is there anything particularly difficult involved in blogging for you? I'm sure time is among the challenging elements.

Yes. But what's really trying is finding something new. Especially now, because the blogosphere has become quite an echo chamber in many regards. And so it's always a challenge, for the best bloggers anyway, because they want to be fresh, they want to contribute something, and there is a lot of rush to try to get the latest thing out. You've got things like Digg that have just truly accelerated the rate at which news spreads. There's no hiding it. And it's very difficult to compete against the hive mind of the thousands of bloggers out there, online all the time.

I have two kids at home, and I can't stay on the computer all day and all night. So I can't compete against some 15-year-old who's stuck in his house all day through the summer.

In short, it's difficult for us to break news. It's difficult for us to contribute something that has not already been discovered.

HOW AGREDA STARTED USING APPLE

Apple is where my heart is, since I was six years old. We got an Apple II at a bicycle shop, back when computers were hobby toys. They had hobbyist tools. My dad was an electrical engineering major, and he brought one home at great expense, with paddles and a cassette deck, and I started from there.

About how much time do you spend blogging?

Well, unfortunately, like a lot of guys who have been moved into middle-management, I'm in a situation where I don't get to create as much as I used to. I make time for it, I would say, just a couple of times a week. But with things like Twitter, which is just micro-blogging, there's another time sink. I've been on there enough that I've already got almost a thousand tweets—which is nowhere near Nick Fletcher, one of our bloggers, who's got like 4,000 tweets. I don't know how you do that.

What takes up a lot of time now is the fractionalization of all these things [social networks]. You've got Pownce [www.pownce.com], Jaiku [www.jaiku.com], Facebook [www.facebook.com], and these other platforms that aren't necessarily blogs, but they certainly have the instant-publishing aspect of blogs. And that ends up taking up a lot of your time. As far as my actual blog, I only post once or twice a week—if I can focus on it.

Do you work every day at blogging, and do you have another job?

Seven days a week, yes. I teach at a technical college. I've taught a lot of different things—Web, multimedia, and even English—all from my personal background.

With all the time you put in, literally every day, what do you get in return that makes it worthwhile—beyond money, that is? What do you find gratifying or fulfilling about blogging?

I think it's really the act of creation, and the act of just getting your words out there, even if you know that only three people that are your friends are going to see what you write. It's like an open e-mail, and anybody can read it if they want to. You are sharing it with your friends, but at the same time, it's for posterity, as well. It's just sort of getting that mind-dump out. And you can refer back to it, on your notes. I'm a terrible notetaker, so it's nice having it backed up online.

> *"I end up having conversations on blogs, and sometimes I have asynchronous conversations online. An example of that would be [Jason] Calacanis picking up a conversation on Twitter where I had left off on his blog."*

Another great thing about the Web in the blogosphere is that I've met people from all over the world, and some of my best friends now live in New York and San Francisco. I get to see them maybe once or twice a year. But we keep in touch all the time, online.

If you're Twittering, I assume you look at other blogs, to see who's doing what. Do you comment?

Yes, I do comment. I find that I comment more often on posts by friends of mine—people who I know, like Ryan Block, C.K. Sample, and [Jason]

Calacanis before he turned his [blog] comments off. I had 130 comments on there before he turned them off. I tend to lurk on blogs I'm not familiar with.

I think it goes back to the concept of blogging as a conversation. It's not just personal media that's being published and left to sink or swim. Interestingly, I end up having conversations on blogs, and sometimes I have asynchronous conversations online. An example of that would be Calacanis picking up a conversation on Twitter where I had left off on his blog.

What advice can you offer other bloggers?

I always struggle with this because I tried to get some of my friends to blog, and I put bulletins on MySpace asking people to blog.

And so I wonder why some of them don't do it. I think it comes down to this: to blog successfully, you have to be passionate about something and stay true to it. And you have to be true to it because that's what blogging is. If you're not passionate, it will very clearly show in what you do and what you say at some point. You may pull it off for a while—kind of like Fake Steve Jobs—but at the same time, blogging is so visceral and publishing so immediate, that you just can't get away with that. That's why things like PayPerPost [PPP] get called out pretty harshly—because that is the antithesis of what blogging is about. Blogging's not about, "I'm going to be excited about this because I'm getting paid." It's more like, "I'm really excited about this, and it would be awesome to get paid for doing this, but I'll do it anyway."

Finally, there is nothing more valuable, and nothing speaks more to how passionate you are about what you do, than just participating in the community.

Points to Review

Victor Agreda, Jr.'s, experience across multiple blogging subjects proves that you don't have to stick with one subject as a blogger. If something new attracts you and you are a fast learner, it's possible to change your role in blogging. No matter what your subject, the following basic axioms and attitudes apply:

- Blogging for free on your own may win the attention of paying blogs.
- Participation in other blogs is one of the key elements to success in blogging.

- The major challenge for bloggers today is to find fresh, original material that is not simply an echo of what other blogs are doing.
- You must write on subjects about which you are passionate. If you are not passionate, it will eventually come out and you'll lose respect and, along with it, readers.
- Participate in the community of blogs and other entities involved with your subject.
- Just about any sort of experience or education can be useful to a blogger.

Steve Garfield
Steve Garfield's Video Blog

29

"The thing about video blogging is you have a video, plus supporting text, and links—in effect, a story."

—*Steve Garfield*

The content of blogs has undergone a logical progression over the past decade. First there was text. Then images were added in supporting roles. Before long, the images were often the main point, with text merely crediting or introducing the graphics. As the use of images grew, audio started appearing in blogs, and a few audio-only blogs cropped up.

http://stevegarfield.blogs.com

The obvious next step in Web content was video. Countless enthusiasts began adding links in blogs, and finally embedding video in blog posts.

A significant portion of Web users were still using dial-up connections at the time, which made viewing difficult. But it wasn't long before communications technology caught up, and watching video in real time on the Web became practical. Before long there were dedicated websites for sharing images and videos, like Flickr and YouTube.

Enough bloggers were using embedded video or running blogs that were totally video that a new term was coined to describe the practice: video blogging, or vlogging. A vlog (video blog) is composed almost entirely of videos, with text and sometimes thumbnail images serving to introduce or catalog videos.

Vlogging is still new enough that it is possible to track down the pioneers, and Steve Garfield is one. He is also a pioneer in blogging; Garfield is one of the few bloggers who can say he was blogging before there was blogging. On November 18, 1997, Garfield hand-coded his first blog in HTML. (He had experimented with this seven months earlier.) The blog was the first daily update for listeners of the *Karlson and McKenzie* (or *K&M*) radio show in Boston. He kept this up five days a week through April 1, 1999.

Garfield also owns the first paid Blogger Pro account, where he established his Off on a Tangent weblog (`http://offonatangent.blogspot.com`) on November 9, 2000.

VLOG Soup

On July 24, 2002, Garfield put his first video on the Web—a short work titled "Inside a Trashcan." The content is what you might imagine, and he has been vlogging ever since.

The vlogging community is a dedicated group, and close. Vloggers enthusiastically share new tools and techniques, and meet as often as possible. "You feel like you already know someone after you've seen them on video," Garfield maintains. "So even new people at get-togethers recognize each other right away."

Garfield has the best job a vlogger could have: he's a video producer.

What sort of blogging did you do before you got into video blogging?

In 1997, I was the producer of a morning radio show in Boston, the *Karlson and McKenzie* radio show. Every day the guests would come in, and I would post on a web page the date and who the guests were, and if they had a product like a CD or a book, I would add a link to it. Then the next day, I would copy all that and paste the HTML in. I changed the date, filled in the new information, and then saved the page.

Each date had a link, and it was like a permalink page to the information about the guest—just what blogging became. In 2000, when Blogger [a blog publishing service] came out, I totally jumped on that right away. I'm still using it.

Your hand-coded blog goes back almost before anyone else.

It is interesting to note that in July, 2007, a story in *The Wall Street Journal* about the tenth anniversary of blogging said someone named John Barger started the first blog in December 1997. I went back and looked at when my first post was, and it was in August 1997—the first kind of blogging thing. So I left a comment on the story: "I'm probably not the first, but at least I was before this guy in *The Wall Street Journal*."

There was a huge firestorm across the Web, about how wrong *The Wall Street Journal* was. They claimed this guy was the first blogger, but he was using software that Dave Winer developed, and Dave Winer had his Scripting News blog [www.scriptingnews.com] up before this guy. It's just another example of how the media can be wrong.

When did you get into video blogging, as such?

That was January 1, 2004. It was my New Year's resolution—that I figure out how to do it, even though it was kind of difficult to share video. I had no idea what I was doing. But I had the blog, and I had been doing video production. So I thought, "I should be able to put video in a blog post. Why not?" I went to Apple, and I learned all the code. I just made it up. And then I started putting video in my blog. That had to be in January.

> "I had no idea what I was doing. But I had the blog, and I had been doing video production. So I thought, 'I should be able to put video in a blog post. Why not?'"

Do you have any difficulties finding material, and keeping the blog going?

Not at all—it just comes naturally. I blog about what's interesting to me and, as it turns out, other people are interested in it, too.

Periodically I put together a clip show of excerpts from vlogs. This highlights video blogs that I find interesting, and that people can go and check out. I've done a whole bunch of those. They are a little lengthy—I highlight five, six, or eight video blogs in one show. I'm now into what I'm calling "Season II" with this, and I'm doing it daily now—highlighting one vlog a day every weekday.

What's the best thing about vlogging?

When reporters or other people look at the landscape, they see YouTube and video aggregation sites, and think, "It's just videos on the Web." If you really spend some time in the community, you'll find that it's about relationships—finding other people, and learning about other people.

> "A side effect [of video blogging] was that you actually got to know the people on an Internet basis more than you get to know text bloggers ... I'm sure it's all psychological, but ... being able to see the other person in the video makes a difference."

One day in April, 2004, this guy, Jay Dedman, made a comment on one of my blog posts. He said, "Hey, Steve, this is cool. Come join us in this Yahoo! Group—we want to talk all about video blogging." So I joined that group, but there were only three people. There was Jay Dedman, a friend of his, and then me. We started talking about online video, and then other people started joining, and we started watching each other's videos to see what everybody else was doing.

Then it got to be 40, 50, maybe 60 people. And we still kept up, and everybody watched everything that everybody else made. People weren't making things every day—they might make one video a week or two a month. So it was still possible to keep up with everything everybody was doing.

A side effect was that you actually got to know the people on an Internet basis more than you get to know text bloggers. We're still figuring out the reasons for that. I'm sure it's all psychological, but being able to see the other person in the video makes a difference.

And one thing that a lot of us were doing was what Jay Dedman calls "moment showing." You pick up the camera, capture a moment, ([like] Dedman with his friends), put it up on the Web, and we get to share in that moment. At the same time, he was building a history for his grandchildren, so when you take all those moments together, they'll tell a story.

When we finally met, we felt like we already knew each other. I don't know if you've experienced that, but with video blogging, it happens over and over again. It's kind of old hat to us, but for new people who are doing it, they come up and say, "Hey, Steve, I feel like I know you! Do you know who I am?"

Oh, yeah! And now there are thousands and thousands of video bloggers. The only bad part is that no one can see everybody's work.

Are the video moments all slices of daily life?

Yes. For example, one of the people in the queue of videos I'm going to highlight is Gogen, a guy in Croatia. He's going to get his car inspected, he's having pizza, and he's taking care of his baby. From his video, I already feel like I know the guy a little bit. It makes the world a smaller place.

A lot of what I shoot is personal, like what my wife and I do on the weekend. I package that into something we call "The Carol and Steve Show." Maybe we go to a wine-tasting in Boston, and I take out my camera and I'm filming it and interviewing the people who are serving the wine. It enhances our experience.

> *"I'm like the guy who's the first early adopter, so every tool that comes out, I give it a run-through."*

Other people ask, "Hey, what are you doing?" And I end up talking to them. The camera has a way of opening people up, so it's kind of fun. I'll take it on vacation, and film little videos of where we go.

Are there any special tools you use?

I pretty much use everything! I'm like the guy who's the first early adopter, so every tool that comes out, I give it a run-through. I'll usually blog about it and tell people what it's like—share my feelings about it.

Right now I use Apple's Final Cut Pro software to edit. I also use iMovie, and sometimes I use QuickTime. It all depends on what the content is.

For shooting video, I have an iSight camera that's right on the Mac, and I'll use a Nokia 93 cell phone that has video in it. I might use a Canon GL2, which is an advanced camera that I use for certain projects.

Something new I'm using is a website called TubeMogul [www .tubemogul.com]. It lets me upload video to nine sites at once. It also provides statistics on all your videos.

That may bring up questions: "Do you really want to load your video up everywhere? Are you losing control of it?" There are a million issues. I'm just testing it out because I think that by putting my videos on a number of sites, I might find an audience that wouldn't have found me through my blog. So now I have them on YouTube [www.youtube.com], Metacafe [www.metacafe.com], Brightcove [www.brightcove.com], and a whole bunch of places. I'm just checking it out to see how it works. I might find an audience that wouldn't have found my blog or wouldn't have gone to where I host my videos.

And I'm writing blog posts about the experience, and what videos and associated posts look like once they get on a site. The thing about video blogging is you have a video, plus supporting text, and links—in effect, a story. And I might give technical details of how I did it all.

A lot of the sites might treat that added information as kind of a side thing, or cut it off, or not put it out there in front. So that's why I'm carefully looking at what's happening with video blogging—what you can and cannot call video blogging, and what it all means.

What kind of traffic are you getting?

On a site called Blogmap [www.vlogmap.org], I'm the second-most-popular video blogger. I have over 6,000 people a day looking at my stuff. That's pretty good for video bloggers.

What's your day job—or night job, as the case may be?

It's video production. Among other things, I produce a video blog for cookbook author Nina Simon called Spices of Life. I have a [Boston] city councilman named John Tobin as a client. From what we know, he's the first elected politician in the United States to have a video blog.

Do you look at blogs and other vlogs?

Yes, I do! I post, comment, link to, and interact with other bloggers. [I] phone and e-mail them.

I do a lot of presentations. I was in a media company and asked, "How many people read blogs?" Everybody does. "How many people comment on blogs?" I'm looking for a show of hands. Out of a crowd of 40, maybe five! I was actually surprised. But that's just what the statistics show: like 10 percent of the people really participate, and maybe 80 or 90 percent just watch.

How many blogs are on your RSS feed?

I probably have about 1,500. No, let me think—I probably have 500. I have some that are in a daily folder, and I have some that are in a media folder, and of those I concentrate on and get through maybe 50 to 100 of them. Then there's another 300 to 500—those I go through at times. But there are certain ones that I watch every day, I definitely want to check every day.

Do you keep track of the time you put into blogging?

I was doing it from 8:00 A.M. until 3:00 P.M. today—straight out. What I was doing today is working on the Spices of Life, capturing video that I shot last week because it's due on Friday.

I'm working on a "Vlog Soup" today, so I'm recording myself doing my intros and grabbing the video from the video blogger to edit that altogether. And then I had a newspaper in England that was on deadline—they wanted to interview me and they wanted video, so I shot a video for them and put it up on the

"[It's important to write] the text along with the videos. Google reads the text. When people are searching for something that's in the context of your video, they can find it if you've written the text properly."

server. Then they e-mailed me and they said, "Can you change where you're sitting in your chair?" I really didn't have time, but I shot it and posted that to them. Today's been a busy day. This interview was a good break. I took a walk around the pond!

I notice that you have a few ads at your vlog.

Yes, there are a few Google ads, but they're not a major focus. I'm not making a lot of money from them,

What do you do to attract readers and viewers?

The way I bring in readers and viewers is just to participate in the blogosphere—reading other blogs and making comments. And I use Twitter, which you could call a micro-blog.

> *"The way I bring in readers and viewers is just to participate in the blogosphere— reading other blogs and making comments. And I use Twitter, which you could call a micro-blog."*

I don't know how many people I have following me lately—almost 400. I just say, "Hey, I just put up a new Vlog Soup." People will go check it out and give me a comment back. Or on my Flickr photos, I'll put up a photo that has a thumbnail of my video, and people who follow my Flickr stream will say, "Oh look, a new video," and go watch.

But I haven't hired any PR companies. I don't do any campaigns to make it happen. It's all organic.

Another way that's organic is to use Google. It points to the importance of writing the text along with the videos. Google reads the text. When people are searching for something that's in the content of your video, they can find it if you've written the text properly. So people who do video and stick it on a page without that important associated text are losing out.

What about SEO (search engine optimization)?

I know about it, and I actually know how to write a descriptive title and first sentence so it tells people what it is I have. And that's mainly how I do it—I write a good description and title automatically.

You mentioned that your growth was organic. This is something I'm hearing from quite a few bloggers: organic growth, and no gaming the system.

No, no way. One quote I have: "I subscribe to people." These are people I'm having a relationship with—that's what so great about it.

Not incidentally, all the people on YouTube are video bloggers. When you look at the definition of a blog—and I'm big on making sure the Wikipedia article is correct!—it's a permalink allowing you to link to an item that everybody can link to. And that's how the whole conversation goes.

So if a blog is a title and an entry made up of whatever it is—audio, text, or video—and then a permalink, which allows people to reference back to the item, that's the whole beauty of blogging! If you look at YouTube, it has that. It has the title, it has the content (which is a video and text), and it has a permalink. That's the big thing about YouTube—and that's video blogging, too.

There's a whole discussion in the Yahoo! Group—you can go to the archives. We've had many discussions of what is video blogging—and I'm always the guy who says, "Video blogging is a technology, it's not a genre."

It's the mechanics of how blogging is done. Video blogging is just adding video to a blog. And then when you look at what the content of a video blog is, you can get into a whole debate. Is it fiction? Is it real? Is it not edited? Could it be a TV show? These are all genres of what a video blog can be.

> *"It's not as hard as it might seem, especially the idea of putting video on a blog. It's really easier than people think."*

In general, it's different from TV because a lot of it is moments from things. One thing that is different from TV—which TV is starting to figure out—the beauty of it is the conversation, the comments, and the interactivity that can happen between the creator and the viewer. And TV just puts it out and people watch.

Do you have some advice for vloggers?

It's not as hard as it might seem, especially the idea of putting video on a blog. It's really easier than people think.

When I do presentations a lot of times, I'll go, "Okay, this is what you do," and if people have a little digital still camera, I show them how they can take that video, pop it up to blip.tv [http://blip.tv], and automatically post it as a blog entry—and they're a video blogger! In five minutes, I can show someone.

If you are capturing a moment, with no editing, you put it on your computer and go to blip.tv. There, you have a link that knows your user name and password to your blog and automatically posts the video moment. You're a video blogger! And the Nokia phone I have makes it even easier than that. You push a button, and it posts it right up to the Vox blog [www.vox.com, a blog picture-hosting site] from the phone if there's Wi-Fi around.

Points to Review

Vlogging is, at present, the apex of blogging. New technology may provide new dimensions to blogging in the future, but for now vlogging is the most intimate and information-rich method of communication bloggers have available. As Steve Garfield implies, many of the rules for conventional blogging also apply to vlogging. There are, however a few new things to be learned:

- To attract readers, you must participate in the blogosphere in your area of interest. Read and comment on other blogs, and use social networking tools like Twitter.
- Common, everyday moments in life are among the most fascinating video that vloggers share.
- Because sharing videos tends to start strong relationships, as a vblogger, you can expect in-person contact.
- Putting video in a blog post is easier than it looks.

Grant Robertson
Download Squad

30

"I think content drives traffic."

—*Grant Robertson*

Download Squad is a Weblogs, Inc. blog for those who use Windows, Mac, or Linux. It offers information on everything from utilities to games. There are lots of tips, scripts, and tutorials, along with news and generous coverage of open source, not to mention Google and the social software space.

The editor of Download Squad, Grant Robertson, is a self-professed Unix geek, having been exposed to it at a young age through his mother's employment

www.downloadsquad.com

with AT&T. His first Unix machine was a Sun 3/60 running SunOS. It was quickly replaced with a PC running first Coherent, and later Red Hat 4.0.

Robertson has held a number of interesting jobs involving computers, first in hardware, and then in network applications, and finally in software. Robertson's software-development credits include web applications based on the LAMP platform since 1997.

He has also founded two companies, and he was editor of the Digital Music blog (`http://digitalmusic.weblogsinc.com/`) until it closed, early in 2007.

At present, Robertson is a full-time blogger, which is a very mobile job for him. He's blogged from Halifax (Nova Scotia), Nashville, Atlanta (his current home), and points between.

If You Build It, They Will Come

Robertson says his most rewarding activities have been advocacy work for first open source software, and later, the Creative Commons family of licenses.

"Sometimes," he notes, "those two things collide, such as the period in which I was program director of Freematrix Radio, a now defunct online radio station that ran entirely upon open source software and broadcast entirely Creative Commons–licensed programming."

What is your background, leading up to blogging?

I was a systems administrator for a long time. I worked in computer support and such, and always had a deep interest in music. I've done some mild production work for small bands, but I eventually got into software development. I was a big open source advocate and user, and I guess those things, all taken together, led me into blogging. It was sort of a natural progression. I've always been into writing, and writing on things I'm passionate about. I would have loved to have been a fiction writer, but nonfiction writing started to appeal to me, and then became more and more a part of my life. Blogging sort of followed.

You were formerly the lead for Weblogs, Inc.'s Digital Music Weblog, but it has been retired. Were you with it from the beginning?

Not from the beginning. Brad Hill was the first blogger there. I started writing for The Digital Music Weblog in April 2006, so I was there for the better part of a year, since the blog closed in [February] 2007. [The Digital Music Weblog is still online as a searchable archive at `http://digitalmusic.weblogsinc.com/`.]

What kind of blogging did you do before that?

My first real serious blog was a political humor blog that was mostly photos and funny captions, during the 2004 election. It was a whole lot of fun! I posted three or four news photos a day, with captions that were sort of over the top—really out there. That was a fun project to do.

After that I started getting into music blogging a bit, and in January of 2006—it was actually before that, but January was the start date—I started a project called Creative Commons 365 [`www.indieish.com`]. It was a music blog, but with a different philosophy. We only posted material that was licensed under the Creative Commons, and freely available to download, keep, and share. We did one song a day, and tried not to repeat artists through the entire year. We did a fairly good job of that. I think we missed a couple of days here and there throughout the year, but we did a fairly solid job of it.

Did you have ads with the Creative Commons 365 blog?

Just Google ads. It wasn't really a for-profit kind of deal—it was more of an activism, Creative Commons promotion sort of thing. It was a fun project. We got a little bit of coverage from BoingBoing.net and from the official Creative Commons blog, and a lot of support from people with the Creative Commons Foundation. It was pretty heartening to see that

> *"If you are publishing solid content and have a reasonable level of traffic, then content will spread and that will draw in a lot of viewers."*

there was that much support behind the Creative Commons. I had been doing some stuff for Creative Commons music previous to that, and I really wanted a project that would allow me take it to a wider audience—so that was why I originally started that blog.

How did you hook up with Weblogs, Inc. and The Digital Music Weblog?

My blog had pretty wide critical acclaim. I think that's how Brad found me originally. He contacted me in March of 2006. He had been following my

Creative Commons blog and asked me if I would write for The Digital Music Weblog.

How many bloggers do you have working with you?

At Download Squad we have, I believe, 18 currently. We're always looking for new people. It's a lot of fun, and we have a really good group going.

Is this your full-time job, or do you have other work?

Since I'm currently in the middle of my move [from Nova Scotia to Georgia], blogging is my full-time thing. It may not always be that way, but it has served me really well as a full-time [job] while I was living in Canada.

Do you make any special efforts to get traffic, or does that just happen?

I think content drives traffic. Most of my effort to drive traffic is put into creating good content. It's sort of a field of dreams: "If you build it, they will come." If you are publishing solid content and have a reasonable level of traffic, then content will spread and that will draw in a lot of viewers.

How do you feel about SEO (search engine optimization) and PayPerPost (PPP)?

There certainly is something to be said for honest search engine optimization–types of things. Tagging, for example, and deeper linking within your own blog are good healthy search engine optimization techniques. When you get into the black hat SEO—paying services to spread your links, get you in links, and that sort of thing—that gets into a very dark ethical place. I'm definitely not a fan of what I would consider black hat SEO, but I think there is certainly something to be learned from the SEO community. There are healthy and ethical techniques to take away from that.

As far as PayPerPost goes, again it's a very dark ethical area. Blogging is really supposed to be about your own perspective, and once you enter into any sort of contract with any commercial entity to write about their products, that takes away from the honesty of conversation.

At Weblogs, Inc., we have a very strict policy where we don't accept anything for free—absolutely nothing. If we are given anything from any company, we give it away to our readers. And we do absolutely zero pay-per posts.

That echoes what a majority of bloggers interviewed here say. Speaking of other bloggers, do you get much chance to look at other blogs, competing or not?

Oh, I'm constantly reading other blogs. I would estimate I have somewhere in the neighborhood of 200 to 250 RSS feeds. I think reading other blogs should be a requirement. You really have to stay in the conversation, because it is a constantly evolving conversation.

Do you pause to make comments on other blogs?

I am not a big commenter. I do comment on other blogs occasionally, but only when I have something absolutely pointed or poignant to say, or something really drives me. I'm not a constant commenter like some people are.

How much time do you spend on blogging and management duties?

Day to day it varies. I would say in any given week, probably somewhere in the neighborhood of 35 to 50 hours reading, writing, and managing other writers, editing, and all of that.

What is rewarding about blogging for you?

There's a lot really. I find it gratifying to hit a chord that resonates with people and put something out, to write something that has legs—I guess that's the best way to put it. I've had many of those moments over the last two years or so. It never ceases to amaze me how, if you put it down and get the right message—saying what everyone else is thinking—so that stories end up having life, it never fails to amaze me, and that is really gratifying.

I'm a big numbers person. I'm constantly watching traffic and trying things to improve traffic or making plans to improve traffic. That's sort of a game for me, just day to day—a "beat this goal, beat this goal" kind of thing. When you hit those goals, it's always very gratifying.

> *"You really have to stay in the conversation, because it is a constantly evolving conversation."*

In the community of bloggers, I find that I really do enjoy a lot of the relationships that I've forged with other bloggers and other people in different walks of life. A good example of that would be Ray Beckerman. He writes Recording Industry vs. The People [http://recordingindustryvspeople.blogspot.com], which is a great blog. Ray is a lawyer, and he's very terse—his explanations are typically not what the average reader will understand. I forged a really great relationship with him in reading his blog, and sort of interpreting the legalese and writing it in ways that appeal to a wider audience. Ray and I have gotten to be fairly good friends over time. This is a relationship that would not exist without blogging. That's a really important thing.

There's sort of a low-level cooperation among blogs with similar themes, isn't there? I've been told that staying in touch with competing bloggers is like joining a community.

There certainly is that aspect to it. It's sort of a big extended family kind of thing in some ways.

What do you find difficult about running Download Squad?

I don't know that I would say "difficult." I wouldn't say difficult enters into it. I love doing what I do, and I don't think that anything about what I do strikes me as difficult.

> *"Constantly engage in the conversation, find the things that you're passionate about, and write about those things."*

There are challenges involved, certainly. Probably the biggest one would be that we've gotten more into covering news items, and that is a very time-critical thing. When you're covering new software and new releases and stuff—when you're covering features—it's not quite as time-critical.

If you've ever read Stephen King's *The Langoliers*, where the monster comes along and eats time, it's like that— you've got to stay one step ahead of it.

Being the lead on a larger blog since The Digital Music Weblog retired, I've learned a lot more about managing writers and how to work with my bloggers. We don't have quotas or anything like that, so our approach to getting writers to write is more positive encouragement, and not a "produce or you're gone" type of thing—which is great. I think you get more honest content that way. You get things that people are interested in. But it's definitely been a change in mindset for me to deal with people's differing styles of productivity. So that's been a challenge.

What would you tell other bloggers about working toward success?

Be dedicated to it, would be the number one thing. Constantly engage in the conversation, find the things that you're passionate about, and write about those things. Just constantly put yourself out there, even when you feel that you're not getting anywhere, or you're not progressing at the speed you would like, or you're not getting more readers—that sort of thing.

You have to plug along at it. I don't want to say it's cyclical, but it is sort of an up-and-down thing. You find that at certain times you won't have the traffic you expect, but at other times you'll have more traffic than you expect. If you constantly plug along, you'll hit those high-traffic levels, but if you let the low times discourage you and back away from conversation, you're squandering opportunities that may come down the road.

Points to Review

One of Grant Robertson's ambitions was to be a "ranking pro-blogger." That ambition was realized when Download Squad broke into Technorati's Top 100 list of Most Linked To blogs. He has amassed much blogging wisdom on his journey to the Top 100, which he has graciously shared here. Here's a summary of the wisdom to be gleaned from Robertson's experience:

- Content drives traffic.
- Although some SEO tricks, such as linking deeper into one's own blog and using tag words, can be effective, it is best to stay away from the darker and more unethical tricks.
- Dedicate yourself to your blogging.
- Constantly engage the conversation in your field or subject area, on other blogs and in forums.
- Find the things that you're passionate about, and write about those things.
- Now matter how little (or how much) progress you are making, just keep working. Things will change.

Further Reading

The Blogging Church: Sharing the Story of Your Church through Blogs
by Brian Bailey, with Terry Storch
(January 2007, Jossey-Bass)

Blogging For Dummies, 2nd Edition
by Susannah Gardner
(February 2008, John Wiley & Sons)

Building a Web Site For Dummies, 3rd Edition
by David A. Crowder
(October 2007, John Wiley & Sons)

Buzz Marketing with Blogs For Dummies
by Susannah Gardner
(April 2005, John Wiley & Sons)

Create Your Own Photo Blog
by Catherine Jamieson
(April 2006, John Wiley & Sons)

Creating Web Sites Bible, 3rd Edition
by Phillip Crowder and David A. Crowder
(coming February 2008, John Wiley & Sons)

The IT Girl's Guide to Blogging with Moxie
by Joelle Reeder and Katherine Scoleri
(October 2007, John Wiley & Sons)

Microsoft 2.0: Life After Bill Gates
by Mary Jo Foley
(coming February 2008, John Wiley & Sons)

Naked Conversations: How Blogs are Changing the Way Businesses Talk with Customers
by Robert Scoble and Shel Israel
(January 2006, John Wiley & Sons)

The New Rules of Marketing and PR: How to Use News Releases, Blogs, Podcasting, Viral Marketing and Online Media to Reach Buyers Directly
by David Meerman Scott
(June 2007, John Wiley & Sons)

Pay Per Click Search Engine Marketing For Dummies
by Peter Kent
(February 2006, John Wiley & Sons)

Podcasting For Dummies
by Tee Morris, Evo Terra, Dawn Miceli (Foreword), and Drew Domkus (Foreword)
(November 2005, John Wiley & Sons)

Starting an Online Business For Dummies, 5th Edition
by Greg Holden
(April 2007, John Wiley & Sons)

We Blog: Publishing Online with Weblogs
by Paul Bausch, Matthew Haughey, and Meg Hourihan
(August 2002, John Wiley & Sons)

Web 2.0 Heroes
by Bradley L. Jones
(coming March 2008, John Wiley & Sons)

WordPress For Dummies
by Lisa Sabin-Wilson
(November 2007, John Wiley & Sons)

Index